Black Woman on Board

Gender and Race in American History

Series Editors

Carol Faulkner, Syracuse University
Amrita P. Myers, Syracuse University
Alison M. Parker, the University of Delaware

Black Woman on Board

Claudia Hampton,
the California State University, and
the Fight to Save Affirmative Action

Donna J. Nicol

UNIVERSITY OF ROCHESTER PRESS

First published 2024

University of Rochester Press
668 Mt. Hope Avenue, Rochester, NY 14620, USA
www.urpress.com
and Boydell & Brewer Limited
PO Box 9, Woodbridge, Suffolk IP12 3DF, UK
www.boydellandbrewer.com

ISBN-13: 978-1-64825-023-1

Please note that some language quoted in this book may be offensive to readers. It is presented as it exists in the original material for the benefit of research. The material reflects the culture and context in which it was created and/or the attitudes of the parties quoted, and not the views of the University of Rochester Press or Boydell & Brewer.

Library of Congress Cataloging-in-Publication Data

Names: Nicol, Donna J., author.
Title: Black woman on board : Claudia Hampton, the California State University, and the fight to save affirmative action / Donna J. Nicol.
Description: Rochester, NY : University of Rochester Press, 2024. | Series: Gender and race in American history, 2152-6400 ; v. 9 | Includes bibliographical references and index.
Identifiers: LCCN 2023047041 (print) | LCCN 2023047042 (ebook) | ISBN 9781648250231 (hardback) | ISBN 9781805432586 (pdf) | ISBN 9781805432593 (epub)
Subjects: LCSH: Hampton, Claudia H. | California State University. Board of Trustees. | California State University—Administration—History. | Affirmative action programs in education—California—History. | Discrimination in higher education—California—History. | College trustees—California—Biography. | African American women college administrators—California—Biography.
Classification: LCC LD729.5 .N53 2024 (print) | LCC LD729.5 (ebook) | DDC 378.1/011092 [B]—dc23/eng/20231204
LC record available at https://lccn.loc.gov/2023047041
LC ebook record available at https://lccn.loc.gov/2023047042

To my mother Wanda, grandmothers Catherine and Maggie,
and othermothers Clarisa and Yvonne.

Contents

Illustrations

Acknowledgments

Shortly after earning *tenure* in Women and Gender Studies at Cal State Fullerton, I took a three-month family leave to assist my mother-in-law with her treatment for breast cancer in Manchester, England. To help pass the time while my mother-in-law underwent chemotherapy sessions, I decided to work on some fiction writing that I had put off for many years. Though I can't say that what I wrote during this period was any good, the process of writing fiction inspired me to embrace my training as an educational historian—a field that I had more or less abandoned while trying to secure tenure. Since I was employed at a comprehensive teaching university rather than a research institution, I was advised by some colleagues to prioritize getting articles into the pipeline as quickly as possible, instead of getting bogged down in trying to write a book.

But after "writing for myself" during my leave, I returned to the U.S. with a renewed determination to do the kind of research that made me want to become an academic in the first place—my love of history. I began researching a community-based organization that my grandmother helped to create in the late 1970s when I stumbled across a digital photograph of Dr. Claudia Hampton. Cliché as it may be . . . the rest is history. Today, I am still amazed at how that simple yet powerful decision to write for myself, utilizing my training as an educational historian, brought me here—writing and publishing one of only a handful of historical monographs that illuminate the role that black women have played in shaping higher educational policy as influential power brokers in the post-desegregation era. But I didn't accomplish this by myself, and I want to thank everyone who has helped and supported me along this journey.

I want to thank my mother, Wanda, who not only gave me life but gave me her quick wit, her passion for justice, and her love of laughter. Thank you for being my mother, and now my friend. To my late father, Paul, I pray I am making you proud. Thanks to my late grandparents Catherine, Everett, Arthur, and Maggie, my great-grandmothers Rosario and Dorothy, my mother-in-law Clarisa, and my godmother Yvonne, who fed my intellectual curiosity, fed my belly, and gave me so many life lessons. I love and miss you all. Thanks for the love and support of my siblings, nieces and nephews, and my extended network of aunts, uncles, cousins, and in-laws from the Gearring, Gough, McLurkin, Nicol, Wall, Washington, and Williams families.

I had a chance encounter with Alison Parker that fundamentally changed the trajectory of my career as a scholar. In her role as an editor for the Gender and Race in American History series for the University of Rochester Press, Alison attended my first conference presentation on Hampton. She invited me to lunch afterward to discuss my plans for my work. She saw the promise and potential of my project and has been nothing short of amazing in terms of offering feedback and encouragement. I also wish to thank the editorial staff at the University of Rochester Press, including editorial director Sonia Kane and assistant editor Chris Adler-France, for their timely response to my queries and their overall support of me as an author. I simply cannot thank Shazia Iftkhar enough for her amazing developmental editing skills, guidance, and encouragement. The attention and care that Shazia gives to her author clients is par excellence!

I am deeply indebted to the staff of the Gerth Archives and Special Collections at CSU Dominguez Hills who helped me locate so many rich primary sources used in this book. For the last six years, Greg Williams and Thom Philo have been exceedingly accommodating in my requests to view materials, granting permissions to use photos, assisting me in contacting the late Dr. Donald Gerth to interview and even granting access to materials to use during stay-at-home orders during the COVID-19 pandemic. Thanks Greg, Thom, Karen, and Beth for the conversations about Hampton that enriched my analysis of the materials contained in the archives. You all are simply the best! Thanks to the late Dr. Donald Gerth, Dr. Herb Carter, and Dr. W. Ann Reynolds for sitting down with me for an interview to share their experiences working with Dr. Hampton.

Sometimes, you are lucky enough to find your tribe where you work. At CSU Dominguez Hills, I have found my place amongst some of the greatest colleagues on this planet. Thank you to all my colleagues in Africana Studies, in particular, Dr. Salim Faraji, Dr. Justin Gammage, Professor Meryah Fisher, Professor Akua TJ Robinson, and the late Dr. Edward Robinson. Thank you to my dear sister friend, Dr. Tiffany Herbert, for helping to bring me to campus and providing opportunities to connect with other Black women on campus through Sisters United. My Lady Write-a-Thon Crew is the best writing group/friendship network that I could ever have. Thank you to Dr. Marisela Chavez, Dr. Laura Talamante, and Dr. Anne "Dial-a-Historian" Choi for the friendship, being sounding boards, and helping me stay on track. You all are inspirations to me.

I also would like to thank my kababayan (fellow Filipina) Dr. Mary Lacanlale, Dr. Helen Oesterheld, Dr. Jenn Brandt, Dr. Corina Benavides-Lopez, and Dr. Siskanna Naynaha for being an amazing group of bad-ass women scholars and mad cool people. I would like to thank all of the members of the Fannie Lou Hamer Queen Mother Society who have embraced me as chair of Africana Studies from day one and offered unwavering guidance and support. Thanks to Dr. Catherine Jermany, LaWanda Gutierrez, Dr. Stephanie Brasley, Dr. Vivian Price, Dr. Kim Costino, Dr. Tim Caron, Dr. John Davis, Dr. Jeff Sap, Dr. Alfredo Gonzalez, Dr. Katy Pinto, Dr. LaTanya Skiffer, Ken O'Donell, Dr. Michael Spagna, Dr. Thomas Parham, Professor Charles Thomas, and my entire CSUDH Toro Family for the myriad of ways you have supported me in words or deeds. Finally, a big thanks to Dr. Anthony Samad and the Dymally Institute for the collaborations on numerous projects and financial support to memorialize the life and accomplishments of Dr. Claudia H. Hampton.

There are a number of colleagues I wish to thank from my days at CSU Fullerton where I began this research: Dr. Terry Synder, thank you for your generosity in sharing insights into the process for securing grant funding to support my writing. Dr. Craig McConnell and Dr. April Bullock, thank you for creating opportunities for me to share my research with your students, for making me laugh, and for being supportive of my move to CSU Dominguez Hills. Thank you, Dr. Jennifer Yee, for being such an awesome friend and writing partner. I love you to the moon and back. Dr. Jodi Davis, I sometimes forget that our friendship started out as a student-professor relationship that has grown and morphed into one of my most treasured friendships. You are an amazing teacher, mom, and friend. Special thanks to Dr. Natalie Fousekis, Dr. Ben Cawthra, Dr. Alexandro Gradilla, Dr. Leila Zenderland, Dr. Becky Dolhinow, Dr. Renae Bredin, Professor David Christian, the HSS Women of Color Lunch Bunch (Dr. Siobhan Brooks, Dr. Patricia Perez, Dr. Eliza Noh, Dr. Tu-Uyen Nguyen, and Dr. Natalie Graham) and my former professor/mentor, Dr. Art Hansen.

Thank you to my sorors in Sigma Gamma Rho Sorority, Incorporated, in particular, those who have supported my work as an academic—Dr. Deirdre Cooper Owens, Dr. Janelle Edwards, Dr. Charlene Fletcher, Dr. Cherisse Jones-Branch and Dr. Michelle Scott. A special word of thanks to some very special sorors who were always enthusiastically supportive of my academic pursuits—Capt. Tracy Isaac, Karen Kimber, Jennifer Barrios, Tiffany Hampton, Mary Bankhead, Dr. Karen Farber, and the late Tamika Nicole Williams-Clark whom I miss immensely.

I wish to also thank all of my sisters from the Harbor Area (CA) Chapter of The Links, Incorporated. I value our friendship and the support you have shown me. I am especially grateful for my cohort sisters—The Honorable Patricia J. Titus, Dr. Tangelia Gentles, Mechellet Armelin-Martin, Dr. Belinda Daughrity, Krystal Thorp Ricks, Dr. Yvette Drake, soon-to-be Dr. Nicole Butts, Dr. Bernadette Lucas along with my sponsor Dr. Gayle Ball-Parker, and mentor Katessa Charles, Esq.

I had so many people who cheered me on, offered a sounding board, and who gave me advice or simply a kind word. Thank you especially to my former OSU classmates, Dr. Derrick White, and Dr. Jelani Favors, who helped me brainstorm this book over drinks at ASALH in Indianapolis. I am forever grateful for academic friends: Dr. Stefan Bradley, Dr. D-L Stewart, Dr. Timeka Rashid, Dr. April Peters Hawkins, Dr. Jamel Donnor, Dr. Raymond Adams, Dr. Stephanie Evans, Dr. Erica Ball, Dr. Patricia Golay, Dr. Maria Malagon, Dr. Jose Alamillo, Dr. Katherine Chu and Dr. Francile Rusan Wilson. Thank you to the Association of Black Women Historians, the Association for the Study of African American Life and History, and Chair at the Table Research Collective for the support and encouragement. Thanks to my fitness friends who helped provide much stress relief and good times—Mychele Sims, Jazmin Gamble, Jess Jackson, Maya Diep, Jacquelyne Ramirez, and Tammy Wrenn and to my very good friends Melvina Young, Darisa Peguero, and Carol Ramos who sent me side-eye texts when I was procrastinating. Love y'all muchly. I want to thank my students and friends who have been eagerly awaiting the final publication of this book. You all have no idea how much your encouragement has meant to me and spurred me on when I felt tired or wanted to throw in the towel.

Last but certainly not least, I want to thank my husband, life partner, best friend, and my biggest cheerleader, Leonard, who has been my rock and my refuge for nearly two decades. I am eternally grateful to him as he spoke life into me, told me when I needed to get up and work, told me when I needed to lie down and rest, and told me that I had something important to share with the world. Thank you for putting up with me talking incessantly about the book, for not always doing my share of the chores because I have been preoccupied with this project, and, for helping me keep some perspective when things did not always go according to plan. Len, I love you, now and forever.

Abbreviations

ACLU	American Civil Liberties Union
ACR 151	Assembly Concurrent Resolution 151 (1974)
AKA	Alpha Kappa Alpha Sorority, Incorporated
APAAC	Asian Pacific American Advisory Committee
ASALH	Association for the Study of African American Life and History
ASI	Associated Students Incorporated
Bakke	Bakke v. University of California (1978)
BOT	CSU Board of Trustees
BSU	Black Student Union (SFSC)
CCC	California Community Colleges
CCCHE	California Coordinating Council for Higher Education
CDIP	Chancellor's Doctoral Incentive Program
CLBC	California Legislative Black Caucus
CPEC	California Post-Secondary Education Commission (formerly CCCHE)
COBA	Council of Black Administrators
CORE	Congress on Racial Equality
CSC	California State Colleges (name used until 1982)
CSEA	California State Employees Association
CSU	California State University System (name used after 1982) (Note: With the exception of the polytechnic campuses [Pomona, San Luis Obispo, and Humboldt], all remaining campuses are California State Universities which utilize "CSU" plus city/location to indicate its name)
EPC	Educational Policy Committee

EOP	Equal Opportunity Program
FSR	Faculty and Staff Relations Committee
HEW	Department of Housing, Education, and Welfare
HBCU	Historically Black Colleges and Universities
LBUSD	Long Beach Unified School District
LAUSD	Los Angeles Unified School District
LA School Board	Los Angeles Unified School District Board of Education
L.A. State	Nickname for CSU Los Angeles
MALDEF	Mexican American Legal Defense and Education Fund
Master Plan	California Master Plan for Higher Education 1960/1973/1985
NAACP	National Association for the Advancement of Colored People
NAS	National Association of Scholars
NOW	National Organization of Women
PCP	Program Change Proposals
Proposition 9	Jarvis II Tax Initiative (1980)
Proposition 13	Howard Jarvis Tax Initiative (1978)
Proposition 187	Save Our State Initiative (1994)
Proposition 209	California Civil Rights Initiative (1996)
Sac State	Sacramento State College
SCJ	Students' Committee for Justice (CSU Los Angeles)
SDS	Students for a Democratic Society
SEEA	Sex Equity in Education Act (California 1982)
SFSC	San Francisco State College
SFVC	San Fernando Valley College (Now CSU Northridge)
SJSC	San Jose State College
TWLF	Third World Liberation Front
UBSA	United Black Students for Action (San Jose State College)

UC	University of California System
UPC	United Professors of California
WEAL	Women's Equity Action League
YAF	Young Americans for Freedom
YBS	Young Black Scholars Program (100 Black Men of Los Angeles)
YMCA	Young Men's Christian Association

Introduction

A Very Fortunate Happenstance

This book traces the history of affirmative action implementation and enforcement within the California State University (CSU) system to its end in California with the passage of Proposition 209 in 1996. It focuses on the black woman on the CSU board of trustees who fought for twenty years to enforce this positive law and prevent anti-affirmative action forces from eliminating these programs designed to increase access to the university for racial minority groups and women. The idea for this book came from a "very fortunate happenstance"[1] while researching another project on a local grass-roots organization started by my maternal grandmother called the Office for Black Community Development in Watts, California, in 1979. While searching through the CSU Dominguez Hills Digital Photo Archive, I stumbled across a photograph of a black woman standing at a podium in academic regalia at the 1976 commencement ceremony at CSU Dominguez Hills. The name was listed as Trustee Claudia Hampton but what intrigued me most about this photograph was a notation at the bottom of the picture with the words "appointed by Reagan." Having written about Ronald Reagan for my doctoral dissertation on conservative philanthropy used to fund the academic culture wars of the 1990s, I knew that Reagan, when he served as the governor of California, had shown great contempt for the efforts made by African Americans to secure their civil rights. In fact, Reagan was a great admirer of Arkansas Governor Orval Faubus, who was at the center of efforts to block the enforcement of the 1954 Brown versus Board of Education

---

1   "A Very Fortunate Happenstance" is how Claudia Hampton described her career as an educator. Hampton said that due to racism and sexism, she could not secure employment in the sciences, so she took the advice of her father to seek out a job in education, which she later came to love. I use the phrase here to also describe my luck in finding a digital photograph of Hampton, as this discovery led to the publication of this monograph. Claudia Hampton (California State University Trustee), interviewed by Sarah Sharp (Bancroft Library Regional History Office), Los Angeles, California, 1984, transcript, California State University Trustee Archives, Carson, CA.

decision. The two men shared a belief that school desegregation was a state's rights issue. Similarly, Reagan opposed the Civil Rights Act of 1964 and the Voting Rights Act of 1965, claiming the latter was "humiliating to the South."[2] He opposed the 1948 Supreme Court decision to overturn restrictive covenants in housing; signed the Mulford Act, aimed at disarming the Black Panthers, into law; and he condemned antiwar and civil rights activists as the "greatest threat to freedom and civility"—actions demonstrating hostility toward the peace and social justice advocacy work taken up by groups like the NAACP, Students for a Democratic Society, and the Black Panthers, among others. Imagine my surprise then at seeing a black woman being appointed by Reagan for any position within his administration.

Aims and Objectives

After learning that Claudia Hampton was appointed as the first black woman trustee[3] in the California State University (CSU) system in 1974, I searched for anything I could find about her. Fortunately, the CSU Board of Trustees Archives is housed at CSU Dominguez Hills in the Gerth Archives and Special Collections, so I had no trouble accessing those records to begin my search. When I started this research in 2016, I had just become the first woman of color to earn tenure and promotion in the forty-plus-year history of the Women and Gender Studies Department at CSU Fullerton, so Hampton's story as the first black woman trustee really resonated with me. During my search through the materials at CSU Dominguez Hills, which contained CSU Trustee meeting minutes, agendas, special reports, and other records, I found a cassette tape at the bottom of a box that had the notation "Claudia Hampton Interview with Sharon Sharp (1984)." I could not believe my luck—that I could hear Hampton in her own words. Over the next couple of days, I transcribed that six-hour interview, and then I knew that Claudia Hampton's story as the CSU's first black woman trustee had to be told.

I soon realized, however, that my focus on Hampton as being a "first" would obscure the depth and complexity of the individual whom such a designation sought to honor. If I only focused on Hampton being the first black woman trustee, I would be ignoring the institutional politics, federal

---

2   Howell Raines, "Voting Rights Act Signed by Reagan" *New York Times*, June 30, 1982. Accessed January 9, 2023. https://www.nytimes. com/1982/06/30/us/voting-rights-act-signed-by-reagan.html.

3   The first Black trustee was Edward O. Lee, who was appointed to the board by Governor Edmund "Pat" Brown, serving from 1966 to 1974.

and state mandates on affirmative action, and black cultural politics, all of which impacted not only the coalitions she built, but also the votes she cast, and her leadership at critical moments on the board. I would do a disservice in telling her story, which fits within the larger narrative of black women's educational activism. To do this project justice, I had to humble myself in how I approached the archives. After transcribing Hampton's interview, admittedly, however, I walked away from the project for nearly six months, because I had challenges reconciling some of the tactics Hampton used to gain access and power with my own black radical political leaning. I was trained as an educational historian in the black radical tradition. For example, I favored W.E.B. Du Bois's liberal arts approach to black education over Booker T. Washington's promotion of manual arts training as the key to black progress. But two things happened that made me rethink my perspective about Hampton.

First, in preparing a list of readings for my Black Women in America class in 2017, I assigned Carol O. Perkins' article, "The Pragmatic Idealism of Mary McCleod Bethune." The article details how Bethune created her own signature approach to black educational and political progress, which merged Booker T. Washington's pragmatism, through his Tuskegee philosophy, with W.E.B. Du Bois's brand of idealism, through his concept of the Talented Tenth.[4] Bethune used this new approach in her work as an advisor to President Franklin Roosevelt as part of the "Black Cabinet" and also in establishing the Daytona Educational and Industrial Training School for Negro Girls in 1904 (later merging to become Bethune-Cookman College). This article reminds its readers that there is "more than one way to skin a cat," so to speak. Second, while attending a conference session on African Americans and philanthropy at the Association for the Study of African American Life and History (ASALH) annual meeting, one of the panelists explained how the African American development officers in her research used sly civility as their approach in courting white donors for contributions to support historically black colleges and universities (HBCUs). Having read and studied Homi Bhabha's work in my graduate program, I was already familiar with the concept of sly civility; but in being reminded of the term, I became filled with excitement, because I knew I had the language to explain how Claudia Hampton operated as a CSU trustee. I reentered the archive with a new perspective—one that embraced and valued multiple approaches and methods to social justice. I was now ready to delve deeper into the history of the CSU's response to demands for greater access, equity, and inclusion of racial minority and women students, with a focus on the work carried

---

4   Carol O. Perkins, "The Pragmatic Idealism of Mary McCleod Bethune" *Sage* 5, no. 2 (Fall 1988):30.

out by Claudia Hampton to ensure that affirmative action programs were given careful and thorough consideration.

Black Woman on Board offers three main interventions within the field of U.S. educational history. First, this book aims to fill in a critical gap in the literature regarding university trustee efforts to eliminate, narrow, or stall the enforcement of affirmative action, thereby attempting to prevent diverse groups from accessing the hallowed halls of academe in the United States. Since its inception in the 1960s, affirmative action has faced fierce opposition, ultimately leading to the policy's dismantling in California and several other states in the early 1990s. Despite the 1978 Bakke decision, having eliminated racial quotas in university admissions, affirmative action is again being contested with more recent cases being brought before the U.S. Supreme Court. Plaintiffs are attempting to do away with affirmative action in the nation's private, elite universities. Few people outside of academe know of the role of the university trustee board in general and even less about efforts to destroy affirmative action from within the university itself. *Black Woman on Board* attempts to correct this omission in the literature. Second, this book focuses on how Claudia Hampton and her allies stood as a bulwark against efforts to undermine affirmative action and other race-based initiatives in the Cal State system. Sonya Ramsey's biography of Bertha Maxwell-Roddy describes how, like Hampton, black women in the post-desegregation era became modern-day "race women," where black women utilized "multifaceted leadership strategies to dismantle discriminatory barriers in the classroom and the boardroom from the 1970s to the1990s."[5] Ramsey describes this particular set of leadership strategies as "charismatic advocacy" in which Maxwell-Roddy and her contemporaries did whatever was necessary to "keep the doors open to not be the only or last one."[6] Similarly, *Black Woman on Board* examines and extends the conversation around Black women's range of leadership strategies within U.S. educational institutions to include "sly civility" to combat their exclusion from the seats of power and decision-making within American institutions. Post-1970s

---

5   Sonya Y. Ramsey, *Bertha Maxwell Roddy: A Modern Day Race Woman and the Power of Black Leadership* (Gainsville: University Press of Florida, 2022), 3. Bertha Maxwell-Roddy was the first black woman principal of a predominantly white elementary school in Charlotte, North Carolina, who would later join the faculty at the University of North Carolina at Charlotte as the founding director of the university's Black Studies Program. She spearheaded the institutionalization of the National Council for Black Studies. In 1992, Maxwell Roddy became the 20th National President of Delta Sigma Theta Sorority, Incorporated, the largest historically African American sorority in the United States.

6   Ramsey, "Bertha Maxwell Roddy," 5.

Black activism has largely been ignored by historians, yet Hampton's story also fills gaps in U.S. civil rights history which sees the 1970s and 1980s as a period of stagnation, or at the very least simply a postscript to the Civil Rights and Black Power movements. And finally, this book demonstrates the need for African Americans and other ethnic minority groups to embrace the full range of methods for achieving social justice within public higher education, rather than being locked into a single approach. It took the 1960s student protests to press the CSU system to broaden its notion of the public good, where equal educational opportunity meant access and equity for all regardless of their race, gender, or income. But it would take people like Claudia Hampton working on the inside to bring lasting structural change, thus ensuring that the gains made through student agitation and governmental affirmative action mandates did not fall by the wayside. Therefore, social justice activists within higher education need to utilize all the tools at their disposal. By working in tandem toward a common goal, radical activists and liberal insiders can have the greatest impact on structural change within educational institutions.

From the Classroom to the Boardroom: The Educational and Professional Journey of Dr. Claudia Hampton

Born in Mississippi in 1917, Claudia Hampton (nee Hudley) and her family relocated to Chicago, where she attended elementary and secondary school. She cited her parents, General and Gertrude, as her most significant influences in furthering her education beyond high school. She said, "My parents are in large measure responsible for whatever I am today. They both had fairly adequate educations for their time. There wasn't much discussion about it. The assumption was that I would get a college education. And there was never any question about this although this was happening in the midst of that awful, awful depression."[7] Hampton would later attend Central YMCA College in Chicago, where she earned a BS degree in chemistry with a minor in physics and biology in 1935.

Founded in 1922, Central YMCA College was one of the few higher education institutions in Chicago where Blacks, women, Jews, Japanese, and Catholics could earn a degree during the 1930s and 1940s. A Christian, liberal, and democratic institution, Central YMCA College offered all students degrees in arts and sciences, commerce, and musics, "unhampered by

---

7   Hampton, interview.

dogma, superstition, or prejudice."[8] The college closed in 1945, when the board of directors voted to cap the enrollment of Black and Jewish students, in direct contrast to the stated mission of the College. In protest, several faculty members and the former college president, Dr. Edward J. Sparling, resigned and established Roosevelt College (now university). Claudia Hampton graduated a decade prior to the closure of the college, yet she would face similar forms of racial and gender discrimination that Sparling hoped to avoid perpetuating at Roosevelt College, as she tried to find work in the sciences. Reflecting on her post-graduate job hunt, Hampton said, "Can you imagine a black woman graduating from college at 18, which I did, trying to find a job in those fields? No! In those days, there was no hesitancy in saying "We don't hire blacks, we don't hire women" They'd be amazed I'd even bother to apply."[9]

Unable to secure a position as a chemist due to racism and sexism, Hampton took a position in a local welfare office, dispensing benefits to women with families. She remained in that position for about six years until she got married and had a child (a daughter, Kathryn). With childcare becoming an issue in her social work job, as she euphemistically described it, Hampton asked her father if he could help her find a teaching job with a schedule that would be more compatible with her childcare needs. Hampton's father, General Hudley, suggested she approach their local ward captain for possible job leads. From that meeting with the ward captain, Claudia Hudley Hampton's career in education began as "a very peculiar but fortunate happenstance."[10]

Hampton worked as a Chicago elementary school teacher for a number of years and did some quasi-administrative work outside of the classroom. In the early 1960s her husband, a fellow teacher, moved the family to Los Angeles, where he was offered a position as a school principal. Hampton continued teaching elementary school, working mostly with Hispanic[11] children in East Los Angeles until her husband introduced her to the Los Angeles Unified School District (henceforth "LAUSD") deputy superintendent. This led to a meeting with the district superintendent, who had heard about her teaching performance in East Los Angeles, working with a large

---

8   Central YMCA College Board of Directors. "Spirit of the College." N.p.: n.p., 1942. Print. Roosevelt University Archives.

9   Hampton, interview.

10   Hampton, interview.

11   The term "Hispanic" refers to a Spanish-speaking person living in the United States, especially one of Latin American descent. Hispanic has been used by government agencies like the U.S. Census as a catch-all term referring to all Spanish-speakers from Latin America regardless of their race or country of origin.

population of children who could not speak English. This in turn led to her appointment in the Child Welfare and Attendance Office, where she directed the district's Compensatory Education program mandated through the federal Elementary and Secondary Education Act of 1965. Compensatory education was part of President Johnson's War on Poverty[12] programming, with a push to require all children aged five through seventeen to receive supplemental instruction in reading, writing, and speaking. Hampton was responsible for the oversight of the federal grants provided by the legislation.

For several years African American teachers and administrators regularly complained about racial discrimination in hiring, funding, and other person-nel-related matters in Los Angeles Unified School District (LAUSD) to the Los Angeles County Board of Education (henceforth Board of Education), which monitored and supervised LAUSD.[13] To address these concerns, The Board of Education mandated LAUSD to create an Office of Urban Affairs in 1963 which would monitor the district's progress in addressing these inequities among LAUSD faculty and staff. Seven years later, in 1970, Los Angeles Superior Court Judge Alfred Gilteson ruled that the district had operated segregated schools and gave the initial desegregation orders with regard to racial and ethnic percentages. On appeal, the California State Supreme Court, while disagreeing with the initial ruling that the district had engaged in de jure segregation, concluded that LAUSD was still required to take steps to alleviate the harms of segregation, arguing that the district needed to look beyond racial/ethnic numbers and look at the overall harms caused by racial isolation. Judge Paul Egly of the California Superior Court identified a list of such harms for which the district would be required to create eradication methods. These harms included: (1) low academic achieve-ment, (2) low self-esteem, (3) lack of access to postsecondary opportunities, and (4) interracial hostility and intolerance.[14]

To address parent, student, and community concerns about racial dis-crimination and segregation, Claudia Hampton was appointed director of

---

12 Johnson's War on Poverty refers to legislation introduced during President Lyndon Johnson's State of the Union address in 1964 in response to the national poverty rate of nineteen percent. The U.S. Congress, in turn, passed the Economic Opportunity Act which established over forty programs to aim at eliminating poverty with a large bulk of the programming addressing educa-tional and health care disparities based on socio-economic factors.

13 Owen Knox, "History of the Council of Black Administrators: Los Angeles Unified School District" http://www.lausd.k12.ca.us/orgs/coba/History.html.

14 Los Angeles Unified School District. "District's Court Ordered Integration Programs" http://achieve.lausd.net/cms/lib08/CA01000043/Centricity/Domain/263/Student%20Integration%20Services%20Programs.pdf.

the newly formed Schools and Community Relations Unit for the Office of Urban Affairs in 1968. This office was set up after the 1965 Watts Rebellion and was developed from the McCone Commission's recommendations, a 101-page report commissioned by Governor Pat Brown and headed by former CIA director John McCone. The commission was established to investigate the causes of the rebellion and make recommendations to prevent future urban unrest. Released to the public on December 2, 1965, the report cited high unemployment, poor schools, and inadequate housing as the root causes for the riot. The creation of the Schools and Community Relations Unit was one of the few McCone Commission recommendations ever implemented. However, had it not been for the agitation of Black teachers and administrators about the discriminatory hiring practices within the district, the low academic performance of Black children, and the unequal distribution of resources throughout the district, the Los Angeles County Board of Education would not have mandated the establishment of Hampton's unit.

This group of Black teachers and administrators began meeting in the early 1960s and formed the Council of Black Administrators (COBA) to serve as a unified voice for Black students and staff in LAUSD. Claudia Hampton was a member of this newly formed organization. Frustrated by the district's inaction to develop a concrete plan of action to address segregation and Black student underperformance, Frederick Dumas, the first president of COBA and a LAUSD elementary school principal, made a presentation on August 18, 1968 before the Board of Education, stating "We intend to take positions on those issues that affect the education of Black children or the services of Black personnel and hope that this may be done within the framework of the institution."[15] District officials were now put on notice that COBA members would be monitoring the district's progress on implementing desegregation orders and providing resources equitably. Without COBA, Black parents and other parents of color would not have had a vehicle to adequately address their children's education concerns. Implementation of the McCone Commission's recommendation to create the Schools and Community Relations Unit was made possible by the agitation of Blacks already experiencing racial discrimination within the district. Therefore the district should not be lauded for creating the School and Community Relations Unit. As Claudia Hampton pointed out, there had been "some allegations that the district was isolated. There was no

---

15   Frederick J. Dumas. Presentation of the Council of Black Administrators.
      1968. Box 421. Board Reports. Los Angeles Unified School District Board
      of Education Records, 1875–2012, Charles Young Research Library, Los
      Angeles, California.

community input. There was no community involvement, and so on. So this office was set up in response to that."[16]

The primary goal of the unit was to assure the district that high-level staff would always have a handle on what the community was thinking regarding education and other related concerns. But this unit's charge went beyond simple information gathering, as Claudia Hampton pointed out: "Whether there was unrest or disruptions or some problem that related to the community, the staff would go out and ameliorate. We had a global charge to go out and do community things but within that context, we were pretty much able to develop our own procedures, practices, and staff activities. We had degrees of freedom that no other unit in the district had."[17] The latitude given to Hampton and her unit gave her the opportunity to develop and hone her leadership skills according to what she thought was best to meet the needs of both district and community.

Hiring and supervising unit staff was one of Hampton's primary responsibilities, and she had the freedom to select staff who demonstrated the ability to relate to the people, based on their knowledge of the community and its resources. These staff members regularly visited school sites to monitor the district's implementation of federal compensatory education regulations and report back to Hampton. She would then attend a standing weekly appointment with the district superintendent. During this meeting, she would brief him and his staff on the progress of the district's compensatory education efforts and would alert the superintendent's office to any potential public relations crises for the district. For example, Hampton says, "I had the responsibility of furnishing to the superintendent, at every first Monday of the month meeting, what the NAACP was jumping up and down about this week: what problems exist in East LA?"[18] Hampton was eventually given the authority to negotiate between minority parents, community groups, and sometimes hostile school principals who did not take kindly to the district sending Hampton and her team of community liaisons to intervene on issues related to desegregation and other race-based concerns on campus. For example, if a principal refused to work with a school advisory council, which was a mandatory component of the compensatory education program, Hampton's unit not only took the complaint but also would ensure that the advisory board was functioning with the cooperation of the principal, who could be written up for insubordination. Being granted this authority to intervene when school site crises arose was particularly important to the specific community for which Hampton's unit was established.

---

16   Hampton, interview.
17   Hampton, interview.
18   Hampton, interview.

As Hampton noted in a 1984 interview, it was the poor minority community served by Los Angeles Unified School District that relied most heavily on her unit for assistance: "The more affluent, even the more affluent black communities, had other ways of dealing with their concerns. They knew very well how you handle a recalcitrant school principal. Most of our work was with the less articulate, the hopeless, the people who didn't know where to go for alleviation."[19] Even after a federal judge ruled that the school district had engaged in de jure segregation and needed to take steps to alleviate the effects of segregation, this ruling could not overcome the sad reality that Los Angeles became even more racially and economically segregated after the Watts Rebellion. The de facto segregation of Los Angeles neighborhoods remained constant and was actually exacerbated by middle-class Black flight from urban ghettos. This segregation pressured the school district to implement an integration plan, even though the city was sharply divided into racial and ethnic enclaves. Claudia Hampton noted how residential segregation doomed district's compensatory education goals from the outset, saying, "I have always said if all of the energy that went into integration went into fair housing, we probably would have never had some of these problems. I don't have data to substantiate this but just by gross observation, I suspect segregation was on the increase."[20]

Hampton's observation about the rise of segregation in Los Angeles in the late 1960s and early 1970s was indeed accurate. White flight from American cities to the suburbs began in earnest during the 1950s, and in California, specifically, this movement of white people from the metropolis was hastened by the Second Great Migration of African Americans out of the American South to locations west of the Mississippi River; this included returning African American soldiers from World War II, who could find auto and defense industry jobs in Los Angeles. However, while white flight contributed to increased segregation, actions taken by the Los Angeles School Board, the seven-member council with oversight responsibility for Los Angeles Unified School District, did not make Hampton's work any easier. In fact, the school board openly rejected Judge Gileston's findings about the district's history of racial segregation and immediately filed an appeal. According to Hampton, "Now at the time we had a very conservative school board. So, I would not accuse them of deliberately increasing this [segregation] but I certainly would not give them credit for giving any attention to that matter. And I am sure at the time, there was some differentiation in terms of services and materials between the two communities [black and

---

19 Hampton, interview.
20 Hampton, interview.

white]. I am certain of that. So the decision [by Judge Gileston] really comes as a shock to a board that was unwilling or unable to accept it."[21]

Not surprisingly, given the school board's unwillingness to address the resource inequities based on race and socioeconomic differences within the district, many white school principals who worked in schools with a sizable racial minority student population felt anxious when Hampton or members of her staff arrived on their campuses. Hampton says such anxiety about potentially having their schools and personnel reported to district officials gave the Schools and Community Relations Office a notorious reputation for being overbearing watchdogs or tattle tales. She explains the main concerns this way, "Sometimes we were quite controversial because sometimes a community concern was a valid concern and that had to be reported. So frequently, when the administrators saw us coming, they thought "Oh God, here comes the CIA."[22] Yet, while school officials felt anxiety about the presence of Hampton's unit on their campuses, civil rights organizations like the NAACP and the ACLU continued to view the district's central office with a fair bit of distrust, even with the creation of Hampton's unit. In 1963 these groups had previously brought a class action suit against the district for refusing to desegregate two district schools, and spent the next five years in unsuccessful negotiations to reach a deal on a comprehensive desegregation plan for all schools, leading to Judge Gileston's ruling charging the district with de jure segregation.

While serving as the Office of School and Community Relations director, Hampton attended the University of Southern California, earning a doctoral degree in education in 1970. Her doctoral thesis, "The effects of school desegregation on the scholastic achievement of relatively advantaged Negro children" utilized her work in school desegregation as both a teacher and an academic administrator. When Hampton retired at the age of 64 from the Los Angeles Unified School District in 1981, she continued teaching education methods courses to pre-service schoolteachers at Pepperdine University.

Prior to retirement, and even more so following her retirement, Hampton was very involved in civic and community groups, most notably with her involvement with the Los Angeles chapter of the National Association for the Advancement of Colored People (NAACP), where she lent her expertise on educational issues facing African American children in the Los Angeles area. In fact, her educational activism on the CSU Board of Trustees was shaped, in part, by her professional and volunteer work around Black education

---

21 California State University Los Angeles Special Collections Archive Blog "A Look Back at School Desegregation and Busing in Los Angeles," February 27, 2018.

22 Hampton, interview.

throughout Los Angeles. Hampton was a founding member and director of Women on Target, a Black woman-led political and educational advocacy organization that worked to help elect Black officials, most notably Mayor Tom Bradley, and held fundraisers to support Los Angeles Public Schools. She also held several board appointments, including the Charles Drew University Scholarship Loan Fund Board, the Los Angeles City Human Relations Commission, and the Los Angeles Police Commissioners' Review Steering Committee. Hampton was elected Director of the Los Angeles Chapter of the Young Women's Christian Association (YWCA) and was a life member of the National Council of Negro Women (NCNW). In 1975, she was initiated into Alpha Kappa Alpha (AKA) Sorority, Incorporated through the Theta Mu Omega Chapter located in Inglewood, California. Within AKA, Hampton served on her local chapter's social action committee, where she helped arrange a forum and reception with then-LAUSD Superintendent Dr. William Johnston and 150 sorority members to discuss current trends and issues in education.

As a result of her work in LAUSD, specifically dealing with sensitive race matters in providing educational access to under-represented groups, as well as her involvement in the Black Los Angeles community, Hampton had a tremendous amount of practical experience to draw on when she encountered challenges while serving as a CSU trustee. This ability to balance competing interests would serve Hampton well as she transitioned from her work in Los Angeles schools to the California State University Board of Trustees later in her professional career.

Black Women's Educational Activism in California

California passed civil rights legislation before any other state; however, white Californians' embrace of a civil rights agenda was short-lived because, as Lisa McGirr notes in *Suburban Warriors*, "the majority of Californians would only tolerate so much liberalism."[23] With the influx of African Americans and other non-white groups into the state with the Second Great Migration from the 1940s through the 1970s, a more conservative approach to civil rights emerged when the state's white majority became increasingly concerned that an aggressive racial minority was usurping their rights. For example, Republican gubernatorial candidate Ronald Reagan opposed the 1963 Rumsford Housing Act, a bill that was designed to end racial discrimination by landlords and property owners who refused to rent or sell property

---

23   Lisa McGirr, *Suburban Warriors: The Origins of the New American Right* (Princeton: Princeton University Press, 2001), 14.

to Black people in the state. In effect, the bill was created to force the state to abide by the Shelley v. Kraemer decision (1948), the landmark U.S. Supreme Court ruling that declared racially restrictive covenants unconstitutional and outlawed their further enforcement, though the practice continued unabated. When Reagan went on the campaign trail in 1964, he claimed that the Rumsford Act violated personal liberty: "I have never believed that majority rule has the right to impose on an individual as to what he does with his property. This has nothing to do with discrimination. . . . It has to do with our freedoms, our basic freedom."[24] Conservatives in the state agreed with Reagan, and the California Real Estate Association used Reagan's comments to drum up support for Proposition 14 (1964), which sought to nullify the Rumsford Act. (Proposition 14 did pass but was ultimately ruled unconstitutional by SCOTUS in 1968.) The furor over the Rumsford Act is just one of many examples where white Californians took the position that Blacks were pushing too hard to enact civil rights legislation, which, in their view, essentially amounted to reverse discrimination. A national Harris poll taken in 1966 found that the number of whites in California who believed that Blacks tried to "move too fast" in pressing for civil rights grew from thirty-four percent in 1964 to eighty-five percent in 1966.[25]

By the 1970s, a vociferous conservative backlash against affirmative action and other civil rights legislation began to emerge in California that would remain strong until the passage of Proposition 187, which prohibited undocumented immigrants from utilizing state services in 1994, and Proposition 209 in 1996, which prohibited the consideration of race, sex or ethnicity in public employment and university admission. This backlash was prompted by a turn toward conservatism in California that was meant to defend "Christianity, family, whiteness, capitalism and tradition," according to historian Jeff Roche.[26] On the other hand, the backlash also galvanized Black women in California into action to protect those hard-fought civil rights victories in housing, poverty alleviation, and welfare reform, and particularly in education.

Black women did not accept a second-class status when it came to the education of Black youth. They mobilized within community-based organizations to organize alternative educational delivery models, lobbied at the

24 Rick Perlstein, *Nixonland: The Rise of a President and the Fracturing of America* (New York: Scribner, 2008), 91.

25 Matthew Dallek, *The Right Moment: Ronald Reagan's First Victory and the Decisive Turning Point in the American Politics* (New York: The Free Press, 2001), 128.

26 Jeff Roche, "Cowboy Conservatism," in *The Conservative Sixties*, eds. David Farber and Jeff Roche (New York, Peter Lang, 2003), 85.

state capital, and filed lawsuits to protect affirmative action. They were met with resistance at seemingly every turn, but this fight was too important for them to give up, so they used a variety of approaches, methods, and programs and adapted to the changing political landscape, which became more hostile to civil rights and affirmative action. It is within this social and political environment that Claudia Hampton became active in California's educational politics, first through her work helping to enforce desegregation orders for Los Angeles Unified School District and through her appointment as the first African American woman trustee on the California State University Board of Trustees in 1974. Hampton's professional work as the Director of School and Community Relations for LAUSD, her volunteer work on the Education Committee for the Los Angeles Chapter of the NAACP, and her twenty-year tenure as the "Affirmative Action Trustee" within the CSU Board of Trustees is part of a long tradition of educational activism by Black women in nineteenth and twentieth century American history.[27] Black women in California were particularly active at the state and local level in holding public education officials and politicians accountable for delivering on the promise of equal educational opportunities for African American children and youth in the post-Civil Rights era. Yet much of this history has been absent from the historical record. *Black Woman on Board* corrects this oversight by centering Claudia Hampton's story, as it provides insight into how race and gender operate in the exercise of university trustee power. However, to fully understand the impact of Claudia Hampton's trustee work, one must understand the political and social context in which she had to operate and maneuver. We can do this by examining the educational activist work of other Black women in California who were Hampton's contemporaries working toward the same goal: to provide access to equal and quality education to Black and other under-represented groups across the state.

Much of the educational activism by Black women in California was carried out through Black women's community work within local and regional chapters of national civil rights and Black nationalist organizations, or grassroots civil rights and legal advocacy groups started and run by Black women. Within these types of community-based organizations, Black women developed their own voices, becoming community leaders in their own right, inspiring what Mary Belenky, Lynne Bond, and Jacqueline Weinstock call the concept of "developmental leadership."[28] In their artic-

---

27   Stephanie Y. Evans, *Black Women in the Ivory Tower, 1850–1954: An Intellectual History* (Gainesville: University Press of Florida, 2008).

28   Mary Field Belenky, Lynne A. Bond and Jacqueline S. Weinstock, *A Tradition That Has No Name: Nurturing the Development of People, Families and*

ulation of developmental leadership, Belenky and others describe this as a process by which "people help each other move out of silence, claim the power of their minds, exercise their leadership and come to have a real say in the way their lives, families and communities are being run."[29] While Belenky, Bond, and Weinstock maintain that this form of leadership enables all women, regardless of race and socioeconomic background, to find their voice to work for change in their communities, these authors do acknowledge that Black women had been doing this community work as "a tradition that has no name" since emancipation, providing the blueprint for other groups of women to model their work. Black women engaged in this type of community work to nurture and care for their families, communities, and themselves. As a result, they developed a race- and gender-informed style of politics and community development that focused on mobilizing the community for political action. At every level of education in California, Black women led the charge to ensure that Black children and young adults had access to a quality education through philosophical and organizational approaches to educational activism in California that was varied and multifaceted. Some utilized an approach to Black educational civil rights that focused on taking their concerns directly to school board officials, as was the case with Virna Canson, the Director of the West Coast Office of the National Association for the Advancement of Colored People. Others, like the directors of the Black Panther Party's Oakland Community School, Ericka Huggins and Elaine Brown, opted to circumvent the public school system and give the community more direct control and input into their children's education. Still others, like Eva Paterson of the California Civil Rights Coalition, used the courts to protect affirmative action in California public higher education.

Black women's role in the fight to protect and extend educational opportunities for Black children and young adults after Brown has largely been obscured in both history and education texts. The focus of the historiography of that period tends to emphasize Black radicalism through the Black Power Movement. As Black radicalism became the dominant political and social ideology within the Black community in the early 1970s, we hear even less about those women who are working to change the system from within. Changing an institution from within is a slow-moving project that involves challenging preconceived beliefs, values, and social norms, often taking several decades to achieve a modicum of success before an actual policy/ procedure is changed. Institutional racism further slows down this process of change as racially embedded beliefs or assumptions prevent institutional

---

Communities* (New York, Basic Books, 1999).
29   Belenky, Bond, and Weinstock, *Tradition That Has No Name*, 4.

agents from making policy changes that benefits all groups. Institutional change, particularly around issues of racial equity and inclusion, is not "sexy" work and it doesn't always capture and hold the public's attention like televised news conferences involving Black Panther Party members holding guns while making demands of the police and other government officials. Even the educational activist work of Black women within Black radical circles has been left out of the discourse, as sexism is another factor in why we know so little about Black women's educational activism in California and across the nation. *Black Woman on Board* aims to give voice to the work of Black women educational activists like Claudia Hampton in the immediate post-Civil Rights era.

Hampton and Racial Uplift Ideology

Hampton was a champion for Black students, but her pro-Black stance should not be confused with black radicalism. Unlike her black radical contemporaries, such as Ericka Huggins and Elaine Brown, Hampton was an upper-middle-class Black woman working in a highly visible and influential position within LAUSD and as a CSU trustee. In fact, Hampton was a long-time resident of the View Park section of Los Angeles, one of the wealthiest African American neighborhoods in the United States. She earned her bachelor's degree in chemistry from YMCA College in Chicago and later earned both a master's degree and a doctorate in education from the University of Southern California. She was active in her sorority and regularly appeared in the society pages of the Los Angeles Sentinel newspaper either as a featured guest speaker or as a guest at a wedding of prominent African Americans in the city.

By any social indicator, Hampton belonged to the African American elite in Los Angeles. Therefore one would not be wrong in suggesting that Hampton subscribed to a belief in what historian Kevin Gaines describes as "racial-uplift ideology"[30] or the belief that educated, elite Blacks had a duty and responsibility for the majority of African Americans. Racial-uplift ideology emerged after the end of slavery, with African Americans' pursuit of full citizenship, education, and economic independence being met with

---

30　Kevin Gaines, "Racial Ideology in the Era of the "Negro Problem," *Freedom's Story*, TeacherServe, National Humanities Center. Accessed 6/17/2022: http://nationalhumanitiescenter.org/tserve/freedom/1865–1917/essays/racialuplift.htm. For a more complete discussion of "racial uplift ideology," see Kevin K. Gaines, *Uplifting the Race: Black Leadership, Politics and Culture during the Twentieth Century* (Chapel Hill, N.C.: University of North Carolina Press, 2nd ed., 1996).

stiff and often violent resistance from white people in power. Wealthy, elite white people were determined to control African American labor even if that meant banding together with poor whites under a new system of "racial caste" whereby whiteness, not social class, became that which united these seemingly disparate groups to prevent African Americans from gaining their full freedom and exercising their constitutionally protected civil rights. A new racist system of Jim Crow, which enforced the complete separation of black and white in nearly all areas of public life, including schools and the workplace, was established, and codified into law. Anti-Black racism and white supremacy were the two ideologies working in tandem to justify this new system of racial segregation. Anti-Black racism held that Black people were mentally, morally, and physically unfit for citizenship because they were lazy, sexually lascivious, and unintelligent. White supremacy, or the belief in white people's moral and intellectual superiority, was defended with claims of Black inferiority. To counter these claims of Black inferiority and negative stereotypes about Black behavior, Black leaders emphasized class differences amongst Black people in which elite Blacks would police and "reform the character and manage the behavior of the black masses."[31] Fast forward to the 1970s, and despite the gains of the Civil Rights Movement and the radical shift toward Black radicalism, influential Black leaders like Hampton continued to emphasize respectability as the means by which Black people could gain access to educational and employment opportunities normally shut off to them because of their race.

Some African Americans leaders responded to white backlash against the gains of the Civil Rights Movement with a new form of black political power that emphasized increasing Black representation in the public sphere to help ensure that African Americans would benefit from the policies they worked so hard to secure during the Civil Rights Movement. In California, specifically, we see a marked increase in the number of Black elected officials by 1980, including Los Angeles Mayor Tom Bradley, Assemblyman Willie Brown, and Lieutenant Governor Mervyn Dymally as well as a host of African American mayors, city council officials, and school board members. As a collective, Black people even embraced a new group label during the 1980s, African American, to signal both a historical and cultural base (African) and a desire to be fully accepted as citizens of the place they now call home (American). To manifest this goal of being included as Americans, albeit with a hyphen, Black elected officials moved away from the Black radical thought of the 1960s and embraced a form of Black pragmatism that embraced electoral politics as the key to Black progress. Claudia Hampton worked and socialized in the same social circles as many of these Black elected officials, so it

---

31   Gaines, "Racial Ideology."

should come as no surprise that she embraced a similar political outlook, even as she took steps to help other racial and ethnic minority groups within the CSU system when the opportunities presented themselves.

To fully understand and appreciate how Claudia Hampton operated in a social environment dominated by wealthy, conservative white men on the California State University (CSU) Board of Trustees, one must be cognizant of the racial and gender norms of this time period. A Black woman's performance of the accepted racial and gender scripts of the era should not be read as an automatic accommodation and acquiescence to white male power. As the *Black Woman on Board*, Hampton was acutely aware of the structure of white racism, which not only pits minority groups against one another but also demands that those tokenized insiders make politically expedient choices for one's survival. Considering the social and cultural environment in which Hampton performed these scripts, where both gender and race were viewed as handicaps to her effectiveness on the board, we might reframe our understanding of her actions from a type of "politics of accommodation" to what postcolonial theorist Homi Bhabha refers to as "sly civility."

Sly Civility and Respectability as Resistance

Sly civility refers to a covert form of resistance in which the colonized deliberately sets out to undermine the authority of the colonizer in such a way that the colonizer is not aware their subordinate has deceived them. In *Location of Culture,* Bhabha provides an analysis of how Western culture is imposed on non-Western (Third World) cultures and societies, creating new categories by which the latter group is redefined in relation to the former. "What is theoretically innovative, and politically crucial, is the need to think beyond narratives of originary and initial subjectivities and to focus on those moments or processes that are produced in the articulation of cultural differences."[32] Thus it is the oppressed Third World subject who develops forms of survival and resistance through what Homi Bhabha describes as hybridity, mimicry, and sly civility.

British colonization of India is a prime example of how Indians are redefined as Third World in their own homeland and subject to British laws and social codes, creating a form of hybridity where the Indian is shaped by both Western (British) and Third World (Indian) cultural values. While Bhabha clearly argues that Western values shape colonial subjects, he also maintains that those same colonized groups can resist the imposition of these values

---

32   Homi Bhabha, *The Location of Culture* (London, Routledge, 1994), 1.

through "The native's refusal to satisfy the colonizer's narrative demand."[33] In other words, the colonizer's imposition of race, gender, class, and sexuality scripts that are at the heart of the colonizer's narrative demand can be subverted with careful planning by subordinated groups who engage in various forms of resistance through "sly civility." The resistance must be strategic, politically, and socially savvy and able to build alliances with individuals and groups with whom you may not have much in common. Furthermore, given the colonizer's penchant for resorting to physical or psychological violence to retain and increase power, the colonized can deploy sly civility as a means of undermining the colonizer's dominance, which eats away at the psyche and self-esteem of the colonized, all while maintaining a facade of civility. The concept of "sly civility" underscores the ability to withstand the psychological warfare imposed by the colonizer.

U.S. women of color face similar struggles against racism, sexism, and class exploitation against Western values and white supremacy as do Indian and other "third-world women" outside of the United States. Chandra Mohanty says that the "third world is defined through geographical location and particular sociohistorical conjunctures. It thus incorporates so-called minority peoples or people of color in the U.S.A."[34] This shared struggle also means that women of color in the United States can use some of the same tools that their third-world women counterparts use to resist, including sly civility. Specifically, sly civility as a concept holds that if colonized or otherwise oppressed people can gain some access within the power centers of Western society, they can deceive those granting them access by pretending to be civil, to change the system from within. The goal is to strategically plan to infiltrate and open these centers of power from within, so that more oppressed people can benefit from the opportunities and resources provided by this system. All actions undertaken by someone engaged in sly civility are meant to give the pretense of civility while slyly undermining the authority and dominance of the colonizer. An interview where Hampton specifically acknowledges and names how she played the "game of boardsmanship" is the most obvious indication of her using sly civility. Claudia Hampton was acutely aware that as a Black woman she must tread lightly in her handling of race or gender issues, so she opted to save and utilize her race or gender capital for those moments when she needed to have very difficult conversations on important issues with her peers on the board. She was willing to use respectability politics to perform sly civility if it meant more diverse groups of people could reap the benefits of an education or employment within the

---

33 Bhabha, *Location of Culture*, 99.
34 Chandra Mohanty, *Third World Women and the Politics of Feminism*. (Bloomington: Indiana University Press, 1991), 2.

California State University system. Drawing on her vast experience working with conservative school board members and district officials, uncooperative school principals, local civil rights groups, and parents in LAUSD, Hampton was able to successfully enact sly civility in approaching her work on the CSU board of trustees.

Evelyn Higginbotham first coined the term "politics of respectability" to describe the community work of African American women involved with the Black Baptist Church during the Progressive Era.[35] Specifically, the "politics of respectability" refers to the promotion of temperance, sexual purity, polite manners, cleanliness, and thrift as behaviors that "enabled Black women to counter racist images and structures." However, Higginbotham also points out that Black Baptist women "condemned what they perceived to be negative practices and attitudes among their own people." Thus their promotion of respectability was aimed at "correcting" bad Black behavior whereby "their assimilationist leanings led to their insistence upon blacks" conformity to the dominant society's norms of manners and morals."[36] Upper-class African American women tended to be the biggest promoters of respectability even as they were also judged by it.

More recently, scholars like Brittney Cooper and Kali Gross have argued that while respectability may have been able to undermine prevailing pseudo-scientific notions of Black inferiority, it did not completely eradicate cultural and social racism.[37] Furthermore, many of these scholars argue that respectability politics has worked to reinforce sharp class distinctions within the African American community. The contemporary critique of respectability politics as a conservative form of resistance sees it as limiting and antithetical to African American progress. The critique holds that respectability politics does indeed promote the notion that only certain types of African Americans are worthy of full humanity. However, respectability politics should not be easily dismissed, since the performance of respectability helps make sly civility an effective counter to discrimination and exclusion in predominantly white male spaces. Claudia Hampton engaged in various forms of respectability

---

35   Evelyn Brooks Higginbotham, *Righteous Discontent: The Women's Movement in the Black Baptist Church, 1880–1920* (Cambridge, MA: Harvard University Press, 1993), 187.

36   Higginbotham, *"Righteous Discontent,"* 187.

37   For a discussion about the negative implications of Black people engaging in respectability politics, see the work of Brittney Cooper, *Beyond Respectability: The Intellectual Thought of Race Women* (Champaign: University of Illinois Press, 2017) and Kali N. Gross, "Examining the Politics of Respectability in African American Studies" *Benchmark Almanac* April 1, 1997, 43, no. 28. Accessed 6/17/2022 https://almanac.upenn.edu/archive/v43/n28/benchmrk.html.

politics by presenting herself as wholly acceptable and "safe" in the public spaces she shared with white people, while working to advance a pro-affirmative action agenda. She comported herself as a respectable lady using polite manners and wearing clean and modest dress, and voiced a type of moderate political stance on many of the issues confronting the CSU trustees. Yet despite having ascended to positions of influence and power within two educational systems, Claudia Hampton never criticized the poor. In fact, prior to her appointment to the CSU board of trustees, she worked almost exclusively with poor and working-class Black and other non-white families seeking better education opportunities for their children in Los Angeles area public schools. Additionally, according to Herb Carter, "She [Hampton] was always concerned about people who didn't have much money, so this campus [Dominguez Hills] became her favorite because it had the most people of color and low-income students in the system."[38] Hampton made use of respectability politics as a means to an end. Based on her success in securing access and resources for under-represented faculty, staff, and students in the California State University system, we cannot wholly discount respectability politics as an effective form of resistance.

Book Organization

Chapter 1, "Shifting Notions of the Public Good," explores the postwar political, cultural, and demographic changes in California, which spawned the rapid expansion of the CSU system but also saw the rise in a new type of student activism, giving voice to students who had been historically excluded from higher education. Refusing to abide by the societal expectation that women and people of color must suffer racism, prejudice, and marginalization in silence, these students used their collective voices to express their displeasure at campus policies that excluded them from campus activities or ignored their claims of discrimination in and out of the classroom. Unprepared to handle these sociocultural shifts, the CSU trustees initially responded to student claims of discrimination by denying such problems existed, and therefore the CSU system had no specific policies or procedures to address these allegations until the early 1970s. By the late 1960s, however, when Black students at San Jose State College ramped up the pressure on campus administrators to deal with several claims of racial discrimination in housing, Greek Life, and athletics, the CSU trustees could no longer ignore this new sociocultural reality on campus.

---

38   Herbert Carter interviewed by Donna J. Nicol, 2018.

While California is often held up as a model for progressive educational policies, much of that can be traced back to student activism and agitation while confronting conservative university officials, namely the trustees. The CSU trustees spent much of their time concerning themselves with the public relations fallout from the campus protests, often ignoring the conditions which led to student discontent in the first place. So instead of hearing from student activists or giving campus leaders the tools needed to quell campus conflicts, such as a systemwide nondiscrimination policy, some of the more hard-liner trustees demanded suspensions and other forms of punishment against these students and the faculty who supported them. CSU trustees responded with increased authoritarianism, for example, when dealing with the conflict over the establishment of the nation's first Black Studies program at San Francisco State College that resulted in the longest student-led strike in U.S. history. Ultimately, these student activists were able to reframe and shape the public's perception of higher education as a public good that should prioritize extending access and opportunities to students from all racial and sociocultural backgrounds, not just for a select few.

While student activists at the various CSU campuses experienced some successes in getting their demands met, the trustees and the Chancellor's Office continued to express their disapproval of the tactics used by protestors. Governor Reagan, who was an ex-officio member of the CSU trustee board, used his veto power to cut funding for the state's Equal Opportunity Program (henceforth "EOP") following the San Francisco State strike in 1969.

Chapter 2, "Misgivings about Affirmative Action," examines the efforts by various segments of both the CSU system and state government that worked against implementing and enforcing federal and state affirmative action laws. In 1965, President Lyndon Johnson signed Executive Order 11246 into law, which prohibited employment discrimination based on race, color, religion, and national origin in public institutions and also required federal contractors (including educational institutions receiving federal student aid) to take affirmative action to promote equal opportunities for women and racial/ethnic minorities. Sex was added as a protected class to the provision in 1967. The Office of Civil Rights within the Department of Health, Education, and Welfare (HEW) was responsible for oversight in the enforcement of this executive order, but many public colleges and universities were left to their own devices as to how to implement this order until a group of feminist organizations pressed HEW to develop specific guidelines for public higher education institutions.

Until those new guidelines were issued, individual CSU campuses enacted their own affirmative action programs, because the CSU trustees were led to believe that the system was already in compliance with federal law. The problem with this assumption is two-fold. First, the CSU never developed a systemwide nondiscrimination policy. Instead, since the system came under the supervision of the state board of education prior to 1960, the general counsel for the Chancellor's Office erroneously concluded that the state board of education's nondiscrimination policy had carried over and automatically protected the CSU. Second, as the new guidelines for the implementation of Executive Order 11246 were released in 1972, many colleges and universities including those in the California State University system, realized that nondiscrimination and affirmative action were two separate policies with completely different aims and objectives.

With neither policy in place, then CSU Chancellor Glenn Dumke hired the system's first affirmative action officer in Herbert (Herb) Carter, in 1974 to help the CSU develop a plan to comply with these orders. On the same day that Herbert Carter was formally introduced to the trustees, Claudia Hampton was sworn in as the system's first African American woman trustee. Carter and Hampton were well acquainted with each other as Hampton served on the board of directors for the Los Angeles Human Relations Committee during Carter's six-year tenure as the director of that unit. This established familiarity with one another made it easy for Carter to rely on Hampton to use her exceptional relationship-building skills to help Carter secure approval for the CSU's proposed employee affirmative action plan. Yet despite having a federal mandate to implement and enforce affirmative action, some campus presidents, trustees, and staff at the CSU Chancellor's Office expressed their disdain for these new policies. Only when individual CSU campuses were awarded federal grant monies to increase the enrollment of low-income and/or racially underrepresented students did these more conservative trustees begin to warm to the idea of affirmative action. Eventually, it would take a legislative mandate concerning student affirmative action, passed by the California Legislature in 1974, for the majority of the board to come around and accept affirmative action as the law, and not simply a recommendation. Approval of the verbiage for the CSU's affirmative action policy was relatively simple; the bigger challenge was in securing funding, which was made more challenging by the conservative fiscal policies of Governor Jerry Brown ahead of the national 1980s economic downturn.

Chapter 3, "The Conciliator Makes Dinner," provides an analysis of how Claudia Hampton used her charm, relationship-building skills, and superior social intelligence to garner the trust and respect of her peers, which she, in turn, used to influence and shape board policy regarding affirmative action programs and procedures. Hampton's approach to "boardsmanship" can be best characterized as "sly civility," where she took calculated and measured steps to ensure that she effectively advocate for underrepresented groups within the CSU. She was acutely aware that her identity as a Black woman might prevent her from gaining the power and influence necessary to lead institutional change regarding affirmative action and other race-based initiatives. Instead, Hampton slowly and methodically built up her social capital by identifying her niche and playing hostess to fellow board members to secure access to the informal networking system that existed where deals were made and votes were traded, ahead of the formal board meetings. Hampton's strategic use of "sly civility" enabled her to lessen the threat posed by her race and gender, presenting herself as flexible and reasonable on issues dealing with race and identity. Through this presentation as a political moderate, Hampton gained the support of most of her fellow board members, regardless of their race or political affiliation, for the initiatives she championed.

This chapter also details Hampton's vetting process before being appointed trustee by Ronald Reagan in 1974. Unlike most other trustees who secured their appointments as a type of political patronage arrangement with the governor who nominated them, Hampton's appointment to the board had nothing to do with her partisan loyalty to Governor Reagan. In fact, Hampton was a lifelong Democrat who co-founded a Black woman-led political action committee dedicated to helping to elect Black Democratic officials in local, state, and national elections. Hampton's appointment to the board was based on the relationship she built with a cabinet member in Reagan's administration. Once again, Hampton's expertise at relationship-building led to yet another very fortunate happenstance, placing her in a position to impact the lives of racial minorities and women in the CSU for many years to come.

Whereas chapter 3 focuses on Hampton's persona and her use of sly civility to gain a seat at the table, chapter 4, "A Hammer in a Velvet Glove," explores the varied ways in which Hampton used the soft power she cultivated amongst her peers to remove barriers that might prevent the implementation, funding, and expansion of affirmative action policies and programming. Hampton relentlessly intervened, negotiated, called in favors, made pragmatic decisions, and otherwise pushed things along to reach her goals. As one of the longest-serving trustees to date, she used her knowledge of board process and procedure to her advantage, even securing revisions to policies and procedures that had been in effect since the creation of the system in 1960.

In 1979, five years into her appointment on the board, Hampton was elected board chair, becoming the system's first woman board chair and one of the nation's first Black women to lead a major university system board. Shortly after the election, Hampton and the board were confronted with a massive state budget crisis that threatened the continuation of the system-wide employee affirmative action program. Though unable to secure funding to backfill the employee affirmative action program, Hampton joined forces with her allies on the board and in the Chancellor's Office to ensure that, once the budget crisis was over, affirmative action remained a board priority. Hampton also expertly handled the potential public relations fallout from her decision to recuse herself during the final voting process for the next president at the CSU Los Angeles campus which came down to two finalists—one African American and the other Mexican American. Hampton was accused of playing racial politics because of her recusal. Ultimately, this selection process exposed the growing tensions between California's Black and Brown communities in light of white backlash against affirmative action in the late 1970s/early 1980s. As conservative forces moved to eliminate affirmative action, any further continuation of interracial coalition politics, which characterized Black and Brown relations during the Black Power Movement, was upended.

Hampton's twenty-year tenure on the board, combined with her service on multiple board committees, special commissions, and search committees, enabled her to stay informed about the upcoming system, state, and national level policy changes. She leveraged this information so she could advocate from a place of strength for the policies and programs she supported. For instance, she spent over a decade as the CSU representative on the California Postsecondary Education Commission, the state's higher education planning and coordinating board comprising public, private, and independent colleges, and universities. In this position, she often learned about important state policy changes or upcoming important legal decisions that would affect the CSU before that information filtered down to the CSU Chancellor's Office for implementation. In one notable example, when Hampton learned that Governor Deukmejian was planning a reduction in education spending, which would likely increase tuition and fees for students, she used that information to propose a "balanced fee policy" where the board's finance committee worked to offset any increases to tuition and fees with additional financial aid for students. Hampton's influence extended beyond policymaking, as she was often called to chair important personnel committees, such as the appointment of a new chancellor for the system.

This chapter also analyzes and provides details of the relationship between Hampton and former CSU chancellor W. Ann Reynolds, the system's first woman chancellor. Reynolds and Hampton forged a solid working relationship and friendship, where Hampton used her charm and influence to help sway her male board colleagues and campus presidents to support the ideas for policies and programs that Reynolds conceived and developed. Where Reynolds sometimes struggled to build consensus on the board, Hampton would run interference and bring the men on board to support expanding affirmative action and strengthening the campuses' teacher education programs. Through the Hampton-Reynolds partnership, there was a marked increase in the enrollment of underrepresented racial and ethnic minority students, even as the CSU adopted more rigorous admission standards. Hampton remained a steadfast ally of Reynolds to the bitter end, when Reynolds was forced to resign in 1990 amid a controversy regarding executive compensation.

The fifth chapter, "The Beginning of the End," provides an analysis of various conjunctural events—the loss of higher education funding, political and cultural shifts, and the onslaught of coordinated conservative media actions—which shifted public support away from affirmative action. Claims of "reverse racism" were used by politicians and news outlets to whip up working- and middle-class white resentment against affirmative action or any program that was thought to have given undeserving and unqualified minorities access to jobs and educational opportunities at the expense of the white majority. In the post-Civil Rights era, particularly in California in the early 1990s, when the state was facing a major economic crisis, this type of racial dog-whistling became a winning political strategy for the Republican Party, says Berkeley law professor Ian Haney Lopez in his book, *Dog Whistle Politics: How Coded Racial Appeals Have Reinvented Racism and Wrecked the Middle Class.*[39] The state's economic slump in the early 1990s, which conservative politicians in the state blamed on liberal economic and social policies, along with white anger over the 1992 Los Angeles riots, had all but sealed the fate of affirmative action. Additionally, California Governor Pete Wilson used racial dog-whistling to great effect in campaign ads, which helped Wilson's bid for re-election and led to the passage of Proposition 187 in 1994, which targeted undocumented Asians and Latinos in the state. This controversial legislation became the California GOP's first test of their ability to translate white racial resentments into substantive policy change. By the time Proposition 209 was placed on the ballot in 1996, the political mood in California had shifted, making it fairly easy to do away with over thirty years of affirmative action law, with over fifty-five (55%) voting in favor of eliminating consideration of race in all sectors of public life in the state. This chapter ends with a substantive analysis of the long-term impact of Proposition 209 on California State University, which continues to affect the system in terms of underrepresented student enrollment and graduation rates, and faculty hiring.

Finally, the concluding chapter, "The Legacy and the Lessons," addresses this essential question: Why does Hampton's story even matter, given that affirmative action was taken away in the end? This chapter argues that knowledge of Claudia Hampton's skillful use of sly civility during her twenty-year

---

39   Ian Haney Lopez, *Dog Whistle Politics: How Coded Racial Appeals Have Wrecked the Middle Class* (Oxford: Oxford University Press, 2014).

tenure on the CSU Board of Trustees can be both educational and revealing for anyone seeking to advance opportunities for underrepresented groups within large institutions, as there are many lessons to be gained from learning about her service on the board. Unfortunately, the issues facing Claudia Hampton as a CSU trustee in the 1970s and 1980s echo those facing Black women education leaders today: the re-litigation of affirmative action as a legal and moral principle; declining federal and state funding for public higher education; lack of representation of women and people of color in key educational decision-making posts; and white academe's long-standing belief in the presumed incompetence of Black women as students, scholars, and administrators. While Proposition 209 represented a step backward for affirmative action advocates and those who could have benefitted from its continuation, Hampton's legacy cannot be erased, as it lives on in the institutions she helped to establish and in the countless students, faculty, and staff who benefitted from her advocacy.

Chapter One

Shifting Notions of the Public Good

It would take the threat of a protest during a football game for university officials in the California State College (CSC and later CSU) system to expand their understanding of "education as a public good" to include students of color. This chapter explores how Black student-led protests at CSC campuses across the system forced the CSC Board of Trustees to confront Black and other nonwhite students' long-ignored claims of racial discrimination and exclusion. These campus protests served as the catalyst for gradual changes within the system, where Claudia Hampton would come to play a key role as a CSC trustee in enforcing affirmative action.

On the evening of September 14, 1967, a headline appeared on the front page of the San Jose News which read "Negro Faculty Member Challenge Claims, San Jose State Race Prejudice Blasted"[1] and in the article, Harry Edwards, a graduate of San Jose State College (SJSC) who had been a star athlete as a student and was now an adjunct sociology professor at the college, was quoted as saying "Segregation is worse here than in Mississippi." Specifically, Edwards referred to housing discrimination by landlords around the college, who posted vacancies but refused to rent to Black students. Elaborating on the problem of housing discrimination against Black students, Edwards said, "I can show you vacancy signs all over but they're not vacant for Negroes."[2]

To San Jose State College President Robert Clark's credit, he quickly mobilized a team under the direction of SJSC executive vice president William Dusel to try to immediately find housing for Black male student-athletes and bring in civil authorities to expose and put pressure on land-lords who discriminated against Black students. Shortly following a meeting between Edwards and President Clark, a notice prepared by the United

---

1   Dick Egner "Negro Faculty Member Challenges Claims, San Jose State Race Prejudice Blasted" *San Jose News*, September 14, 1967.

2   Egner, "Challenge Claims."

Black Students for Action (UBSA), went out to faculty soliciting their support for the principles for which Black students planned to protest and contained a list of demands that included public deliberations of all problems and solutions related to Black students, increased admission and enrollment of minority students, and public statements from the athletics office, housing, and the office of Greek life, denouncing racism.[3]

Once made aware of the list of demands now circulating around campus, Dusel approached Edwards in his office to question him about the basis of the protest and to persuade Edwards to call it off. To add to Dusel's consternation about UBSA notices being sent to faculty, the evening edition of San Jose News ran a story in which Edwards said, "If this doesn't work, we'll keep it up and do whatever is necessary. We intend to end discrimination here and now."[4] According to the article, Edwards and eighty-two members of the UBSA planned to formally present their demands to the college administration on the following Monday. If the listed goals weren't sufficiently met by the following Friday, Edwards said that Black students from San Jose State College and San Jose City College would "picket, disrupt and bring a halt" to the SJSC versus University of Texas El Paso football game.[5] Suddenly Edwards and the UBSA had the university's full attention. So important is sports to the American college experience for both students and spectators that any disruption to the game is often met with anger, hostility, and sometimes even threats of violence against those causing the disruption.

As if anticipating that the UBSA threat of a strike during the football game might be met with violent retaliation from other students or off-campus spectators, Edwards' comments in the San Jose News article further suggested that UBSA protestors would respond to violence directed against them with violence when he said, "Let me make one thing very clear, Edwards said. I'm not asking the people who picket to remain non-violent if they have bottles and garbage thrown at them as if they were dogs. We're seeking help in this, because if you have discrimination in the elite sub-culture of this College campus, then how can you hope to eliminate it in places like Detroit, Newark, Hunter's Point and East Palo Alto."[6]

The growing militancy of Black students caught many SJSC campus administrators by surprise. By taking their protest to the football field, Black

3   United Black Student Demands, 15 September 1967. Series 3 Correspondence, Box 31: Racial Discrimination. San Jose State University Office of the President, Robert D. Clark Papers. San Jose State University Special Collections and Archives.

4   Dick Egner (b). "Militant Anti-Prejudice Move Threatens San Jose State Sports Program" *San Jose News*, September 15, 1967.

5   Egner, "Militant Anti-Prejudice Move."

6   Egner, "Militant Anti-Prejudice Move."

students at SJSC were forcing campus administrators to take drastic action to prevent a public relations disaster. At the Black student rally that following Monday, September 18, 1967, with over 500 people present, Harry Edwards, speaking on behalf of the UBSA, aired charges of racial discrimination in campus activities.[7] Following the presentations of their list of grievances, UBSA members called for a "lie-in" during the Saturday night football game against the University of Texas El Paso. They reiterated Harry Edwards' earlier comments that violence would be met with more violence. In so doing, these black students were saying they unequivocally refused to abide by the racial status quo, where black people would suffer the physical and psychological pain and sit idly by and do nothing in response. To drive home the point that violence against protestors would not be tolerated, a self-identified member of the Black Panther Party who attended the rally said his group would help with non-violence or violence, with Edwards adding, "You heard what the Panther had to say. That's where it's at. If things don't get better than this, Uncle Tom won't be able to cool it any longer."[8]

What is so striking about this incident is not only the quick and comprehensive response of SJSC officials to enter into direct talks with students about these specific grievances but also in how university system officials, namely Governor Ronald Reagan and State Superintendent of Public Instruction Max Rafferty, who were voting members of the California State College Board of Trustees, reacted to President Clark's handling of the situation. In being dismissive of black student grievances and demands at San Jose State College, which they believed to be illegitimate and politically motivated by external forces, Rafferty and Reagan set in motion a Black student movement that challenged the prevailing idea that students of color were not deserving of a quality college education. Harry Edwards and the UBSA were challenging the very notion of education as a public good by illuminating how the college and the system rendered Black and other underrepresented students invisible until those students ratcheted up the pressure to be heard. If the California State Colleges were supposed to

---

7   SJSC Chronicle of Events in Racial Incident, 15 September 1967. Series 3 Correspondence, Box 31: Racial Discrimination. San Jose State University Office of the President, Robert D. Clark Papers. San Jose State University Special Collections and Archives, p. 4. These charges included: (1) the administration was tolerating discriminatory practices in the recruitment, housing, and treatment of black athletes, (2) residents of the community whose listings were carried by the campus housing office discriminated against black students (3) fraternities and sororities were guilty of discriminatory practices in pledging and (4) not enough effort was being made by the college to recruit racial minority and low-income students.

8   SJSC, "Chronicle of Events," 4.

provide educational access to all of the state's residents, Black students at SJSC held campus and system officials accountable for doing just that. The condemnation of these students' efforts, however, saw Rafferty labeling SJSC's handling of UBSA concerns and demands as "educational appease-ment" when he wrote, "A college president who knuckles under to either one (violence or threats) is simply laying up a vast store of rapidly escalating woe both for himself and for his entire profession. Seriously brother school-men, when some goon walks into your office from here on in and threatens to burn down the place if you don't pay him educational blackmail, tell him to get lost. Whether he's black, white, brown, red, or yellow."[9]

Echoing many similar sentiments as Rafferty when asked about the racial incident at San Jose State, Governor Reagan was widely reported to have said that the college was "yielding to a threat of force" and should have called out enough law enforcement to protect anyone attending the game.[10] These comments, which focused primarily on canceling the football game as an inconvenience to players and fans and not the specific grievances made by the United Black Student Association, only reinforced why Black students at San Jose State College felt they had to take decisive action to be heard. Several local and state newspapers ran editorials blasting Rafferty and Reagan's comments as ill-informed and irresponsible, with the Los Angeles Times leading the morning news, chastising Max Rafferty in particular for his lack of leadership in his role as California State College (later University) trustee: "As a member of the colleges' Board of Trustees, Dr. Rafferty could provide useful leadership in seeking ways to ease tensions on the 18 cam-puses where 140,000 students are enrolled. So could Gov. Reagan, who was also critical of the game cancellation."[11] Instead of aiding SJSC President Clark, Reagan, and Rafferty took the opportunity to politicize what was a very tense campus situation.

Yet despite Reagan and Rafferty's disapproval of Clark's actions, other California State College (henceforth CSC) trustees, including CSC Chancellor Glenn Dumke, praised Clark for taking "preventive actions to avert the possibility of a public disturbance stemming from racial

---

9   Max Rafferty, "Educational Appeasement" *Oakland Tribune*, November 26, 1967.

10 Themis Chronopolous, "Racial Turmoil at San Jose State: The Incident of the 1967 University of Texas at El Paso vs. San Jose State Football Game" Paper Presented to the Annual Meeting of the Popular Culture Association/ American Culture Association, (Philadelphia, PA, April 12–15, 1995).

11 Los Angeles Times Editorial Staff, "The Real Issue at San Jose State" *Los Angeles Times*, September 28, 1967.

misunderstandings and/or disagreements on campus."[12] In commending Clark, the California State College trustees passed a resolution that among other things criticized the governor and state superintendent of instruction: "Resolved, that the irresponsible statements by Governor Reagan and Dr. Rafferty counseling the use of force to solve a potentially explosive racial problem be deplored as not in the best interests of the college, the State, or the issue involved."[13] In other words, the majority of the CSC trustees condemned two of its own members for whipping up fear, potentially leading to racial violence.

The racial incident at San Jose State College ended rather peacefully, despite the potential for violence at any given moment, especially with trustees Reagan and Rafferty only exacerbating campus racial tensions. Yet it should be noted that despite the remaining trustees and Chancellor Dumke applauding President Clark for his prompt action to get the situation under control, their continued silence on the UBSA's list of grievances speaks to a larger problem, that of university and campus leaders being dismissive of hostile campus environments facing many Black students. The silence that led to this incident at SJSC galvanized Black and other students of color to agitate even further to bring about change within the CSC system—a shift in attitude and belief about issues of access and equity. The UBSA at SJSC took cues from larger social justice movements organized principally by youth and young adults during the 1960s, including the 1964 Mississippi Freedom Summer Project organized by the Student Non-Violent Coordinating Committee (SNCC), the student lunch counter sit-ins and Freedom Rides organized by the Congress on Racial Equality (CORE), and the burgeoning Black Power Movement that was launched in nearby Oakland. These youth-led social justice movements emphasized a type of black radicalism that focused on challenging white supremacy directly and without equivocation. At San Jose State College, this meant confronting campus and university system officials in ways that would draw attention to their cause by airing a list of demands and being willing to risk expulsion rather than politely asking or begging for consideration of their complaints. While the incident at SJSC ended without any bloodshed, arrests, or expulsions, these brave Black students gave other students the courage to challenge the way the

---

12　Office of the Chancellor, Resolution and Commendation of President Robert Clark San Jose State College, 23 October 1967. Series 3, Box 31: Racial Discrimination. San Jose State University Office of the President, Robert D. Clark Papers. San Jose State University Special Colleges and Archives, 1–2.

13　A Resolution of Commendation for President Robert Clark, San Jose State College, 18 October 1967. Series 3, Box 31: Racial Discrimination. San Jose State University Office of the President, Robert D. Clark Papers. San Jose State University Special Colleges and Archives.

institution worked. Influenced by the UBSA, CSC student activists of all races and backgrounds at SJSC and other CSC campuses began openly protesting U.S. involvement in Vietnam on campus, by publishing and circulating trustee biographies, including information about trustees with personal or professional ties to Dow Chemical corporation, the makers of Napalm and Agent Orange, which were used as weapons against the Viet Cong during the war. Now student activists were beginning to understand just how powerful and influential the trustees were in regard to day-to-day campus operations due to the San Jose State racial conflicts. Less than a year later, students at San Francisco State would see just how far the trustees would go to crack down on anyone who would disrupt the existing social order.

Race and the Redefining of the Public Good

In the late 1960s and 1970s, as David K. Wiggins noted "Boards of trustees, university presidents, provosts, deans and other administrative support personnel, were faced with a myriad of problems that threatened the basic structure of higher education in this country."[14] Greater demands from a more politically engaged and outspoken group of students, including groups like Students for a Democratic Society (SDS) and more socially conscious faculty demanding more transparency and accountability from campus officials threatened the stability of America's colleges and universities. Campus protests over America's involvement in wars, debates about campus free speech, and faculty strikes for better wages and working conditions are just some of the various challenges confronting university officials, but none was more alarming than demands from students of color.[15] University and campus administrators were not accustomed to having their power and authority challenged on so many issues.[16] They certainly were not prepared for the type of pressure brought on by minority student demands to increase

---

14   David K. Wiggins, "The Future of College Athletics Is at Stake: Black Athletes and Racial Turmoil on Three Predominantly White University Campuses, 1968–1972" *Journal of Sport History* 15, no. 3 (1998): 304–333.

15   For the purpose of this study, *students of color* refer to all non-Caucasian American students including but not limited to African American, Asian American, Hispanic American and American Indian students, unless otherwise noted.

16   *University administrators* refers to university system chancellors, provosts, legal counsel, and system-wide university trustees. The California State University is a multi-campus system comprising 23 individual campuses and 8 off-campus centers. *Campus administrators* refers to specific individual campus presidents, provosts, deans, ombudsman, legal counsel, and campus boards of trustees.

the enrollment of minority students, hire more racially diverse faculty and staff, include ethnic studies into the university curriculum and provide additional campus support services to aid students of color, including financial aid and tutoring assistance.[17] Race and diversity issues were never a central concern for governing boards at the nation's colleges and universities until the 1960s, when students of color began challenging the traditional notion of education as a public good. As a public good, higher education serves essential functions in society. It is said to produce several benefits, including but not limited to (1) the development of new knowledge, (2) the training of qualified personnel, (3) The provision of service to society, and (4) the ethical function, which implies social criticism. Since society benefits from an educated populace, so the popular thinking goes, the financial burden of higher education should be borne by all who benefit from it. Thus the very notion of higher education as a public good, a resource that benefits and should be made available to the masses, centers on the question of access and equity. Over time, affirmative action would become the vehicle used to expand this idea of higher education as a public good in the nation's public higher education institutions. Within the California State Colleges, trustee Claudia Hampton helped to ensure that the system lived up to its promise of providing equitable education and employment opportunities to all California residents by proudly becoming the "affirmative action trustee," using her skills at relationship-building, negotiation, social intelligence, and strategic compromise to stand against any anti-affirmative action forces which sought to limit access for underrepresented groups.

Before the 1960s student protests across the country, the role and function of university governing boards could be best understood as a group of individuals who manage colleges and universities ". . . charged with ensuring that the public trust in the institution is maintained; the board is also responsible for ensuring that institutions appropriately exercise their responsibilities."[18] To this end, the primary duties of university governing boards were to make sound fiscal decisions and policies for the institution and provide some modicum of oversight on academic issues. Social and political concerns over equity were less important to governing boards. As Brian Pusser notes, "In the post-World War II period, the debate over the public good in higher education moved away from consideration of postsecondary education as a right or entitlement. The debate has been fundamentally

---

17 Wiggins, "College Athletics," 304.

18 David A. Longanecker, "Reconsidering Higher Education and the Public Good: The Role of the Public Spheres." In *Governance and the Public Good*, ed. William G. Tierney (Albany: State University of New York Press, 2006), 95–115.

reframed around two issues: finance and access."[19] The reason for this focus on finance and access following the war was largely due to the growing pressure on states to expand public higher educational access from new groups of students, including war veterans (following the passage of the GI Bill in 1944), and baby boomers who would soon be old enough to attend the nation's colleges and universities. Likewise, as racial segregation in American public education (including elementary, secondary, and postsecondary schools) began to come to an end in the 1950s, many states scrambled for the resources to build new facilities to educate a new generation of students. To respond to this growing student demand, the California State Colleges established eleven new campuses within the span of eighteen years (1947–1965), long before federal financial support for public higher education vis-à-vis the Higher Education Act of 1965 was available to the states. Five doctoral universities and comprehensive colleges and twenty-five community colleges were built within the same period in the State University of New York system. With such tremendous growth of public post-secondary institutions in such a short span of time, governing boards and trustees across the country focused largely on the fiscal management of taxpayer dollars, as oversight of these funds was associated with upholding the "public interest." In exchange for state and federal resources for higher education, governing boards would ensure that colleges and universities would provide research for the common good and training for teachers, engineers, and public servants. Therefore governance in the form of university boards of regents or trustees was equated with contributing to the "public good."[20]

Opponents of the idea of higher education as a public good, namely many economists, say that since only a small number of citizens can meet the admission criteria of colleges and universities, or indeed are even able to afford the costs of a college education, we should not refer to higher education as a public good but as a private commodity that only benefits a small minority of the population. A third group maintains that "both sides of the argument (public good versus private commodity) is essentially about finance, and neither public monopoly nor unrestricted market competition is by by itself ways of providing the best higher education for all."[21] Yet, regardless of how one views who should benefit from higher education, it was the promulgation of higher education as a public good that is largely

---

19   Brian Pusser, "The 'New' New Challenge of Governance by Governing Boards." In *Governance and the Public Good*, by William G. Tierney (Albany: State University of New York Press, 2006), 9–15.

20   Pusser, "Governing Boards," 15.

21   Gareth Williams, "Higher Education: Public Good or Private Commodity" *London Review of Education* 14, no. 1, (April 2016).

responsible for the rapid growth and expansion of California's public higher education system starting in the late 1800s, with the establishment of the University of California as a public trust.

According to John Aubrey Douglass, government corruption and political instability that plagued California due to rapid population growth and the resulting economic troubles from the Gold Rush years to the 1880s led to a proposal that called for a new constitutional convention whereby "the University of California would be elevated from a statutory provision to the status of a "public trust" under the new 1879 state constitution.[22] Under this new status, the University of California would receive the bulk of its funding directly from the California Legislature, while governance of the university would be removed from state legislative control and turned over to a board of regents. This new legal status thus gave the University of California a great deal of autonomy over its internal management, academic programs, and the type of research its faculty and students could be engaged in.

The California State Colleges, by contrast, were established in response to a statutory provision to provide teacher education for the state's fast-growing population of students under the age of fourteen in the 1860s. With a narrowly focused mission centered on teacher training, the California State Colleges were subject to strict governance and control from the California State Board of Education, the agency responsible for managing public elementary and secondary schooling and the primary employer for the state's ever-growing class of teachers. Unlike their University of California counterparts, who enjoyed a great deal of autonomy over the day-to-day management on their campuses, the California State Colleges had little autonomy and control of their management and operations, nor were the state colleges assured the same level of financial support from the California State Legislature. This tight control relegated the California State Colleges to a second-tier status. It would eventually come to impact how the state colleges would be governed once they were allowed to have a say over their own affairs, establishing the system-wide California State Colleges Board of Trustees in 1960.

When students of color began protesting and making explicit demands at campuses across the State College system in the late 1960s, the notion of education as a public good was severely tested and called into question. California State College trustees were ill-prepared to deal with the issues of access and equity based on race and gender. The racial conflict at San Jose

---

22   John Aubrey Douglass, "Revisionist Reflections on the California's Master Plan @50" *California Journal of Politics and Policy* 3, no. 1 (January 2011):1–36.

State College in 1967, and student protests at San Francisco State College in 1968, resulting in a five-month closure of San Francisco State College, became critical flashpoints where university and campus administrations within the California State College system could no longer ignore demands for greater access, inclusion, and representation of diverse students, faculty, and staff. However, the impact of these racial-cultural conflicts was not limited to just the California State College system.

As one of the most populous states in the Union, California often serves as an important bellwether regarding public higher education policy. John Aubrey Douglass has noted that California developed the nation's first coherent system of mass higher education—the public tripartite system of the Universities of California, California State Colleges (later renamed Universities), and California Community Colleges—due in large part to the progressive political culture in the state that began in earnest at the turn of the twentieth century.[23] The nation's first Black Studies program was established in 1968 at San Francisco State College (now university). Cal State LA established the nation's first Chicano Studies program in 1968. San Diego State College (now university) created the nation's first Women's Studies program in 1970. Formal institutionalization of these interdisciplinary studies programs in California public universities continue to serve as a blueprint for those seeking to include women and racial minorities in their university and its curriculum. Today, the student strike at San Francisco State College, along with the Free Speech Movement, which originated at the University of California Berkeley, is still studied by historians and education scholars, inspiring students who continue to grapple with exclusionary race and gender practices, hate crimes on campus, and the defunding of programs aimed to promote access and inclusion.[24] Even the U.S. Supreme Court decision in the *University of California v. Bakke* case, which upheld affirmative action but eliminated racial quotas in university admissions, significantly impacted university admission of students of color across the country.

Most of these unprecedented changes within American higher education dealing specifically with race and gender can be traced back to student protests. Despite California's reputation for being a bastion of progressive and liberal politics, as Martha Biondi notes, "this dramatic explosion of militant activism set in motion a period of conflict, crackdown, negotiation, and reform that profoundly transformed college life. At stake was the very

---

23 Douglass, "Revisionist Reflections."
24 Carie Rael, *Taking Back Our Education: How Students Shaped California's Public Higher Education System, 1960–1996*. (M.A. Thesis, California State University Fullerton, 2015).

mission of higher education."[25] Trustees at the California State Colleges were no different than trustees or regents at other major colleges and universities across the country in their resistance and sometimes vocal opposition to social changes in American society, which fueled student activism calling for redefining the notion of the public good in higher education to include people of color and women.

The California Master Plan and the Absence and Presence of Diversity

The California Master Plan for Higher Education of 1960 has been lauded for its promotion of the California tripartite system of public research universities, comprehensive four-year undergraduate campuses, and open-access community colleges, which has been highly influential with other states imitating this structure. The plan has been touted for its progressive vision of higher education: "Anyone from California could, if they worked hard enough, get a bachelor's degree from one of the best universities in the country (and, therefore, in the world), almost free of charge."[26] Yet through a closer examination of the plan itself, issues dealing with race and/or gender diversity are essentially absent, which raises the question of why these issues were ignored in light of the predictions by state legislators and academic administrators of a looming enrollment surge.

Worried baby boomers coming of age by the 1960s would put considerable strain on taxpayers' financing of the state's public higher education system.[27] State legislators passed Assembly Concurrent Resolution No. 88

---

25 Martha Biondi, The Black Revolution on Campus (Berkeley: University of California Press, 2012), 1–2.

26 Aaron Bady and Mike Konczal, "From Master Plan to No Plan: The Slow Death of Public Higher Education," Dissent, Fall 2012, accessed May 30, 2023, http://www.dissentmagazine.org/article/from-master-plan-to-no-plan-the-slow-death-of-public-higher-education.

27 According to T.C. Holy, Special Consultant to the University of California and the American Association of Collegiate Registrars and Admissions Officers "Between 1940 and 1959, the number of births in the United States rose from 2,360,399 to 4,298,000, an increase of 82 percent. During that same period, the births in California increased from 114,483 to 355,288, or 210 percent." These population increases would undoubtedly affect higher education across the country and particularly in California, where the number of native-born and immigrants to the state would soon translate into full-time enrollments in California's higher education system. For more discussion on California's postwar population boom and its impact on public higher education, see T.C. Holy, "California's Master Plan for Higher Education, 1960–1975: A Factual

in 1959, which mandated the Liaison Committee of the State Board of Education and the Regents of the University of California "to prepare a Master Plan for the development, expansion, and integration of facilities, curriculum, and standards of higher education in junior colleges, state colleges, the University of California and other institutions of higher education of the States, to meet the needs of the State during the next ten years and thereafter."[28] The ultimate goal of the plan, says Douglass, was "to quickly formulate a document that would shape an orderly and cost-effective expansion of the state's rapidly growing higher education system."[29] It is important to note, however, that the impetus for this legislation came solely from the new president of the University of California, Clark Kerr, who was alarmed by the rapid expansion and growing political power of the State Colleges, as lawmakers had approved these new campuses without seeking the approval of the State Board of Education—the constitutionally mandated body responsible for managing the State Colleges. Likewise, Kerr was worried that expansion of the State Colleges would encroach upon the "academic territory" of the University of California as the state's premier research institution. To protect resources for the University of California, including its doctoral degree-granting function, Kerr conceived and wrote a resolution mandating the creation of what would become known as the California Master Plan that Assemblywoman Dorothy Donahoe offered nearly verbatim to the legislature.[30] The California Master Plan for Higher Education was the result of six months of intense negotiations between various public higher education entities, including representatives from the California State Colleges, the University of California, California Community Colleges, California's independent, private colleges and universities, and the California State Board of Education. The public postsecondary institutions, in particular, had a special incentive to be cooperative with this seemingly rushed process, according to Gerth and Grenier, who maintained that "a sympathetic governor (Edmund 'Pat' Brown), elected in 1958, who was willing to support higher education with increased state funding, as well as consider new ideas in the organization. was essential to the changes that occurred in the early 1960s."[31] Biographer Ethan Rarick points out that although the

Presentation of an Important Development," *Journal of Higher Education*, 32, no. 1, (January 1961): 9–16.

28 Journal of the State Legislature of the State of California, 1960 Regular Budget Section, p. 35–35.

29 Douglass, "Revisionist Reflections," 12.

30 Douglass, "Revisionist Reflections," 12.

31 Donald R. Gerth and Judson A. Grenier, A History of the California State University and Colleges, (Carson, CA: California State University Dominguez Hills: Office of University Relations, 1981), p. 21.

California Master Plan was touted as a large part of Brown's legacy, "Brown did not conceive the overall plan, or negotiate it, or write it. Rather, he midwifed it. He prodded and pushed and urged. He helped the idea when it was in trouble, left it alone when it was flourishing. And then, he made sure the state would spend the money to complete the vision."[32] Cooperation and compromise were critical to ensure continuous funding support from taxpayers through governor's annual budget proposal to the state legislature.

Among the primary areas of concern and compromise for higher education officials to reach some agreement on were (1) open access and cost controls, and (2) the function and mission of each segment of the tripartite system. In addressing each of these concerns across the three tiers of public higher education in California, members of the Master Plan Survey Team (and their respective study groups) had to grapple with this central question: How can the tripartite system best deliver quality postsecondary education to all eligible residents of California while controlling future costs to the taxpayers given the rapidly expanding and changing population of the state?

Controlling costs while continuing to provide access and quality was a tough balancing act. In an early compromise proposed by Glenn Dumke, then-president of San Francisco State College, who would later become the Chancellor of the California State College system from 1962 to 1982, they helped to shift costs to the California community colleges, whose operating costs were significantly lower than at the State Colleges or the University of California. Under Dumke's proposal, the public four-year institutions would raise their admission standards, whereby the State Colleges would guarantee admission to students graduating in the top one-third (33.3%) of their graduating high school class. The University of California would admit students graduating in the top twelve and a half percent (12.5%) of their class. The California Community Colleges would absorb the remaining students, constituting approximately sixty percent (60%) of California's entire public higher education population.[33] While some education scholars such as Benjamin Bowser have claimed that the California Master Plan "was unique for its provision for virtual open access," others such as John Aubrey Douglass believe that the plan "did not expand California's commitment to mass higher education. The Master Plan shifted future enrollment demand to the California Community Colleges, actually reducing access to the University of California and California State Colleges."[34] This was

---

32   Ethan Rarick, California Rising: The Life and Times of Pat Brown (Berkeley: University of California Press, 2005), 138–139.

33   Douglass, "Revisionist Reflections," 7.

34   Benjamin P. Bowser, The Abandoned Mission in Public Higher Education: The Case of the California State University, (New York: Routledge, 2017), 21; Douglass, "Revisionist Reflections," 3.

mainly done to help keep down costs as a means of securing support for the future expansion of these institutions from state lawmakers. Representatives from the various constituencies involved in the drafting of the Master Plan understood "open access" largely vis-à-vis a utilitarian perspective, whereby California's tri-partite public higher education system would enroll the greatest number of students so long as the costs to educate these students remained palatable to voters and legislators. Race, gender, and other social factors that affect admission, enrollment, and matriculation was never part of the 1960 Master Plan Survey team's discussion of "open access" as evidenced by the document's absolute silence on these issues.

While the Master Plan has been lauded for its important progressive vision of American higher education by seeking to broaden access to the state's three-tiered public higher education system, the plan did not at all address the looming questions about race and gender that were rapidly becoming important issues with the shifting demographics in California and around the rest of the country. In his book *The California Idea and American Higher Education: 1850 to the 1960 Master Plan*, John Aubrey Douglass suggests that despite California officials pursuing a progressive vision of public higher education for all, the issues of racial discrimination and segregation were important caveats left out of the original Master Plan of 1960. He says, "Until the 1960s, however, the specific issue of enrolling 'historically underrepresented minority groups' had not entered the lexicon of California policymakers. The 1960s California Master Plan for Higher Education, for instance, made no mention of racial or ethnic representation."[35] Instead, policymakers focused on disparities in the quality of local schools, and obstacles to college access and preparedness related to economic factors. Thus the absence of a discussion on enrollment concerns for "historically underrepresented minority groups" in light of simultaneous concern for local school quality, poverty, and economic class among the members of the Master Plan survey team is quite telling about how many Americans are taught to disentangle race from social class when it is often the case that one's social class is largely impacted by one's racial identity. In this way, despite the discussion of diversity being absent from the Master Plan deliberations, its authors were signaling its presence by ignoring the importance of race and gender in how American society functions, particularly for historically underrepresented minority groups that try to enter into the nation's hallowed halls of academia.

---

35 For an in-depth historical analysis of the California Idea, that is, the notion of post-secondary education as a right and not a privilege accessible only to the elite few, see John Aubrey Douglass, *The California Idea and American Higher Education: 1850 to the 1960 Master Plan* (Palo Alto: Stanford University Press, 2007), 93.

The document's silence on racial and gender diversity would have reverberations that would be felt for years to come, with campus and system officials initially being caught off guard when students began demanding greater attention to their concerns about discrimination in university admission, on/off campus services, and in the general campus climate. Without a plan for addressing these types of student concerns, campus officials were often left scrambling to respond, with some university leaders taking a hard stance against student protests, as was the case with the San Francisco State College strike of 1968 over the formal institutionalization of Black Studies. It would be another fourteen years before the question of student diversity is addressed in an updated Master Plan at the insistence of state legislators, rather than academic administrators, within the tripartite system. Meanwhile, the predicted demographic shifts in the state had been realized, and this new generation of students was far more vocal about their concerns.

Between 1965 to 1973, nearly every CSC campus had some form of student protest focused on pre-college preparation, admission and enrollment, financial aid, academic support and curricular concerns, and student services for underrepresented students. So, instead of proactively addressing the question of diversity, the Master Plan Survey Team simply ignored these issues until students forced campus and university officials to confront them head on. This left people like Claudia Hampton to confront often hostile campus presidents, fellow trustees, and the public at large in an effort to both implement and enforce federal and state affirmative action mandates.

CSC Programs for "Culturally Deficient" Students

Even though the Master Plan did not address the looming concern of student diversity, California State College Trustees had to adopt policies to respond to allegations of racial discrimination at state colleges campuses as early as 1961, shortly after the Donahoe Act created the three-part California public higher education system, each with its own governing board. Records indicate that in January 1961, the CSC Trustee Committee on Educational Policy voted to adopt a resolution that prohibited state college students from participating in any intercollegiate activity that subjected students directly or indirectly to discrimination or segregation based on race, national origin, or religion.[36] A similar policy was adopted regarding discrimination in col-

---

36 Agenda of the Trustees of the State College System, January 11, 1961, Board of Trustees of the California State University Collection, Courtesy of the California State University Archives. California State University, Dominguez Hills.

lege fraternal groups two months later. The origin of both resolutions stems from a State Board of Education policy that was initiated by the Regents of the University of California in 1959. In August 1959, "the Regents, upon the recommendation of President (Clark) Kerr and all of the chief campus officers, adopted a policy statement which will require the elimination by recognized student groups, including fraternities and sororities, of rules and regulations that impose discrimination on the basis of race, religion, and national origin."[37] In fact, it was at the urging of the University of California Regents and the State Board of Education that the state college trustees were encouraged to adopt similar non-discrimination policies regarding fraternal organizations and intercollegiate athletics.[38] It is important to note how much earlier the University of California began addressing the question of non-discrimination on campus than the State Colleges. While it is not clear from archival materials whether the trustees were either reluctant or oblivious to the issue of non-discrimination, the fact remains that State Colleges trustees did not address the issue until they were called upon by their more powerful counterparts at the University of California to adopt policies that, in effect, were limited to students' extra-curricular activities.

For the next few years, individual state college campuses grappled with the question of student racial and gender diversity and the impact of this diversity on teaching and learning, without much assistance or input from the State College trustees. However, in 1963 State College trustees adopted a motion requiring the newly appointed State College Chancellor, Glenn Dumke, to advise the board on ways the State Colleges could provide a teacher education component that addressed the "special problems of the culturally handicapped." According to State College trustees, the "culturally handicapped" were primarily Black students who lived in congested urban areas attending public elementary and secondary schools, where recent school desegregation created problems for students' adjustment to a new integrated school environment. Some trustees, including Louis Heilbron, the first chairman of the California State Colleges Board of Trustees, held firmly to the belief that these Black students demanding access and admission to the State Colleges were "culturally deprived" and as such had no right to make such demands. In his words,

---

37   University Bulletin (University of California), August 3, 1959, Board of Trustees of the California State University Collection, Courtesy of the California State University Archives. California State University, Dominguez Hills.

38   Agenda of the State College System, March 3, 1961, Board of Trustees of the California State University Collection, Courtesy of the California State University Archives. California State University, Dominguez Hills.

There is a far greater number of blacks who come from the ghetto poor, who do not find books in their homes, who come from families who are relatively inarticulate, providing neither the facilities nor the encouragement for students, or speak a language peculiar to the ghetto. These culturally deprived students have difficulty verbalizing and counting; they cannot read, write, or do arithmetic. To throw them into general and qualified competition with white students would be manifestly unfair. The only way that they can be brought into a competitive position is to undergo training for their cultural handicaps.[39]

Heilbron argued against the liberalization of the California State Colleges' admissions policy and argued for time limits on special academic support programs for culturally handicapped or deprived students, claiming that, "it takes considerable financial assistance from federal, state, and local grants. Special large-scale efforts in remedial work for higher education should end in ten to twenty years."[40] Heilbron's suggestion for time limits for such programs flies in the face of his own acknowledgment of the nation's long history of denying blacks and other minorities access to quality education over many generations when he asks, "How long should this special assistance continue? Viewed in light of the unhappy history of blacks in the United States, for as long as necessary."[41] Yet in the following sentence he maintains, "But it is quite obvious that the task is not fundamentally that of higher education. The duty to equip black students is in the public school system. I do not underestimate the public-school problems in dealing with desegregation, with large classes, and with non-cooperative parents."[42]

Ironically, as Heilbron spoke of the need for time limits for remedial programming due primarily to the financial costs involved, the California State College Trustees passed a motion to direct the chancellor to advise the board about the problems of culturally deprived and culturally handicapped students. However, college campuses were not provided with any additional resources to help faculty and teacher education students better understand and solve problems related to "inter-group relations."[43] Instead, San Fernando Valley College (now CSU Northridge) had to seek federal funding

---

39   Louis Heilbron. *The College and University Trustee: A View from the Board Room* (San Francisco: Jossey-Bass, 1973), p. 51–52.
40   Heilbron, "Board Room," 52.
41   Heilbron, "Board Room," 52.
42   Heilbron, "Board Room," 52.
43   Minutes of the Meeting of Trustees of the California State Colleges, September 6, 1963, Board of Trustees of the California State University Collection, Courtesy of the California State University Archives. California State University, Dominguez Hills.

to establish a statewide research center to study methods for dealing with the problems of the "culturally handicapped."[44] These students were believed to have accounted for most of the high school dropouts in California. With the endorsement of the trustees, Chancellor Dumke advised the State Colleges to offer teacher education curricula in "inter-group relations" to better serve these students but again provided individual campuses with no additional resources to carry out this directive.

With the passage of the Higher Education Act of 1965, the federal government began to provide federal educational resources to colleges and universities and financial assistance to students to pursue higher educational opportunities. These resources were aimed primarily toward ethnic and racial minority students as well as low-income students attending public colleges and universities and minority-serving institutions, including historically black colleges and universities. The most popular of these federal resources available to institutions were the TRIO programs: a collection of three grant-funded programs that "primarily served individuals who are or would be low-income, first-generation college students, they also serve students with disabilities, students at risk of academic failure, veterans, homeless youth, foster youth, and individuals underrepresented in graduate education."[45] TRIO Programs included Talent Search, Upward Bound, and Student Support Services (SSS) programs out of which the Educational Opportunity Program (EOP) was later developed. These federal grant programs had a significant impact in opening up educational opportunities in higher education for students who were deemed "culturally handicapped" by California State College trustee standards. Thus it was a change in educational policy at the federal level that forced these same trustees, who had taken a hands-off approach to the challenges of inter-group relations a few years before, to now consider alternative means for the state colleges to provide a quality education for these students as well.

In the early part of the 1960s a varying degree of attention was paid to the enrollment of ethnic and racial minority students at individual state college campuses. With the influx of African Americans moving to California to take advantage of defense and automobile industry jobs in the 1940s through the 1970s, some state college campuses, such as those in the Los Angeles area, saw a dramatic increase in applications from African Americans seeking admission into either Los Angeles, Long Beach, or San Fernando Valley State

---

44   Minutes of the Meeting of Trustees of the California State Colleges, September 6, 1963, Board of Trustees of the California State University Collection, Courtesy of the California State University Archives. California State University, Dominguez Hills.

45   Congressional Research Service. *The Higher Education Act (HEA): A Primer.* Washington, D.C., January 2, 2014.

College. To address the concerns and challenges brought on by these racial demographic changes in urban centers of the state, California State College Chancellor Dumke established an Advisory Committee on Human Rights in 1964 and an Advisory Committee on Compensatory Education in 1965, with the hope that both committees would be able to advise the state colleges on the best way to move forward in addressing the needs of "minority groups and the culturally handicapped."[46] According to Dumke's report to the trustees, the purpose of the Advisory Committee on Human Rights' was to "develop the optimum capacities of persons from racial minority backgrounds" while the Advisory Committee on Compensatory Education's goal was to "recognize the special social and educational needs of this segment of American society" and to provide appropriate programs and services to meet these needs.[47] Presenting their groups' activities to the trustees with the hope of garnering support for the continuance of these committees' work, the report included a copy of the program from the first of its kind conference and workshop on The Role of Higher Education in Compensatory Education, sponsored by the California Teachers Association in conjunction with the California State Colleges, the California State Department of Education, and the National Education Association. Likewise, the report also provided a list of compensatory education projects at California State College Los Angeles. These projects included a college work-study program under the Economic Opportunity Act of 1964, funded by the Bureau of Higher Education, a program called "Project Teach," designed to create a new curriculum for teachers of children residing in "culturally deprived" areas, funded by the U.S. Department of Health, Education and Welfare (HEW), programs for deaf children, blind youth, and emotionally disturbed youth, and research programs analyzing the employment problems of minority youth.[48] For the 1964–1965 academic year, for example, California State College at Los Angeles received over $1.1 million dollars in federal and state grant monies to address the needs of the "culturally handicapped."[49] It should then come as no surprise that the State College trustees began to pay much closer attention to the needs of racial minority groups and the disabled when the availability of federal and private grant support increased.

---

46 State College Activities Concerned with Problems of the Culturally Disadvantaged in the Los Angeles Area, August 1965, Board of Trustees of the California State University Collection, Courtesy of the California State University Archives. California State University, Dominguez Hills.

47 "Culturally Disadvantaged," 2.

48 "Culturally Disadvantaged," 7.

49 "Culturally Disadvantaged," 7–8.

By the fall of 1965, the state colleges initiated the first major change to its admissions policy as part of the agreement outlined in the California Master Plan for Higher Education, whereby students graduating in the top one-third of their high school class in California would be guaranteed admission into the State Colleges. Originally proposed in 1960 and initially drafted by the California State Colleges Chancellor's Office, in consultation with the Educational Policy Committee of the Board of Trustees in 1963, these new standards not only raised the eligibility of admission to new first-time freshmen to the upper one-third of their graduating high school class but for the first time required both grade point averages on transcripts and scores on standardized tests for admission. This proposed change to include a weighted combination of grade point average and test scores was incorporated into the new standards, "to achieve equal opportunity for males and females."[50] According to a 1963 Admissions Study conducted by the Technical Advisory Board of the Chancellor's Office, a recommendation to "minimize the unbalance of the sexes in colleges, that at least one plan of admission be adopted that takes into account patterns of aptitude and achievement differentially associated with the sexes."[51] In other words, the consideration of gender in these newly revised admission standards was based on the sexist assumption that young women routinely performed poorly on aptitude tests such as the SAT and ACT and by establishing a formula for weighing high school grades with standardized tests, the California State Colleges could allay concerns of a sex imbalance for future entering classes of freshmen students.

Nevertheless, these raised admission standards had the net effect of sending the majority of California's high school graduates to the California community colleges and not the State Colleges or the University of California, which according to Douglass, was the intent of CSC Chancellor Glenn Dumke and U.C. President Clark Kerr.[52] By diverting a majority of students to the lower-cost California Community College System through these raised admission standards at the public four-year institutions, the state politicians could claim that as a result of the legislatures' support of the California Master Plan for Higher Education, a greater number of students in the state were pursuing higher education than ever before. However, the real effects of these policies were that these new admission standards

50   "Admissions Standards for First Time Freshmen" Committee on Educational Policy Minutes of the Meeting of Trustees of the California State Colleges, December 3, 1964. Board of Trustees of the California State University Collection, Courtesy of the California State University Archives. California State University, Dominguez Hills.

51   "Admissions Standards," 2.

52   Douglass, "Revisionist Reflections," 4.

simply shifted academic and fiscal responsibility to the lowest tier segment of the system, where transferring from the community colleges to one of the state's public four-year universities did not always happen. Furthermore, these newly instituted admission policies worked as a form of gatekeeping, preventing students of color, African Americans, and Mexican Americans in particular from entering the State Colleges and Universities of California, as many of these students attended racially segregated, poorly resourced schools situated in urban ghettoes where access to decent housing and jobs were scarce. Many of these students of color arrived in California with the Second Great Migration from the Jim Crow South only to be forced into inner-city ghettoes, with the largest concentrations in Los Angeles and San Francisco. As Donald Gerth noted in *An Invisible Giant: The California State Colleges*, a collection of essays about the multi-campus system, "The admissions cutbacks of the early 1960s in some measure contributed to the tension of the late 1960s, for unplanned, they tended to reduce access for minorities and the poor to state college freshmen classes."[53] The 1960s Master Plan's reduction of access to the state's four-year public universities thus became the impetus for the rapidly developing student movement that engulfed the San Francisco State campus in a five-month battle between students, trustees, and a "law and order" governor.

CSU Trustees Respond to the Fight for Black Studies at San Francisco State[54]

Despite landmark state (Shelley v. Kramer) and federal (Brown v. Board of Education) court decisions outlawing restrictive covenant and racial discrimination in elementary and secondary schools, de facto segregation in housing, employment, and education continued to plague California, coming to a head in a series of racial conflicts that were played out in the streets of Watts. The Watts Rebellion of 1965, and later, the Long Hot Summer of 1967, which saw over 150 race riots across the country, had a tremendous impact and "the values of the higher education community changed

---

53   Donald Gerth, "History of the California State Colleges" in *An Invisible Giant: The California State Colleges,* ed. Donald Gerth (San Francisco: Jossey-Bass, 1971), 19.

54   This section is adapted from Donna J. Gough (Nicol), "*Ideas Have Consequences: Conservative Philanthropy, Black Studies and the Evolution and Enduring Legacy of the Academic Culture Wars, 1945–2005.*" (Ph.D. dissertation, Ohio State University, 2007). Donna J. Gough is the maiden name of the author of this monograph.

dramatically from a traditional academic emphasis to one focusing on access and a concern for race and poverty."[55] Racial conflicts in the California State Colleges were major factors in a new conceptualization of "access" in American higher education, focusing more on racial inclusion and racial equity rather than in years past, where access was only associated with keeping educational costs down. Students made demands and pushed for change, and the trustees in the California State Colleges were forced, often begrudgingly, to respond.

The development of Black Studies coincided with the rise of the Black Power Movement of the late 1960s and early 1970s. Johnetta Cole has referred to the Black Studies Movement as the intellectual arm of the Black Power Movement.[56] Unlike traditional disciplines that were created and supported by academia, Black Studies was influenced by protest marches against segregation and police brutality against Black people. The revolutionary, counterculture spirit of the 1960s reached American colleges and universities, and the Black Studies movement was just as much a political revolution as it was an intellectual one. The political nature of Black Studies impacted how campus and university administrators viewed this emerging discipline. Black Power ideology undergirded Black student protests in historically Black and predominantly white colleges and universities alike.

Black students were actively involved in the development of the first Black Studies program in the country, and they also demanded several other measures be made available to help promote their psychological and emotional well-being and academic success. Black Studies served to help Black students ". . . alleviate their alienation, facilitate their resiliency, increase their retention, enhance their chances of school success and make education more relevant to the Black experience."[57] Black students were actively involved in the development of the first Black Studies program in the country, and they also demanded that several other measures be made available to help promote their psychological and emotional well-being and academic success. Black students called for the creation of Black student unions and separate campus facilities for Black students as well as tutorial services, department organizations such as the Black Pre-Law Society, and academic advising services, such as the Minority Advising Program at The Ohio State University, which began in 1970.

---

55   Gerth, "History" p. 19.

56   Johnetta B. Cole, "Black Studies in Liberal Arts Education, " in Cole, Butler, and Walter, *Transforming the Curriculum: Ethnic and Gender Studies*, 131–149. Albany, NY: State University of New York Press, 1991.

57   Joy Ann Williamson, "In Defense of Themselves: The Black Student Struggle for Success and Recognition at Predominantly White Colleges and Universities. *Journal of Negro Education*, 68, no. 1 (1999): 92–105.

The impetus for the creation of a Black Studies program at San Francisco State College was initiated by the college's Black Student Union through the campus's Experimental College, in which students could offer non-credit courses on topics that were not being offered through the traditional curriculum at SFSC. This program represented an educational playground for students who were bored or alienated by the regular curriculum and it inadvertently absorbed much of the growing political and social discontent with local and national politics, as well as university administration.[58] Floyd Hayes notes that the push for Black Studies "converged with mass movements of protests against the brutalizing effects of social injustice, socio-economic inequality, racial antagonism, the Vietnam War and university paternalism."[59] Black students were actively engaged in such protests as noted in a 1968–1969 American Council on Education study that found that Black students were involved in fifty-seven percent of all campus protests.[60]

SFSC's Black Student Union felt sensitive enough about the virtual lack of courses that dealt specifically with the Black experience that they utilized the Experimental College as the vehicle to create the Black Arts and Culture series, which enrolled over two hundred students in the 1966 fall semester. Made up of a series of seminars on topics ranging from "Black Psychology" to "The History and Social Significance of Black Power," the Black Arts and Culture Program, William Orrick argues, sought to "reeducate Black students along more black-oriented lines" by using Carter G. Woodson's 1933 publication of *The Mis-Education of the Negro* as the principal text for the program. The book took the position that Blacks have been educated to perpetuate a racist power structure destructive to Blacks rather than to fight against it as a community.[61] By Spring 1968, seventeen courses were taught under the newly named Black Studies Program through the Experimental College, including course offerings such as *Mis-education of the Negro, Ancient Black History,* and *Sociology of Black Oppression.*[62] It is through the

---

58   William Barlow and Peter Shapiro. *An End to Silence: The San Francisco State College Movement in the 1960s.* New York: Pegasus, 1971.

59   Floyd W. Hayes, "Taking Stock: African American Studies at the Edge of the 21st Century," Western Journal of Black Studies 18, no. 3 (1994); 153–163.

60   A.W. Bayer and A.E Astin. "Antecedents and Consequents of Disruptive Campus Environments." *Measurement and Evaluation in Guidance,* no. 4 (1971): 18–30.

61   William H. Orrick, *"Shut It Down! A College in Crisis: San Francisco State College."* (Washington, D.C.: A report to the National Commission on the Causes and Prevention of Violence, 1969).

62   SFSC Black Student Union, Black studies curriculum, spring 1968, from SFSC Black Student Union. (Box: Black Student Union) SFSC Strike Collection at J. Paul Leonard Library, San Francisco State University Archives.

Experimental College that the initial idea of creating a comprehensive Black Studies curriculum originated.

Some CSC trustees became alarmed at the rapid growth and popularity of courses taught through Experimental College to the extent that at the July 25, 1968, meeting of the Educational Policy Committee of the Board, members initiated a review process of all Experimental College curricula, funding, and staffing. While the committee found that the experimental colleges were, in general, a valuable educational enterprise and offered a meaningful extension of academic life at the colleges, others, like Trustee Dudley Swim, accused the committee of "soft-pedaling" in their criticism of the Experimental College.[63] Instead, Swim expressed his concern for what he called "current abuses in the experimental colleges which are instigated by members of worldwide conspiratorial networks whose ulterior motive is to undermine the youth and to upset present society in this country."[64] To address this concern, Swim actually called for the State Colleges to renovate "stale courses" and incorporate new courses into the curriculum so that SFSC could have greater oversight of the content of the courses as well as those in attendance in what amounted to a push for racial control. Chancellor Dumke, Trustee Louis Heilbron and Sol Buchalter from the Academic Senate Executive Committee of the California State Colleges all raised concerns about the Swim definition of "stale courses" to be revamped. Nevertheless, the trustees unanimously passed a resolution requiring the Chancellor's Office to develop preliminary plans to conduct a curricula study for all State College campuses. This review set in motion the beginning of the end for the Experimental College Movement at San Francisco State.[65]

While the trustees were looking for ways to close the Experimental College, the demand for an autonomous Black Studies program came about due to a series of conflicts between the Black Student Union (BSU) and Associated Students Incorporated (ASI) legislature over issues of funding

---

63   Minutes of the Meeting of Trustees of the California State Colleges, July 25, 1968. Board of Trustees of the California State University Collection, Courtesy of the California State University Archives. California State University, Dominguez Hills.

64   Minutes of the Meeting of Trustees of the California State Colleges, July 25, 1968. Board of Trustees of the California State University Collection, Courtesy of the California State University Archives. California State University, Dominguez Hills.

65   For more information on the history of the Experimental College Movement, see Alexander Meiklejohn, *The Experimental College* (New York: Harper &Brothers, 1932); also see Jon N. Hale, *The Freedom Schools: Student Activists in the Mississippi Civil Rights Movement* (New York: Columbia University Press, 2016).

for the BSU-led tutorial program and the Black Arts and Culture series. Eventually, in 1967 one of the confrontations between BSU members and the Associated Students legislative board turned into a free-swinging brawl that became known as The Gater Incident. BSU members alleged that members of the Daily Gater staff (the SFSC student newspaper) began running a series of slanderous articles and opinion columns that intended to portray the BSU as having misappropriated ASI funds.[66] Relations between the BSU and the ASI legislature were permanently damaged as a result of the incident, yet it did open the door for the BSU to enter into direct talks with university administrators instead over the possibility of establishing a separate, autonomous Black Studies program.

Word of the conflicts between the BSU and ASI legislature resulted in a series of open meetings between the BSU leadership, select faculty, and college administrators in 1966. It was during these meetings that talk of establishing a formally recognized Black Studies program first began after the administration had taken notice of the extraordinary growth and popularity of the tutorial program and the success of the Black Arts and Culture series through the Experimental College. These initial meetings did not result in a solid commitment to develop a Black Studies department, however. Instead, it was the university's handling of the Gater Incident that added fuel to the fire of Black students' demands for better inclusion in the curriculum and campus community as a whole. The nine black students involved in the incident were placed on temporary suspension, while white students who were involved in the brawl were neither suspended nor given a disciplinary warning. The delay in approving the initial Black Studies proposal led to the dissemination of a press statement from Open Process, a campus weekly newspaper supported by the BSU and Students for a Democratic Society (SDS), claiming that SFSU President Summerskill found BSU members involved in the incident to be guilty without due process.[67]

---

66   For further information on the Gater incident, see Helene Whitson, "*Strike! A Chronology, Bibliography, and List of Archival Materials Concerning the 1968–1969 Strike at San Francisco State College.*" Washington D.C: Educational Resources Information Center, 1977, and Helene Whitson, "*On Strike! Shut It Down: A Revolution at San Francisco State; Elements For Change,*" edited by Joan Borrelli. San Francisco: J. Paul Leonard Library, San Francisco State University, 1999. Helene Whitson was the Special Collections Librarian/Archivist for San Francisco State College at the time of the SFSC Strikes.

67   The initial Black Studies proposal was written and disseminated by SFSC student and activist James Garrett. The proposal, though approved by the Faculty Senate for implementation, languished in Council of Academic Deans where it stayed until it was re-written by Dr. Nathan Hare, who was hired for the express purpose of establishing a formalized Black Studies program at SFSC.

Summerskill was summoned to go before the trustees at the December 9, 1967, meeting to explain his actions regarding the Gater Incident. Worried about being reprimanded by the chancellor and the Trustees, Summerskill also brought a prepared statement from Thomas J. Cahill, Chief of the San Francisco Police Department, to reiterate the fact that the Gater Incident had not reached riot level, as some media outlets had claimed. There was indeed a brawl and some broken windows, and one photographer had his camera taken, but upon reflection, Summerskill noted that while SFSC's disciplinary procedures and techniques needed improvement, he claimed: "The power of immediate suspension, I think, would be helpful, but I think there are a lot of individuals involved and that doesn't mean much."[68] In his statement to the trustees, Summerskill further pointed out that in lifting the suspensions, he created even greater anger among the members of the Black Student Union because "the students would now proceed before a disciplinary panel for a hearing and recommendations to [him] for final disposition of the matter."[69] In essence, Summerskill's statement amounted to "passing the buck" to other campus officials so as to avoid being labeled racist for the actions he took against BSU members involved in the Gater Incident. Summerskill was so sensitive to the charge of racial discrimination implied in a press statement that he became more directly involved in the day-to-day operations of the campus and as tensions involving the BSU grew, he began making promises to different groups regarding the establishment of a formally recognized Black Studies Program without necessarily having the full support of the Council of Academic Deans or the faculty.

At the BSU's urging, Summerskill put his credibility and reputation on the line and pushed through the BSU recommendation to hire Dr. Nathan Hare as the Special Curriculum Supervisor for the Black Studies program at the rank of lecturer, despite unfavorable recommendations from Devere Petony, Dean of the School of Behavioral and Social Sciences and the sociology department faculty.[70] Hare had the requisite academic credentials for the job, but his dismissal from Howard University due to his "radical" racial politics raised concerns for many search committee members. Despite this, Hare arrived on campus in January 1968 and was assigned to the staff of

---

68 Minutes of the Meeting of Trustees of the California State Colleges, December 9, 1967. Board of Trustees of the California State University Collection, Courtesy of the California State University Archives. California State University, Dominguez Hills.

69 Minutes of the Meeting of Trustees of the California State Colleges, December 9, 1967. Board of Trustees of the California State University Collection, Courtesy of the California State University Archives. California State University, Dominguez Hills.

70 Barlow and Shapiro, "End to Silence."

Academic Vice President Donald Garrity. Hare began drafting the second Black Studies proposal in hopes of addressing two of the most pressing questions that faculty and administrators had about the proposed program: why Black Studies was necessary and whether the program would perpetuate "racial separatism." On April 29, 1968, after being at SFSC for nearly four months, Hare submitted "A Conceptual Proposal for a Department of Black Studies" to both the Instructional Program Committee of the Academic Senate and the Council of Academic Deans.

The proposal was written to address the need for the Black Studies curriculum and outlined Hare's vision for the implementation of such a plan. Divided into six sections, the proposal dealt with issues of community involvement, admission criteria, and course scheduling, but focused primarily on why such a program was necessary.[71] The final section of Hare's proposal outlined his implementation plans, which he titled "The Black Studies Curriculum—A Five-Year Plan." Hare described two phases of program implementation, beginning with pulling together all of the Black Arts and Culture series courses offered through the Experimental College into a single Black Studies department by September 1968. The second phase would take place a year later and involved the "the inauguration of a major consisting of an integrated body of black courses revolving around core courses such as black history, black psychology, black arts, and the social sciences."[72] However, by the summer of 1968, Hare came to realize what the BSU already knew. The administration had no real intention of honoring the "commitment" to help him (the Negro student) find his place in American society."[73] Though SFSU made some efforts at inclusion in which President Summerskill played a role, the institution did not make enough changes, as far as Hare and BSU were concerned. After three years of false promises and politicking along with countless hours drafting his conceptual proposal, Hare allied himself completely with the students and attended their BSU Central Committee meeting in August 1968. It is suspected that from this meeting the idea of organizing a massive strike of the college was born.

While Hare and the BSU Central Committee were contemplating their next move, with the possibility of a strike on the table, the Council of Academic Deans and Instructional Personnel Committee of the Academic Senate approved the establishment of a Black Studies program at SFSC

71　Hare, N. (1968). A Conceptual Proposal for a Department of Black Studies. SFSU Strike Collection, J. Paul Leonard Library, San Francisco State University Archives. (Box: Nathan Hare).

72　Hare, "Conceptual Proposal," 6.

73　Orrick, "Shut It Down," 137.

based on the conceptual proposal and timeline proposed by Nathan Hare on September 17, 1968. The new program would be implemented in September 1969. Given the nature of how colleges and universities function, it is quite an extraordinary feat that the Black Studies program was approved by the Academic Senate and Council of Deans as quickly as it was. Academic Vice President Garrity said that the steps that SFSC had taken "moved with unusual speed in the implementation of the Black Studies program."[74] Yet, if we delve a bit deeper into the politics of establishing new academic programs, we will see why the Black Student Union with the aid of Dr. Hare, the Third World Liberation Front (TWLF), and eventually members of the California Faculty Association (CFA) joined in a five-month long protest at SFSC beginning in November 1968. [75] Beyond merely getting the approval of the faculty, department chairs, and deans of the college, academic programs had to be approved by the Trustees of the State College System, faculty and staff had to be hired, and the department needed an operating budget with which to run the day-to-day affairs of the program. Since there was no infrastructure in place when the Black Studies program was finally approved in September 1968, the courses that Nathan Hare had set up with other departments could not be transferred to Black Studies as they had no funds with which to maintain the faculty already teaching these courses for other departments. By September 30, 1968, Academic Vice President Garrity made an oral agreement with Nathan Hare to commit 1.25 faculty positions for immediate use but in order for Black Studies to operate as a program, Hare needed a minimum of three positions. [76] Now

---

74   Orrick, "Shut It Down," 122.

75   The Third World Liberation Front began in 1967 when a group of Black, Mexican, and Asian American students formed an organization that would serve as a unified political arm that pushed for the educational needs of Third World students. The BSU at SFSC was one of five organizations that comprised the TWLF and took the lead on the student strike of 1968 although all of the remaining groups were very active participants and supported the BSU's push for the establishment of a Black Studies program. The remaining groups included the Latin American Students Organization, the Mexican American Student Confederation, the Philippine American Collegiate Endeavor, and the Intercollegiate Chinese for Social Action and the Asian American Political Alliance.

76   In the California State College system, full time faculty are designated at a 100% time-base (which includes a full semester load of courses, research, and service responsibilities) and lecturer faculty work on a 25% time-base for each course they have been assigned to teach. A typical teaching load within the CSC system is four courses per semester per full-time faculty member. To determine how many full-time faculty positions a department has been given is indicated by whole numbers and decimals. So, 1.25 faculty positions means

that Black Studies was formally recognized at SFSC, the next obstacle that had to be overcome was the issue of budgeting and personnel. However, involvement of the Trustees and then Governor Reagan would delay Black Studies getting the resources needed to become a fully functional program by September 1969.

One of the major hurdles that the BSU and Nathan Hare faced in trying to establish a fully autonomous Black Studies program lay in the fact that SFSC had serious problems with structure and governance. From 1960 to 1968, the college had seven presidents, which is akin to having no presidential leadership at all.[77] The problems began when Glenn Dumke took over as president in 1960 and intended to increase the share of college governance given to the faculty, but because he was engrossed in developing the California Master Plan for Higher Education, he was absent a great deal of the time and proved to be an ineffectual campus leader. The California Master Plan also, in effect, weakened the authority of the college president by making this person accountable not only to faculty, staff, and students but also to the chancellor, trustees, and governor, who often used education as a political tool. Paul Dodd was said to have not asserted the power of his office. John Summerskill became SFSC's seventh president in 1966. Robert Smith took over for Summerskill when he resigned in February 1968 but left before his official September resignation date. Lastly, S.I. Hayakawa, though serving as acting president, was handpicked by the trustees, chancellor, and the governor, which lent him little credibility with the faculty and students, who viewed these entities as meddling in the day-to-day operations of the college for their own political gain.

This heavy turnover, coupled with the weakening of the presidential authority under the California Master Plan, made it difficult for any campus leader to enact change. Academic program decisions now had to be approved by the board of trustees, which meant that Academic Senate approval was only one step in a long, arduous process to get new, innovative academic programs on the books. Furthermore, the California Master Plan also strengthened the power of the governor to hold the state colleges accountable to the interests of California taxpayers, who were now supporting a large state

---

that a department can hire one full time faculty member and offer one course to a lecturer (or a max of five classes) to be offered to students that semester.

77   The following is a list of SFSC presidents who served from 1960–1968: Glenn Dumke (1960–1961); Frank Fenton (acting president, 1961); Paul Dodd (1962–1965); Stanley Paulson (acting president, 1965–1966); John Summerskill (1966–1968); Robert Smith (1968), S.I. Hayakawa (acting president, 1968–1972).

college system through taxes by making the governor an ex-officio member of the board of trustees.[78]

Ronald Reagan was elected governor of the state of California in 1966, just as SFSC was faced with several challenges brought on by changes in American society, including the Cold War, the Civil Rights Movement, and the Vietnam War. Reagan became directly involved in the day-to-day operations at SFSC in 1967 after a campus demonstration against the suspension of a student newspaper turned violent and the president closed the campus. Summerskill was forced to defend his actions before the board of trustees, while Glenn Dumke, now Chancellor of the California State College System, issued a statement meant to quell trustee fears that the state colleges were headed toward a state of emergency. Additionally, since recently elected governor Ronald Reagan was in attendance, his tough stance on crime and lawlessness dictated the content of the speech. The chancellor stated: "Force will be met by special force on any of these eighteen campuses without hesitation; . . . the day is past when ANY student, professor, or administrator will be asked to operate in a climate of fear and intimidation; or when any of our overwhelming majority of serious, responsible students cannot face the school year with an absolute guarantee of uninterrupted, undisturbed study."[79]

Summerskill's appearance before the trustees is important for two compelling reasons. First, Reagan's speech ultimately undermined CSU presidential authority when the trustees appointed a task force of five to evaluate Summerskill's "stewardship" and handling of the December 6 incident, and second, this appearance and, more specifically, the speech delivered by Dumke, gave Reagan the mandate he needed to attack "liberal" policies regarding higher education. On February 22, 1968, John Summerskill announced his resignation as president of SFSC effective in September of that year. In his statement, Summerskill charged "the Reagan administration with political interference and financial starvation of the State college system."[80]

Two months later, Summerskill's words seemed almost prophetic, when in April 1968, Reagan used a line-item veto against a proposed increase for the Educational Opportunity Program (EOP) programming budget by $250,000 and further ignored a trustee recommendation of $2,472,000 to be included in the state budget for 1969–1970. With the help of the trustees

---

78 California State Department of Education. (1960). A master plan for higher education in California, 1960–1975. Sacramento: California State Department of Education. Available from the Online Archive of California; http://ark.cdlib.org/ark:/13030/hb9c6008sn.

79 Orrick, "Shut It Down," 25.

80 Orrick, "Shut It Down,"27.

and other state college presidents, Summerskill had attempted to relieve some student discontent by admitting minority students under the newly formed Educational Opportunity Program (EOP). This program was created to deal with one of the shortcomings of the California Master Plan: the reduction of minority student enrollment at the state colleges through its admission policy of limiting spaces to the upper one-third of the high school graduating class. The EOP program sought to increase the number of students admitted under these special guidelines from two to four percent. The EOP was grossly under-funded and therefore unprepared to handle some four thousand students admitted through EOP statewide. Reagan's veto further drove a wedge in already strained relations between the governor and the faculty and students at the state colleges.

Furthermore, as the nation became more deeply involved in the Vietnam War and race riots across the country became more numerous, the governor and the trustees attempted to tighten their hold on the California campuses, making it nearly impossible for any SFSU president to establish credible leadership. Summerskill predicted what would happen to the college should the trustees continue with its hardliner course of action in response to student and faculty protests saying, "This whole system is going to break down if the trustees and politicians are going to hire and fire professors. I couldn't say what I'm saying now as president, but somebody had better start saying something about these problems. The issue is: are we going to let the educational establishment be taken over essentially by people who are running for political office?"[81] Summerskill's assessment was amazingly accurate insofar as his successor, Robert Smith, faced similar challenges in working under the directives of the California State Colleges Board of Trustees.

Robert Smith assumed the presidency of San Francisco State College in June 1968 and faced not only a group of restless student activists but also a board of trustees that were hostile to faculty governance and presidential leadership. Smith was ordered by the trustees to fire George Murray for comments he made upon his return from a trip to Cuba that was sponsored by the Black Panther Party. Murray was a black graduate student and teaching assistant in the English department who was a participant in the 1967 Gater incident. Upon his return from Cuba, Murray "was quoted as saying that every American soldier knocked out by the Vietcong in Vietnam meant "one less aggressor" to deal with here at home."[82] Smith refused to honor the trustees' request, citing that Murray had a contract with the university which could not be broken without following proper procedures. Furthermore, he

---

81   Orrick, "Shut It Down," 27.
82   Orrick, "Shut It Down," 27.

maintained that "the public statements and political philosophies of faculty members are not grounds for punitive action."[83]

Though Smith won this round with the trustees, Murray's October 24, 1968, speech at Fresno State College ended any further restraint on the part of the chancellor, governor, and trustees in the local affairs of the college. Not only was there a general lack of concern for diversity from the start, but the trustees were also actively repressive of these political opinions. In this speech, Murray was quoted as saying, President Lyndon B. Johnson, Chief Justice Earl Warren, and Governor Reagan were "slave masters." He called on third-world peoples to organize ". . . an old fashioned black-brown-red-yellow-poor white revolution. That's the only way we're going to change things in the U.S. Political power comes from the barrel of a gun. If you want campus autonomy, if the students want to run the college, and the cracker administrators don't go for it, then you control it with a gun."[84] Even after this speech, Smith refused to take any action on Murray despite being ordered to suspend him by the trustees and the chancellor claiming that, "I decided I wasn't going to act until the following week for the good of the college, for the community, and because of the politically laden operation."[85]

Smith's decision to wait a week only made the trustees more anxious for him to take swift and decisive action against Murray and made the faculty and student leaders even more wary of the trustees' involvement in the daily operations of the college. For example, on October 12, 1968, the CSC Student Presidents Association passed three resolutions calling for the trustees to (1) recognize campus autonomy and due process procedures concerning personnel in response to the handling the George Murray case, (2) support a policy of full student representation in the selection process of college presidents, and (3) support the budget for the recruitment and financing of college capable "minority culture students," including a requirement that all students must take at least one course in "minority culture" or "minority studies' as a prerequisite for graduation.[86] By the time Smith was ready to take action on October 31, 1968, the decision was taken out of his hands as the BSU announced their intention to stage a campus-wide strike on November 6, 1968.

83 Orrick, "Shut It Down," 32.
84 Orrick, "Shut It Down," 33.
85 Orrick, "Shut It Down," 36.
86 Minutes of the Meeting of Trustees of the California State Colleges, October 24, 1968. Board of Trustees of the California State University Collection, Courtesy of the California State University Archives. California State University, Dominguez Hills.

A delegation of Black faculty, students, and staff met with Smith on November 5, 1968, to present him with their list of ten non-negotiable demands. Chief among these demands was that all Black Studies courses being taught through various departments be immediately made part of the Black Studies Department and all the instructors in this department receive full-time pay. This particular demand was most likely conceived of by Dr. Hare as the Black Studies department was approved in theory but functional in name only, due to the lack of financial and personnel resources. At the beginning of the BSU strike, Hare was the only person authorized and financed to teach a course in the Black Studies department, and his teaching appointment only constituted twenty-five percent of his total job duties. In order to gain program status, Black Studies needed three full-time hires, and to be considered a department, eleven full-time positions were needed.

The staffing and financing of the Black Studies program was the primary reason for the BSU call to strike. Among the other issues that the BSU sought to redress was the trustees' involvement in deciding which Black programs and personnel would be retained at SFSC. In explaining this demand to the wider campus community, the BSU claimed that "On November 22–24, the California State College Trustees will meet at the request of Pig Dumke to dissolve the Associated Students on all State College campuses throughout the state. This means that we cannot create and maintain programs on and off campus. Everything we do will be controlled by the Pig Dumke. All programs such as the Associated Students, CSI, EC, etc., will have to have Pig Dumke's o.k. If the Trustees destroy our creativity on and off campus, we will use our creativity in a prolonged and protracted war against them."[87]

There was indeed some truth to these claims as the Board chair, Theodore Meriam, did call a special meeting of the board to discuss the strike. Governor Reagan and Norman Epstein, General Counsel for the CSC Chancellor's Office, were among those present at this meeting, even though they were typically absent unless there was a controversial topic to be discussed. In this meeting, President Smith made a statement explaining his decision to close the campus, reminding the trustees that he was following procedures that were previously followed as a result of a racial incident at San Jose State College only a few months before: "Although the Mayor of San Francisco and the Police Department indicated that they were prepared to offer their assistance, I decided to halt instruction after consultation with the Academic Senate, the general faculty, academic deans, and Black administrators and

---

87   Black Student Union (1968b). Demands and explanations. SFSC Strike
       College at J. Paul Leonard Library, San Francisco State University Archives
       (Box: Black Student Union).

staff members."[88] Records do not indicate any discussion of plans to dissolve the Associated Students Incorporated, the student government body on all CSC campuses. However, Donald Garrity, Academic Vice President at SFSC, assured the trustees during this meeting that campus officials would not give into BSU demands that only Black people run the Black Studies Program, including its off-campus community projects. He was quoted as saying that "all courses approved in the Black Studies Program would meet high academic standards; the students in this program would not have charge of the employment of faculty for these courses or prescribe curriculum. Classes would not be restricted on a racial basis and instruction in these courses would seek the objectives of education and would not be propaganda."[89] Yet, despite these assurances, Governor Reagan made it a point to bring up a televised interview with George Murray the previous day in which Murray advocated for the Black Studies Program to be run by Black personnel only.

Though Black Studies has been charged with being heavy on political aims and weak on academic and conceptual rigor, it is interesting to note how much the trustees and politicians like Ronald Reagan, with little or no collegiate research or teaching experience, used the fight for Black Studies at San Francisco State to take advantage of California white voters' fears that the passage of the 1964 Civil Rights Act gave Black people the license to commit random acts of civil disobedience in an effort to have their demands met.[90] The California State College trustees, with the aid of Governor Reagan undermined the authority of the office of the president at SFSC, abused political power by involving themselves directly in curricular decisions of the college, and used the situation at SFSC to closely scrutinize, deny funding, and otherwise crack down on activities designed to help integrate students of color into the academy. The demands for access and inclusion from students of color in the California State Colleges forced the trustees to scramble to establish new policies, re-examine old practices, and consider new ways to negotiate with an active and informed student body that refused to abide by the old social order, thus shifting the notion of the public good to be inclusive for all.

---

88 Minutes of the Meeting of Trustees of the California State Colleges, November 18, 1968. Board of Trustees of the California State University Collection, Courtesy of the California State University Archives. California State University, Dominguez Hills.

89 "Minutes, November 18, 1968," 2148.

90 Kurt Schuparra. "A Great White Light": The Political Emergence of Ronald Reagan, in *The Conservative Sixties*, ed. D. Farber and J. Roche, 93–107 (New York: Peter Lang, 2003).

Chapter Two

Misgivings about Affirmative Action

Campus protests up and down the state did not soften most CSU trustees' attitudes toward the plight of people of color and women within academia. In many ways, white board member attitudes hardened because of the perceived disruption to the "status quo," as it did with many ordinary white Californians. In this chapter I examine the varying levels of resistance and opposition to implementing affirmative action within the California State University system from trustees, Chancellor's Office staff, and elected officials. Despite federal and state laws that opened access to insure racial and gender equity in the nation's public colleges and universities, it would be necessary for pro-affirmative action forces to challenge this resistance to guarantee the success of these policies and programs. Even after the loud, rancorous student protests on campuses across the CSU system in the late 1960s, trustees continued to slow-walk enforcement of affirmative action policy until the appointment of Claudia Hampton as the system's first Black woman trustee in 1974. Hampton's appointment to the board was one of several factors that forced the trustees to fully comply with the law after nearly a decade of obfuscation and overt delays.

On the heels of politicized campus protests at San Jose State and San Francisco State, Ronald Reagan, for example, in his position as governor and as a member of the CSU Board of Trustees, used these events as opportunities to pressure the state legislature and trustees to enact policies that greatly expanded the role of law enforcement in the day-to-day operations of the university. Reagan also used his line-item veto power to dramatically cut the State College budget, denying requests to increase support for the Educational Opportunity Programs (EOP) which directly benefited racial minority and economically disadvantaged students needing academic counseling, mentoring, and tutoring services in preparation for admissions and retention in the California State Colleges. In 1970, for example, the Governor's budget included only $1.6 million of the trustees' proposed $4.1 million as compared to the previous year's appropriation of $3.3

million. Trustees' notes from that period reveal how the reduction in funding to EOP had a devastating impact on disadvantaged students the public was demanding that the State Colleges serve. Reagan's budget cuts to EOP programs also impacted the coordination of existing EOP programs, according to a March 25, 1970, report of the California Coordinating Council for Higher Education (CCCHE) which noted that "Agenda Item #6, Coordinating of EOP programs, was being taken off the agenda because of the numerous conflicting calls the council had received from various members of government. It was discovered yesterday afternoon that there is a lack of unanimity on the part of the Executive Branch of (state) government as to what it is that they want the Coordinating Council to do in connection to EOP programs."[1]

The governor, trustees, and university officials' lack of clarity about the funding and coordination of race and gender-based programs such as EOP initiatives on college and university campuses contributed a great deal to campus tensions that began in the 1960s. These tensions led the American Council on Education (ACE) to recommend "greater diversity of age, occupation, and other salient individual characteristics" in the representation of college and university trustee board membership.[2] However, it was not until the late 1970s that university boards across the country began to diversify slowly and incrementally. A 1985 Association of Governing Board Special Report noted that across the United States, twenty percent (20%) of trustee board members were women, and ten percent (10%) were non-white.[3] The racial and gender composition of most university boards in the United States has virtually remained unchanged since 1985.[4] A 2023 report on university board diversity found that most data on the race and gender of college boards of trustees was not publicly posted or readily available. However, as an initial step in determining the demography of college and university

---

1   California Coordinating Council for Higher Education Report (later renamed "California Post-Secondary Education Council"), March 25, 1970. Board of Trustees of the California State University Collection, Courtesy of the California State University Archives. California State University, Dominguez Hills.

2   American Council on Education, *Campus Disruption during 1968–1969*, ed Alan Bayer and Alexander Astin. (Washington D.C.: American Council on Education, 1969).

3   Association of Governing Boards of Universities and Colleges. *Composition of Governing Boards.* (Washington, D.C.: Association of Governing Boards of Universities and Colleges, 1985).

4   Association of Governing Boards. *Composition of Governing Boards of Public Colleges and Universities.* (Washington, D.C.: Association of Governing Boards, 1997).

boards, *Washington Monthly* examined the websites and public records information of a representative sample of one hundred (100) institutions from across the country. Their report found that only nineteen percent (19%) of institutions had a board that was well-aligned to match the diversity of the student body. In other words, most of the college trustees in this sample were white and male, even if the majority of the students attending these institutions are people of color and women.[5]

Back in 1989, former University of California Chancellor Clark Kerr, along with Marian L. Gade, former Deputy Director of the University of California, Berkeley's Center for the Study of Higher Education, argued that "many boards were once like 'clubs' made up of 'establishment' types but are now more like 'rainbow coalitions.'"[6] Such a description of university board composition belied the fact that within these seats of power, the appointment of people of color and women was and continues to be the exception, not the rule. The language choice of "clubs" and "rainbow coalitions" is notable for how heavily coded they are for race, while managing to leave race and racism unnamed. Until the appointment of the CSU board's first Black woman trustee, Claudia Hampton, in 1974, trustee discussions about affirmative action focused primarily on creating policy to satisfy minimum requirements set by federal and state laws, not because trustees necessarily viewed affirmative action or nondiscrimination policy as a moral imperative.

Nondiscrimination versus Affirmative Action

Starting in 1972, the federal Office of Civil Rights issued new "Higher Education Guidelines" requiring universities to develop a plan to implement affirmative action regulations outlined in President Johnson's Executive Order 11246 (1965) or risk losing access to federal contracting monies. According to Martha S. West,

> Affirmative action has played a role in higher education both in the employment practices of colleges and universities, and in the admission of students. In employment, educational institutions were not brought under Title VII's prohibitions on discrimination until Title VII was amended in 1972. Theoretically, educational institutions that had federal contracts

---

5   Raquel M. Rall, Demetri L. Morgan, and Richard Chait, "Does Your Board of Trustees Reflect Your Student Body?" Washington Monthly, August 27, 2023.

6   Clark Kerr and Marian L. Gade. The Guardians: Boards of Trustees of American Colleges and Universities: What They Do and How Well They Do It. Washington, D.C.: Association of Governing Boards of Universities and Colleges, 1989.

were covered by Executive Order 11246 when it was issued in 1965, but little notice was paid to colleges and universities as federal contractors, until discrimination against women was included in the Executive Order by its revision in 1967.[7]

Taking advantage of the revision of Executive Order 11246, women's organizations such as the Women's Equity Action League (WEAL) began filing complaints in 1971 about the lack of women on the faculty in America's colleges and universities. WEAL became one of several activist constituent groups that pressured higher education institutions to change and reform or risk losing their federal funding. Formed in 1968 as a conservative response to the "militant tactics" of other women's groups such as the National Organization for Women (NOW), the Women's Equity Action League focused its activities on ending workplace gender discrimination. After WEAL's founder Elizabeth Boyer published an article in a popular women's magazine about sex-segregated job advertisements, the group was flooded with thousands of letters from women who believed they were subject to discrimination based on their sex. Boyer personally responded to each of these letters which, in turn, helped the organization grow its membership.[8] WEAL's specific interest in sex and gender discrimination in higher education, however, came in 1970 after WEAL member Bernice Sadler experienced what she believed was sex-based discrimination that prevented her from successfully securing a tenure-track faculty position at the University of Maryland College Park, where she had worked as a part-time instructor for many years.[9] Sadler, who would later become known as the "Godmother of Title IX" worked as an education specialist for the Special Subcommittee on Education for the U.S. House of Representatives. She floated the idea of using the revision of Executive Order 11246 (which was renumbered as Executive Order 11375) to press for the implementation of affirmative action programs based on colleges and universities' failure to address sex discrimination in the hiring of women faculty and staff in higher education institutions. By researching legal tactics similar to those that African Americans had used to end segregation in public schools, Sadler found a way to use the courts to enforce the law on behalf of women.[10] In 1970, WEAL filed the first of a series of complaints under the newly revised

---

7   Martha S. West, "The Historical Roots of Affirmative Action" *Berkeley La Raza Law Journal*, 10, no. 2 (2015): 607–630.

8   Karen O'Connor, *Women's Organizations' Use of the Courts* (Washington D.C.: Lexington, 1980), 105–106.

9   Bernice Resnick Sadler, "Title IX: How We Got It and What a Difference It Made" *Cleveland State Law Review*, 55, no. 4 (2007): 473–474.

10   Sadler, "Title IX," 474–475.

Executive Order 11375 against every college and university in the country that received a federal contract, totaling more than 350 higher education institutions named in the complaint. Approximately forty institutions named in the complaint experienced a delay in receiving federal contracts because of WEAL's complaint. In response, the Department of Housing, Education and Welfare's (HEW) Office of Civil Rights, issued new "Higher Education Guidelines" in October 1972, which sent many colleges and universities scrambling to establish new faculty affirmative action plans for their individual campuses.[11] Of note is the role that women's rights organizations, even those mainly comprising middle-class white women, played in enforcing affirmative action in higher education. Although it was never WEAL's intention to use their activism on behalf of people of color, religious minorities, or immigrants seeking employment within the nation's colleges and universities, their campaign had a net positive effect for all who had been historically and systematically denied employment in America's hallowed halls of academe. To be clear, these new higher education guidelines only applied to employment; affirmative action for student admissions would come many years later.

The Office for Civil Rights had begun signaling that these guidelines would be forthcoming with a speech by J. Stanley Pottinger, Director of HEW's Office for Civil Rights, during the annual meeting of the American Association of University Professors on May 5, 1972. Pottinger's speech made a point of distinguishing between affirmative action and nondiscrimination saying, "Nondiscrimination requires the elimination of all remnants of discriminatory treatment whether purposeful or inadvertent. Affirmative Action requires the contractor to go beyond a purely passive stance of not discriminating by requiring him to seek to employ members of groups which have traditionally been excluded, thereby mitigating the effect of discrimination in society at large."[12] Pottinger's insistence on distinguishing between affirmative action and nondiscrimination was particularly important, because

---

11 Herma Hill Kay and Martha S. West, *Cases and Materials on Sex Based Discrimination* (Eagan, MN: Thomson West, 2005).

12 J. Stanley Pottinger, *"Remarks at the Panel on Affirmative Action and Faculty Policy"* (New Orleans, LA: American Association of University Professors, May 5, 1972): 1–24. Pottinger goes further to explain how affirmative action should be enacted to address underutilization of certain classes of employees. "The premise of the affirmative action concept of the Executive Order is that systemic discrimination in employment has existed, and unless positive action is taken, benign neutrality today will only preserve yesterday's conditions and project them into the future. The affirmative action concept requires a contractor to determine whether women and minorities are "underutilized" in its employee workforce, and, if that is the case, to develop as part of its affirmative

most colleges and universities up to this point, had established a practice of nondiscrimination in faculty hiring. Still, most had no clearly articulated affirmative action policy or practice, which also meant that institutions often overlooked qualified minority faculty applicants due to implicit bias by hiring committees.

Although their counterparts from their Regents for University of California had established a systemwide nondiscrimination policy in 1959, the Trustees for California State Colleges had neither a nondiscrimination nor affirmative action policy in place when the Office for Civil Rights issued its new guidelines in the later part of 1972. Yet despite this lack of policy, CSU Vice Chancellor C. Mansel Keene as well as CSU trustees on the Faculty and Staff Affairs Committee were convinced the California State Colleges were already in compliance with the federal mandates of affirmative action policy because of their misunderstanding (or misrepresentation) of the distinction between affirmative action and nondiscrimination. To illustrate this point, one only needs to go back to 1971, when Vice Chancellor Keene told the CSU trustees that racial minority employee numbers rose from 6.4% in 1964 to 13.5% in 1971, giving the impression that the CSU had enacted a systemwide affirmative action program which would explain this growth. However, no such plan existed before the federal government mandated that higher education institutions develop such plans.[13]

---

action program specific goals and timetables designed to overcome that underutilization."

13   Keene, Mansel, C. "Affirmative Action Information," July 11–12, 1972. Box 2C9 (1972). CSU Board of Trustees Minutes of the Meeting of the Board of Trustees, Board of Trustees of the California State University Collection. Courtesy of the California State University Archives. California State University Dominguez Hills. P. 1–6 plus Attachments A1 and B1–5. Among CSU minority employment trend for all occupational sub-groups, the largest increase to minority employment occurred in the labor and custodial classes. Two important caveats about these figures should be noted. First, the CSU Chancellor's Office defined employment in these survey figures as "all of those employed at least half time or more." Second, the exclusion of women from the category of minorities makes it difficult to discern how women of color have been factored into these figures. All that is known about the employment of women within the CSU from these survey reports is that women's wages at the $10,000 or more earning level remained virtually flat from 1970 to 1971 while 70% of white males earned over $10,000 per year in 1971. There was an 8% increase of the number of minorities who earned over $10,000 per year in 1971 (36% compared to 28% in 1970). Vice Chancellor Keene explains this pay difference as "the tendency for minorities to be more prevalent in the lower skill categories." There was no evidence contained within this report of any concerted efforts to conduct outreach and recruitment for qualified

A closer look at these numbers reveals that the most significant increase in minority employees occurred in the labor and custodial fields. Notes from the meeting where this employment survey was shared with the board pointed out the CSU Chancellor's Office defined employment in these survey figures as "all of those employed at least half time or more" such that the formula for counting employees is far more likely to explain this increase in numbers rather than a special outreach or recruitment efforts undertaken by the campuses.[14] Keene made the false assumption that qualified minority candidates in the faculty, executive, and supervisory classes did not exist nor was it the responsibility of the Chancellor's Office and individual campus presidents to go beyond simply not discriminating against minority candidates. The leadership within the CSU, most notably the Chancellor, and trustees, seemed to readily accept at face value Keene's observation that "the dilemma facing any equal opportunity employer—the preponderance of minorities who have not had as much education, training or experience bulking in larger relatively unskilled occupations."[15] These comments gave the impression that the problem with affirmative action falls squarely on the shoulders of the people the policy was intended to assist—minority candidates—instead of institutional barriers that have worked to keep women and minority candidates out of the system. Institutions looking to side-step their responsibility to conduct targeted outreach and recruitment programs for prospective minority candidates all too often relied on blaming the victim like this, instead of increasing their efforts to recruit a more diverse applicant pool.[16]

As the California State University and other colleges and universities across the country were grappling with how to implement affirmative action policy, many university and campus officials from these institutions relied on victim blaming to divert attention from an institution's structural factors, which prevented the inclusion of underrepresented groups as faculty, staff, and students. Instead, racial and ethnic minorities and women were held responsible for their own exclusion from these institutions. The victim-blaming tactic continues to be the popular way that opponents of affirmative action use to justify their opposition to this type of policy. As time went

---

minority candidates for positions in the faculty, administrative, or supervisory classes. The CSU did not have an actual system-wide affirmative action program that would meet the HEW Higher Education Guidelines.

14   Keene, "Affirmative Action Information."

15   Keene, "Affirmative Action Information."

16   Victim-blaming was a common way to justify racism direct against Black people in the United States according to psychologist William Ryan who coined the phrase "blaming the victim" in his book of the same name in 1971. See William Ryan, *Blaming the Victim*. (New York: Pantheon, 1971).

on, Claudia Hampton, with the help of others on the board of trustees and among select staff within CSU Chancellor's Office, would fight against this type of victim-blaming, particularly regarding student affirmative action.

On the issue of diversifying the student body, it would take a mandate and pressure from the state legislature to compel the trustees to address the issue of student affirmative action. In 1973, the Joint Committee on the Master Plan for Higher Education of the California Legislature released the draft of their report in 1973. It analyzed where the tripartite system was in order to reach its goals so that educators and politicians could begin planning for the next decade. Two of the most distinct features of the 1973 draft of the California Master Plan compared to the 1960 version were (1) the racial composition of the committee and (2) their specific attention to issues of access and retention for racial minorities. By the mid-1960s, California had elected its first African American representatives, including Assemblyman Willie Brown and State Senator Mervyn Dymally, who both served on the Joint Committee. Likewise, the presiding chairman of the Joint Committee was John Vasconcellos, known throughout the state as a champion of civil rights and author of several pieces of legislation aimed at ensuring equal opportunities for underrepresented groups within California's public higher education systems. Though the document casually mentions "equal and universal accessibility for persons of both sexes and all races, ancestries, incomes, ages, and geographies" as a critical objective for California public higher education, the draft and final document explicitly addresses all of the aforementioned identities except for sex (or gender) in its recommendations. [17] This oversight was likely related to the absence of women on the Joint Committee. Nonetheless, the inclusion of a considerable discussion on the sociocultural identity of students beyond finance was a marked departure or shift away from the previous iteration of the Master Plan, which was silent on these concerns. In the 1973 Master Plan, the report authors were critical of the 1960s recommendation to divert approximately fifty percent of all high school graduates to the California community colleges, seeing no intellectual rationale for such admission practices. The 1960s admission recommendations were based primarily on economic considerations and not "institutional match" for students.

To correct this, the 1973 Joint Committee recommended a more integrated admissions approach, one that included a flexibility option for the California State University and the University of California, where these

---

17   Report of the Joint Committee on the Master Plan for Higher Education. California Legislature. September 1973, p. 1–2. Board of Trustees of the California State University Collection, Courtesy of the California State University Archives. California State University, Dominguez Hills.

campuses could utilize non-traditional criteria for accepting up to 12.5% of students, who might be short on one or more traditional criteria for admission. Over time, this flexible option became known as the "special admit" policy (later known throughout the CSU as the 4% plan[18]), where students would be accepted and given additional academic support services to make up for any academic deficiencies which might hold them back. Within the CSU, this particular special admit policy was used to help a high number of students of color gain admission into the system. Without the California Legislature's call for a flexible option, many of these students would have been denied an opportunity to get a college education. Previously, these students might have been poorly advised or tracked not to take the requisite college prep courses needed for admission into the CSU. Or some of these students might not have met the baseline ACT or SAT scores required for admission. Regardless of why students were admitted under this special program, this policy helped to address one of the major concerns of the Joint Committee, which was the racial imbalance within the state's public colleges and universities. Additionally, the Joint Committee recommended that "each segment of California public higher education . . . strive to approximate by 1980 the general ethnic, sexual, and economic composition of the recent California high school graduates."[19] The aim of this recommendation was to force these institutions to make specific outreach and admission goals for underrepresented student groups. This recommendation eventually became state policy with the passage of Assembly Concurrent Resolution 171 (1974), which called for the development of a statewide student affirmative action plan within the California State Universities and Universities of California. The passage of ACR-71 is yet another example of the type of pressure needed to compel CSU officials to embrace and endorse affirmative action fully.

The fact that the California legislature specifically mentioned race, age, geography, and income meant that the trustees could not ignore these issues if the system wanted to continue receiving favorable funding from the state legislature. A reciprocal relationship between the state legislature and the Public Affairs Committee of the board existed where each consulted each other for input and support on new legislative policies and board resolutions. Ignoring such important provisions from this document could have a tremendous impact on the long-term functioning and day-to-day operations

---

18   While the California Legislature recommended up to 12.5% of students could be admitted under this special admit policy, CSU campuses customarily never accepted more than 4% of students using non-traditional admissions criteria. Hence the plan came to be called the "4% plan" throughout the system.

19   Joint Committee, "Master Plan," 38.

of the California State Colleges. It would be political suicide for the trustees and the Chancellor's Office to ignore the state legislature on these issues. Following the release of the final draft of the updated Master Plan in September 1973, the Chancellor's Office of the CSU and the Board of Trustees got to work on drafting a policy that would address the system's lack of a unified nondiscrimination policy as well as the federal government's demand that the nation's colleges and universities implement affirmative action as a standard employment practice.

Alex Sherriffs had been appointed Vice Chancellor of Academic Affairs by September 1973, and he was given the task of developing affirmative action and nondiscrimination policies that addressed the hiring of faculty, curriculum policy, and student learning. While the historical record is silent as to Sherriffs' true feelings on affirmative action, given his center-right political leanings that included an embrace of the ideas posited by Black conservative economist Thomas Sowell and his work as an education advisor to Ronald Reagan, it is most likely that Sherriffs was simply following orders. In his role as CSU Vice Chancellor for Academic Affairs, he was the designated advisor for the Ad Hoc Committee on Affirmative Action for the board that was formed in September 1973 as part of his duties as Vice Chancellor. This ad hoc committee was established in response to the findings contained in a 1973 draft of the Master Plan with its goal of developing an affirmative action framework for the system.[20]

By the November 1973 board meeting, the Committee on Faculty and Staff Affairs, which worked directly with Sherriffs and was part of the ad-hoc committee, presented a Statement on Non-Discrimination and Affirmative Action for the California State University as an action item. Broken up into three broad categories, including policy, general principles, and administration, this statement defined nondiscrimination and affirmative action as distinct policies wherein the concept of nondiscrimination referred to

> personnel practices which assure applicants are employed, and employees are treated during their employment, without regard to their race, color, religion, national origin, or sex. Affirmative action means that a 'benign neutrality' under which no particular effort is made is not enough. Affirmative action requires identification of areas where minorities and women are underutilized in occupations, at certain salary levels or in organizational units. It requires that specific good faith efforts be made to enhance op-

---

20   Minutes of the Faculty and Staff Affairs Committee, September 1973. (1973).
CSU Board of Trustees Minutes of the Meeting of the Board of Trustees,
Board of Trustees of the California State University Collection. Courtesy
of the California State University Archives. California State University
Dominguez Hills, 1–2.

portunities for employment and advancement for those who, on the basis of their abilities, merit such opportunities.[21]

Making such distinctions between nondiscrimination and affirmative action was critical in ensuring that CSU hiring managers could not use the mere existence of the nondiscrimination policy to side-step their responsibility to make good faith efforts to recruit and hire qualified minorities and women, which was at the heart of the 1972 federal HEW guidelines for affirmative action.

Early Roadblocks to Affirmative Action

In the early rollout of affirmative action within the CSU, there were many roadblocks, limitations, restrictions, and narrow thinking that stood in the way of this policy being fully embraced and implemented by trustees, Chancellor's Office staff, and CSU campus officials. Racial animus and hostility toward affirmative action policy was often on display during CSU trustee meetings. For example, during the September 1973 board meeting, the idea of a quota system or racial preferences was rejected by the Ad Hoc Committee on Affirmative Action chaired by Sherriffs, but allowed "preferential treatment in the sense that special efforts would be made to seek out and find qualified members of minority groups and women."[22] The committee reached this decision after consulting with the regional director of the Anti-Defamation League of B'nai B'rith, Milton Senn, who approached the Chancellor's Office Staff to "minimize misunderstanding on the part of campus representatives in the development of their implementation program."[23] The Anti-Defamation League believed that some CSU campuses were misinterpreting affirmative action as preferential hiring for women and racial minorities. Hence, the organization contacted the Chancellor's staff and the ad-hoc committee to provide counsel. Senn

---

21 "A Statement on Nondiscrimination and Affirmative Action for the California State University and Colleges," January 23, 1974. (1974). CSU Board of Trustees Minutes of the Meeting of the Board of Trustees, Board of Trustees of the California State University Collection. Courtesy of the California State University Archives. California State University Dominguez Hills, 3030–3035.

22 Minutes of the Faculty and Staff Affairs Committee, January 23, 1974. (1974). CSU Board of Trustees Minutes of the Meeting of the Board of Trustees, Board of Trustees of the California State University Collection. Courtesy of the California State University Archives. California State University Dominguez Hills, 4.

23 Faculty and Staff Affairs Committee, "Minutes" 4.

cautioned the Ad Hoc Committee on Affirmative Action to encourage and emphasize using traditional recruitment methods while expanded recruitment efforts should be conducted simultaneously. The committee considered Senn's advice.

But some of Senn's suggestions went too far. He advised the board to not implement surveys requiring employee identification by race or ethnicity. Also, he asked for the complaint procedure to include the words "majority as well as minority persons" who alleged discrimination against them. Senn's suggestions were problematic because (1) the federal government required the collection of race and ethnicity data in the HEW guidelines, and (2) CSU trustees concluded that the collection of race, ethnicity, and gender data was critical in determining the utilization of under-represented groups in various employment classifications throughout the system and (3) the complaint procedure was to be applied to everyone so there was no need to include "majority or minority" language in the policy explicitly. A review of both Senn's prepared notes as well as sidebar notes written on the typed copy of the board meeting minutes shows that an unidentified person present questioned whether the CSU's proposed affirmative action policy would usurp the rights of the white majority over the needs of the non-white minority. This line of questioning reveals some resistance and resentment toward affirmative action within the California State University system.

On the other end of the spectrum, notes from the January 1974 board meeting reveal general support for affirmative action policy from different constituencies within the system, most notably from the faculty and staff unions. However, many of these groups questioned or took issue with the implementation aspect of the policy and, in so doing, put pressure on the trustees and Chancellor's Office to step up the enforcement of this federal and state-mandated policy. A representative for the United Professors of California (UPC) supported the policy but asked how independent campus affirmative action officers would be able to implement affirmative action programs on their respective campuses. The California State Employees Association (CSEA), which spoke for 9,000 academic and non-academic employees throughout the system offered general support for the document. As noted in their comments entitled "Misgivings about Affirmative Action," the CSEA took issue with what they called "a New Year's Eve Resolution," which created promises but "leaves implementation for a later day."[24] Specifically, the CSEA was concerned that the proposed policy delegated

---

24 "Misgivings about Affirmative Action: Remarks by George Clark, California State Employees Association January 22, 1974. (1974). CSU Board of Trustees Minutes of the Meeting of the Board of Trustees, Board of Trustees of the California State University Collection. Courtesy of the California State University Archives. California State University Dominguez Hills, 1–3.

responsibility to campuses to draft their own policies and procedures for implementing affirmative action. Furthermore, CSEA was concerned that there was no mention of faculty and staff consultation in drafting these affirmative action plans in the trustees' proposed document. In response to concerns about implementation, trustee Winifred Lancaster, one of the few women trustees on the board before the appointment of Hampton, stated that "the concerns of and fears being expressed by groups and individuals should be properly raised at the campus level rather than before the Trustees who develop policy but do not implement it."[25] While it was true that the trustees developed and approved policy, the refusal of Lancaster and other trustees to accept feedback aimed at strengthening policy was highly problematic, especially when one considers the varying levels of resistance to the very notion of affirmative action. Lancaster's comments could be likened to "kicking the can down the road," which, in effect, served as yet another roadblock in implementing this important policy. Likewise, since the proposed policy called for the hiring of a system-wide affirmative action officer and campus affirmative action officers, it would seem logical that the trustees would also seek the requisite funding for these new positions simultaneously to implement the policy. Yet some months later in July 1974, Leo Cain, president of the Dominguez Hills campus, sent an inter-office memo which read "Affirmative Action, Look at the budget. Committed to do them without the money" (see below).[26]

Reviewing the "Status Report on the 1974–1975 Support Budget" reveals that the trustees did not submit a Program Change Proposal (PCP) for affirmative action.[27] Program Change Proposals are budgetary items for developing or improving new programs within the CSU. The Finance Committee solicits PCPs from other board committees to fund new policies

---

25 Minutes of the Faculty and Staff Committee, January 23, 1974. (1974). CSU Board of Trustees Minutes of the Meeting of the Board of Trustees, Board of Trustees of the California State University Collection. Courtesy of the California State University Archives. California State University Dominguez Hills, 5.

26 Leo F. Cain, Inter-Office Memo. (1974). CSU Board of Trustees Minutes of the Meeting of the Board of Trustees, Board of Trustees of the California State University Collection. Courtesy of the California State University Archives. California State University Dominguez Hills (Folder Marked Agenda Attachments, July 9–10, 1974.)

27 Status Report on 1974–75 Support Budget and Capital Outlay Program, CSU Board of Trustees Minutes of the Meeting of the Board of Trustees, Board of Trustees of the California State University Collection. Courtesy of the California State University Archives. California State University Dominguez Hills (Folder Marked Agenda Attachments, July 9–10, 1974).

from the desk of . . .

LEO F. CAIN, *President*

CALIFORNIA STATE COLLEGE, DOMINGUEZ HILLS

*Affirmative
Action*

*look at budget
Committed to do
them without
the money.*

Leo Cain, Inter-Office Memo. July 1974. California State
University Archives. Board of Trustees Meeting Agendas
and Minutes Collection, Carson, California. Reproduced
with permission from CSU System Archives.

or programs. It creates a comprehensive budget request that is submitted to
the Governor's Office and the California Legislature for review and approval.
While the trustees did not include affirmative action in their budget request,
the California Legislature requested $520,000 to serve as seed money
for the CSU's affirmative action program, but that request was denied by
Governor Reagan. Given Reagan's denial of the legislature's request for
funding of affirmative action, his denial of a trustees' request for affirmative action funding would have been automatic. Reagan also denied three

separate trustee requests for increased funding for the Equal Opportunity Program, forcing CSU Chancellor Dumke to establish extended education units at various campuses as the for-profit side of the CSU to make up for EOP budget shortfalls. However, by not even including affirmative action funding in the budget from the start, the trustees signaled a general lack of concern for the success of the policy they developed.

The Politics of Funding Affirmative Action

When California State University Board of Trustees formally adopted a resolution to establish a systemwide affirmative action and nondiscrimination policy in late 1974, the trustees also authorized Chancellor Dumke to pursue funding from the state legislature to hire one systemwide and several individual campus affirmative action officers. These affirmative action officers would facilitate and oversee the implementation of a comprehensive affirmative action plan for faculty and staff hiring. Yet, despite the passage of this resolution, getting the funding to implement affirmation action programs was a herculean task that was made more challenging by Governor Brown's fiscal conservatism, coupled with the 1978 passage of Proposition 13, which capped property taxes across the state, resulting in severe budget cuts to the California State University system.

Before Brown was elected governor in 1975, several individual CSC campuses had initiated their own affirmative action programs out of necessity, because the Chancellor's Office and Board of Trustees refused to take up the issue until federal mandates prompted the board to act. For example, CSC Long Beach established a Minority Faculty Development Program in 1967, which provided budgetary support to relieve minority faculty of two of their four courses per semester so that they could work toward the completion of their terminal degrees. The program began with nineteen in the initial cohort, and despite budget restrictions in 1970–1971, eleven minority faculty participants earned their degrees and were offered permanent employment within the College.[28] During the October 1971 Board of Trustees meeting, Stephen Horn, president at CSC Long Beach, formally requested a systemwide affirmative action program like the program he spearheaded at his campus. His rationale for the request was simple, "Since many campuses

---

28   Stephen Horn. "Minority Faculty Development Program." October 28, 1971, Box 2C9 (1971). CSU Board of Trustees Minutes of the Meeting of the Board of Trustees, Board of Trustees of the California State University Collection. Courtesy of the California State University Archives. California State University Dominguez Hills, 1–3.

within the California State College system have recently adopted affirmative action programs which require that over the next few years a major effort be made to attract minority members to the faculty, it is essential that the Board of Trustees seek appropriate changes in law and system policy as well as request necessary budgetary support so that these goals can be attained."[29]

Stanford Cazier, President of California State College Chico, summarized his feelings on affirmative action in a letter to all board members of the Faculty and Staff Affairs committee ahead of the July 1972 meeting entitled "Accolades for Affirmative Action." In this letter Cazier said, "A frequent response in academe to HEW's affirmative action program has been righteous indignation. . . . However, insensitive as HEW may be to the complexities of implementation of an affirmative action program, to focus on those complexities is to be casuistic."[30] Inaction on the part of the Chancellor's Office and the Board of Trustees made campuses vulnerable to the loss of federal contracts and other sources of funding, apart from the fact that the individual campuses themselves were best able to develop a specific affirmative action program to meet the needs of the faculty, staff, and students in their own area. In a system as large and as complex as California State University, many of whose campuses existed before the system was even formed, implementing such a massive and complex program such as affirmative action would be no small feat. Likewise, given the Chancellor and Board of Trustees' hands-off approach toward individual campus implementation of federal and state-mandated programs related to race and the socioeconomic background of students, such as Upward Board and EOP, it is no wonder that individual campuses saw fit to begin developing their own affirmation action programs without consulting systemwide administrators.

However, after the San Francisco Student Strike of 1968, CSU trustees wanted to be more involved in developing and monitoring of affirmative action and nondiscrimination policy due, in part, to the politics surrounding federal and state race-based policies and programs. On the one hand, the trustees were seemingly resistant to the very premise of affirmative action to rectify past discrimination by giving underrepresented groups special consideration for university admission and employment opportunities. On the other hand, the trustees also wanted to play a major role in how these policies would be structured, administered, and evaluated. Despite their objections to the entire idea of affirmative action, the CSU trustees wanted to

29 Horn, "Minority Faculty Development," 3.
30 Stanford Cazier. "Accolade for Affirmative Action." July 7, 1972. Box 2C9
    (1972 Supplement Documents Folder). CSU Board of Trustees Minutes of
    the Meeting of the Board of Trustees, Board of Trustees of the California State
    University Collection. Courtesy of the California State University Archives.
    California State University Dominguez Hills, 1–6.

have the power to monitor the program to narrow its scope as much as legally possible.

It would have made the most logical sense for the Chancellor's Office to take the lead on developing a systemwide affirmative action policy. However, it would take a federal mandate to galvanize university systems to take more decisive action on these issues during this time, not only in California, but in most colleges and universities in the United States. The CSC trustees requested presentations and reports on the system's affirmative action programs' status for both the July and November 1972 board meetings. However, instead of rolling out new policies that would meet the HEW Higher Education Guidelines, Vice Chancellor Keene provided the trustees with copies of letters of protest from white applicants for faculty positions who believed they were denied these positions because of what Keene calls "over-zealousness and heavy-handedness" in the implementation of individual campus affirmative action efforts. The Chancellor's Office squandered an opportunity to take the lead on the issue. Instead, it offered a reactive approach, creating unnecessary confusion and tension between individual campus administrators and system-wide administrators. One of these letters from a campus hiring officer went as far as to deny a white applicant a position who was the campus's top candidate because "your ancestry does not qualify you as an oppressed minority."[31] Although there were never any directives from the system or campus general legal counsels to deny top white candidates for positions and instead hire less qualified minority candidates, Keene's decision to highlight these grievance letters by white applicants foreshadowed the tenor and tone of the upcoming debates that trustees, the Chancellor's Office, campus presidents, and the statewide Academic Senate would have once the new Higher Education Guidelines were released. These grievance letters were "weaponized" by the Chancellor's Office with the net effect of torpedoing trustee support for affirmative action in faculty and staff hiring. It is within this fraught environment that Claudia Hampton and other supporters of affirmative action would be operating.

Given the trustees' stance on the funding of EOP, it is no wonder that the debate over the funding and implementation of affirmative action would become so contentious. At this juncture, it is vital to acknowledge the role that the California State Legislature would play in this debate, as the California State Colleges depended on the legislature for funding. Prior to the issuance of the HEW Higher Education Guidelines, individual members of the State Legislature authored several bills and resolutions to firm up support for affirmative action and nondiscriminatory policy. In March 1972, for example, Assemblyman Willie Brown introduced Assembly Bill 1703 (AB

---

31   Keene, "Affirmative Action Information," Attachment B5.

1703), which called for continuous funding of Educational Opportunity Programs (EOP) through an open-ended appropriation formula similar to one used to provide aid to K-12 schools. Brown was part of a group of African Americans elected to the Assembly in 1965 along with Mervyn Dymally, F. Douglass Ferrell, and Byron Rumford. Yvonne Braithwaite Burke became the first African American woman elected to the Assembly in 1966. This was the first time the Assembly had more than a single African American legislator at once, which meant these members could come together to increase support for legislation that would be of great interest and benefit to African Americans. The election of these five African American Assembly members increased legislation to either establish or protect the interests of Californians of color, women, and the poor.

Assembly Bill 1703 was in fact designed to reduce the annual process of battling over EOP appropriation, giving students a greater sense of security and eliminating any excuses for program ineffectiveness. However, when this legislation was presented to the Public Affairs Committee of the CSC Board of Trustees in April 1972, some trustees objected to the legislation on the grounds that it would ". . . reduce Trustee authority over a significant portion of the total budget," not to mention some objected to the "singling out of a single program for special budgetary consideration."[32] Given how the EOP budget has always been subject to the funding priorities and whims of the governor and state legislators, one would think the trustees would welcome Brown's bill to put the program on firmer financial footing.

Instead, what we see from these raised objections is a type of racial dog-whistling in opposition to EOP from some trustees. The largest beneficiaries of the EOP programs were racial minority students. Yet members of the Public Affairs Committee went on the record in opposition, stating, "We recommend therefore that the bill be amended so as to make the funds appropriated solely on the basis of level of need. In this way, we would not find ourselves in the awkward position of passing over a poor but otherwise qualified and eligible student for a less needy student who happens to also be enrolled in a special program of academic assistance."[33] This statement was an attempt to slowly chip away at one of the system's most successful pre-college programs by narrowing the scope to financial need only and disregarding the actual intent of the program, which was to expand access

---

32 CSU Board of Trustees Public Affairs Committee "Attachment: AB 1703, Brown, Higher Education Opportunity Programs," April 26, 1972. Box 2C9 (1972). CSU Board of Trustees Minutes of the Meeting of the Board of Trustees, Board of Trustees of the California State University Collection. Courtesy of the California State University Archives. California State University Dominguez Hills, 1.

33 Public Affairs, "AB 1703," 1.

to educationally disadvantaged, low-income, racial and ethnic minority, and other under-represented groups of students. This type of indirect dog-whistling—where class is put before race as the sole qualification to special programs and/or scholarships—was a power play by CSC trustees to limit access by students of color, implying these students were not as needy or deserving as their white counterparts.

These attempts at limiting the scope and reach of EOP programs by CSC trustees were deeply concerning for Chancellor Dumke and his staff, who had been warned by state legislators that student affirmative action would soon be the next priority for the system, with the release of a draft copy of the 1973 Master Plan for Education by the Joint Committee of the California Legislature. This draft report clarified that "By 1980, each segment of California public higher education shall approximate the general ethnic, sexual, and economic composition of the state."[34] Where the 1960 Master Plan was silent on the issue of student access and equity, this new Master Plan would make it clear that the state legislature expected the state's public higher education institutions to prioritize equal educational opportunity for underrepresented students through affirmative action programs. Not long after the release of the final report of the Master Plan, this recommendation became state law with the passage of Assembly Concurrent Resolution 151 (ACR 151) in late 1974, which required state higher education institutions to produce a comprehensive student affirmative action plan or risk losing state funding to operate.[35]

CSC Assistant Executive Vice Chancellor Lee Kerschner was given the opportunity to present a statement about the draft report of the Master Plan, in which he conveyed that the CSU agreed in principle with the recommendation but asked the Joint Committee to revise the language to read "shall approximate the general ethnic, sexual, and economic composition of those high school graduates who are eligible to attend higher education." Kerschner said that achieving this objective would require the full cooperation of elementary and secondary schools and, with his suggested revision, would make it clear that higher education was not solely responsible. However, considering how the trustees' attempts to limit funding for EOP pre-college programs, which also depended on cooperation with elementary and secondary schools, this requested revision seemed like nothing more

---

34   Draft Report of the Joint Committee on the Master Plan for Higher Education. March 1972 CSU Board of Trustees Minutes of the Meeting of the Board of Trustees, Board of Trustees of the California State University Collection. Courtesy of the California State University Archives. California State University Dominguez Hills.

35   California State Assembly. Assembly Concurrent Resolution 151 – Relative to public higher education. September 11, 1974.

than an attempt to deflect responsibility for the recruitment and retention of diverse student groups within the CSC. It is a foregone conclusion that any student seeking admission into the CSC would be a high school graduate, so Kerschner's request seem unnecessary and deliberately disingenuous.

Although the original language of the recommendation was revised to include part of the CSC's requested phrasing of "high school graduates," the final report went further in delineating exactly how the CSC, UC, and community colleges were expected to fulfill this policy with (1) affirmative efforts to seek qualified students, (2) experimenting with alternative ways to assess student potential, (3) special financial assistance programs and (4) counseling for disadvantaged students. The Joint Committee wanted to clarify that public higher education institutions in California had a responsibility to take demonstrative steps to ensure that diverse students (including women) had access. This state legislative mandate, through the 1973 Master Plan and ACR-151, therefore, became that seminal moment when the CSC trustees and Chancellor's Office could no longer obfuscate, stall, or halt the enforcement of affirmative action as they had attempted in the early days of this federal policy. It became essential for system administrators (trustees and Chancellor's Office staff) to embrace affirmative action as bound law and not simply a series of suggestions.

Prompted by the release of the 1973 Master Plan, Claudia Hampton made her first official appearance as a member of the CSC Board of Trustees at the March 1974 board meeting. She was placed on the Educational Policy, Finance, and Organization and Rules committees. At the same meeting, Herbert Carter was introduced as the CSC's first systemwide affirmative action officer. In a 2018 interview, Carter, who is African American, described his first meeting with the CSC Council of Presidents, in which one of the campus presidents stated, "That's fine if you want to hire him [Carter], but I don't want him on my campus. So that was the beginning of my tussle with the Council of Presidents." Carter's direct experience in working as a negotiator between campus presidents and student activists at the Northridge and Pomona campuses in the late 1960s and his early recollection of the racial attitudes held by the CSC system and campus leadership is essential, because it gives some insight into the opposition that both Hampton and Carter would face.

Campus administrators took an aggressive and hostile stance against Black student protests calling for Black Studies programs, more support services and aid to Black students, and increased enrollment of students of color in the university. Carter saw first-hand how resistant CSC campus and system administrators were to Black student concerns and, because of this resistance, Carter says that when Chancellor Dumke approached him about becoming the system's first affirmative action officer, his initial response was,

"Not really. My real response to Glenn Dumke was no, I don't know if I want to work with you guys because you're a bunch of racists, anyway. I'm not all that excited about being here. But he [Dumke] was nice about it and said, well if you think that about us you ought to be concerned to help us try to change that." With Carter's appointment as the system's first affirmative action officer and Hampton's appointment to the system's board of trustees at the March 1974 board meeting, they became some of the system's earliest African American appointees directly associated with the Chancellor's Office. As such, they both experienced and witnessed racism first-hand and used their positions to change the system from within. Yet despite the open hostility from campus presidents and many of the conservative trustees, Carter secured federal approval for all then-nineteen campuses' affirmative action plans within eighteen months. The CSC needed someone to coordinate and monitor the development of these plans between multiple campuses. Carter shepherded this process through, with Hampton running interference by defending the affirmative action plans that Carter proposed to the board of trustees.

Unlike the faculty plan devised by Carter and coordinated within the CSC, ACR 151 mandated that the student affirmative action plan would be coordinated by the California Post-Secondary Education Commission (CPEC, formerly the CCCHE), the state's higher education coordinating council. Representatives from the state's higher educational institutions, including independent and private colleges and universities, provided input on the student plan. Claudia Hampton had a tremendous influence over the plan's content, structure, and tone while she served as the primary CSU representative on the CPEC from 1977 to 1988. There was less resistance to the student affirmative action plan for two reasons: the state mandate and because CPEC handled coordination of the plan. However, less resistance should not be confused with more support. Affirmative action would continue to face challenges and obstacles despite systemwide statements of support for the general principle.

Case in point: implementing of affirmative action within the CSU was at a virtual standstill for nearly a year after trustees voted to approve the faculty affirmative action policy in early 1974. The trustees submitted no specific budget requests for affirmative action hiring or special programs to the state legislature or governor until March 1975, when Democrat Jerry Brown assumed the governorship of California. One possible explanation for why the trustees delayed making budgetary requests was Ronald Reagan's vocal opposition to affirmative action which he called "reverse racism." Reagan also used his line-item veto power to strike down a state legislature request for half a million dollars to support affirmative action hiring in the CSU. Throughout his term as governor, Reagan voiced his opposition to any race-based policies and initiatives such as the state's Equal Opportunity Program (EOP). Trustees likely figured it would be easier to wait until Brown assumed office, given his vocal support for affirmative action. However, there was a difference between supporting affirmative action in principle and using one's position to make those policies a reality. Affirmative action faced challenges even from its professed supporters.

Jerry Brown: Liberal in Name Only?

Jerry Brown attended the March 1975 trustee meeting for the first time as governor of the state. During that time, he expressed concern about the lack of women and minorities in the faculty, signaling his support for affirmative action. He further commented that faculty responsibility, student consultation, affirmative action, and prevention of political interference were the principles for promoting faculty.[36] Yet despite the Committee on Finance introducing affirmative action as a Program Change Proposal (PCP) for the first time in 1975, Brown removed this funding request from the budget presented to the state legislature for approval. Even more, Jerry Brown moved to reduce the number of teachers in California due to his assumption of an "oversupply" of teachers in what would become part of Brown's attempt to save costs for the state. Unfortunately, Brown's assumption about teachers in California ignored that data that showed that students of color and students living in low-income areas needed more teachers to help combat their lower retention rates. Campus presidents and deans felt compelled to raise the alarm to the trustees about the potential harm caused by Brown's cost-cutting schemes, which directly impacted the CSU's implementation of affirmative action policy.

Early into his tenure as governor in the late 1970s, Brown gained a reputation as a fiscal conservative that contradicts his reputation as a "flamboyant liberal."[37] Jerry Walker, for example, writing in *The American Conservative,* states that "Governor Brown was much more of a fiscal conservative than Governor Reagan . . . Reagan raised taxes several times and boosted spending by an average of 12.2 percent a year. In his first year as governor, by contrast, Brown increased spending by just 4.6 percent, less than the rate

---

36 March 1975. CSU Board of Trustees Minutes of the Meeting of the Board of Trustees, Board of Trustees of the California State University Collection. Courtesy of the California State University Archives. California State University Dominguez Hills.

37 Jesse Walker. "The Five Faces of Jerry Brown," *American Conservative,* November 1, 2009.

of inflation."[38] In fact, Brown's cost-cutting measures resulted in the state's largest budget surplus in the state's history. Yet one could argue that Brown's thrift came at the expense of affirmative action programs, which were severely negatively impacted.

By 1976, Brown had begun emphasizing Educational Opportunity Programs (EOPs), which had been in place within California's public community colleges and universities since 1969 with Senate Bill 1072. Educational Opportunity Programs were designed to improve access and retention of historically underrepresented students by facilitating their matriculation into the CSU through several support services, including pre-college advising and mentoring, outreach, tutoring and financial support. Compared with affirmative action, which dealt with faculty and staff employment, by the mid-1970s, EOP programs were not controversial; in fact, each CSU campus had some form of EOP programming already in place. Brown proposed a 50% increase to the overall EOP budget to the tune of a 3.4 million dollars while continuing to veto the CSU trustees' request for faculty and staff affirmative action funding. Why Brown continued to deny trustee requests for affirmative action amidst a federal mandate for these programs is unclear. What is known is that in refusing to finance affirmative action programs in the CSU, Brown left the program vulnerable and conservative opposition to the policy saw this lack of funding as an opportunity to limit or eliminate the program altogether.

As early as 1974, the Supreme Court began hearing cases challenging the constitutionality of affirmative action, following President Kennedy's Executive Order 10925 which called for the Equal Employment Opportunity Committee to provide access and equity to minorities in programs utilizing federal funding.[39] Later cases, most notably, the *Regents of the University of California v. Bakke* (1978), upheld the use of affirmative action for university admission. Still, it outlawed the use of racial quotas, affecting not only the CSU system but all public higher education institutions in the United States.

---

38   Walker, "Five Faces."

39   *Defunis v. Odegaard* (1974) was the first case to reach the Supreme Court challenging the constitutionality of affirmative action in higher education admissions. While placed on a waiting list and subsequently denied admissions into the University of Washington Law School in 1971, the plaintiff Marco Defunis Jr. filed a lawsuit against the law school by claiming its admissions policy had set-aside a specific number of admissions slots for minority applicants with significantly lower test scores and grades which violated the Equal Protection Clause of the Fourteenth Amendment. The state Supreme Court found that the law school's affirmative action policy would enable officials to attain a racially diverse student body. The plaintiff sought further review from the U.S. Supreme Court, but as the plaintiff had since been admitted and was finishing the last year of law school, the Court vacated the case as moot.

Critics of affirmative action and racial quotas as a practice claimed that affirmative action hindered racial reconciliation, undermined the achievements of minorities, and perpetuated "reverse racism" against the white majority. Although conservative opposition to affirmative action had been unsuccessful in eliminating affirmative action completely in *Bakke*, they were able to cast enough doubt about the inherent "fairness" of the policy. The *Bakke* decision led to the eventual elimination of affirmative action not just in the CSC but in higher education across California less than two decades later.

The CSU Trustees continued making budget requests to fund affirmative action programs with the Committee on Finance noting:"The most difficult aspects of affirmative action are the necessary changes in attitude and behavior."[40] It seems a bit ironic that the trustees would make such a statement about the need for change in attitudes and behavior given the board's past resistance to affirmative action. However, several factors might explain this shift from outright hostility to more favorable support of the policy. From a legislative perspective, the federal requirement for public colleges and universities to develop an approved employee affirmative action plan and the state mandate for California colleges and universities to create a student affirmative action plan meant that trustees had to prioritize affirmative action. Another critical factor in the CSU's gradual move toward support for affirmative action came from other CPEC member institutions, most notably the University of California, which fought hard to protect affirmative action to ensure equal educational opportunity. In essence, the University of California, given its more stringent admission requirements than its CSU or community college counterparts, would have had very few ethnic minority and women students had it not been for affirmative action. With the University of California at the center of the affirmative action debate with the *Bakke* case, the CSU and other CPEC institutions looked to the UC for guidance on protecting their existing affirmative action programs. Finally, the presence of Claudia Hampton as a trustee and Herb Carter as the system's first affirmative action officer put a face to affirmative action in ways that made the policy real, tangible, and understandable for the white trustees on the board, who were unfamiliar with the lived experiences of racism and sexism. Combined, these factors moved even the most conservative trustees away from outright hostility toward a general willingness to compromise, though this shift did not happen overnight.

It should also be noted that Chancellor Dumke was neither a proponent nor an opponent of affirmative action; he was more of a pragmatist whose investment in affirmative action had more to do with protecting the system

---

40   Committee on Finance Report. October 1976. CSU Board of Trustees Minutes of the Meeting of the Board of Trustees, Board of Trustees of the California State University Collection. Courtesy of the California State University Archives. California State University Dominguez Hills.

more so than a genuine belief in the value of affirmative action. As one of the chief architects of the 1960 Master Plan, Dumke was always attuned to the state legislature's demands rather than the political whims of the governor. Since the passage of the Donahoe Act, which codified the 1960 Master Plan that Dumke helped to develop, it has been the legislature where the CSU found most of its loyal support, particularly from Assembly Members Teresa Hughes and John Vasconcellos who authored hundreds of bills in support of the CSU through affirmative action programs. From a fundamental political standpoint, it simply made sense for the Dumke and the CSU to try to court favor with the legislature by expressing support for affirmative action, since the legislature's most ardent supporters of the CSU had already embraced the idea.

As a result of Governor Brown's continued refusal to authorize funding for affirmative action, CSU Chancellor Glenn Dumke created an affirmative action task force made up of trustees, Chancellor's Office staff, and campus presidents to look for alternative admission methods even as the Office for Civil Rights approved the CSU affirmative action plan in 1977. One of the proposals regarding student admission to gain traction was an admissions exception provision known throughout the system as the four percent rule, which enabled campuses to admit a small percentage of "disadvantaged" students as exceptions to the regular university admission criteria. Both the California State University and the University of California approved such provisions. Since additional funding was not needed to implement this provision, the four percent rule was not impacted by the funding debate between the governor and the CSU.

For her part, Claudia Hampton was serving as Vice Chair of the Educational Policy Committee (EPC) when the debate over affirmative action funding started to reach a boiling point. The board's Educational Policy Committee sought input from various campus entities about funding priorities around affirmative action as early as 1976, with this information being shared with the newly formed task force the following year. In a CSU systemwide ranking of funding priorities, affirmative action was ranked as a top priority byforty-two percent of all campus presidents, forty-six percent of the systemwide Academic Senate, and sixty percent of students in late 1976.[41] Despite this broad support for the implementation of affirmative action, Brown continued to veto trustee budget requests. Frustrated with Brown's continued vetoes, but desperate to secure even a miniscule

41   CSU Board of Trustees Meeting Minutes, May 1976, CSU Board of Trustees Minutes of the Meeting of the Board of Trustees, Board of Trustees of the California State University Collection. Courtesy of the California State University Archives. California State University Dominguez Hills.

amount of funding to implement and maintain a special recruitment and selection program for minority faculty, supervisory staff, and administrators, the Trustee Finance Committee cut their estimated program maintenance request from $350,000 to $150,000, in hopes of increasing the likelihood of this program being supported by the governor and legislature. Yet Brown also vetoed this request, including a remedial student writing skills program. It would be another two years before Brown finally relented and approved funding for affirmative action, but this only came after pressure from United Professors of California (UPC) released press releases condemning Brown's neglect of the entire CSU system.[42]

Brown's delay in approving the funding foreshadowed the numerous challenges still facing affirmative action advocates like Hampton, who then had to contend with the fallout from the passage of Proposition 13, which capped the tax rate on real estate in California. According to the Howard Jarvis Taxpayers Association, authors of the ballot measure, "Prior to Proposition 13, property taxes were out of control. People were losing their homes because they could not pay their property taxes, yet government did nothing to help them."[43] On June 6, 1978, more than two-thirds of California voters passed Proposition 13, which limited property taxes for residential and commercial properties to one percent (1%) of the full cash value of a property. Over time, new homeowners end up paying significantly more than their fair share of taxes for real estate because of the wild fluctuation of home values in California. Proposition 13 effectively made it tougher for the state to pass taxes, because this new legislation required any state tax to be approved by two-thirds of both houses of the California legislature.[44] Likewise, any new city or county taxes had to have the approval of two-thirds of voters for projects with a special purpose, such as building schools, roads, or parks. This legislation immediately put the "California Idea," that

---

42 United Professors of California News Release, January 11, 1978. CSU Board of Trustees Minutes of the Meeting of the Board of Trustees, Board of Trustees of the California State University Collection. Courtesy of the California State University Archives. California State University Dominguez Hills.

43 Howard Jarvis Taxpayer Association "Proposition 13." Accessed September 8, 2022. https://www.hjta.org/propositions/proposition-13/?gclid=C j0KCQjwpeaYBhDXARIsAEzItbEqGuxaG4DKMmaiAEBj3a3FWVs6J_ 9VAT6TjJjInxkgkyJxkvT1XBMaAqj0EALw_wcB.

44 Matt Levin. "What is Proposition 13? Your Prop. 13 Cheatsheet" Prop. 13 The California Dream Series/CALMatters. Accessed September 8, 2022, https://projects.scpr.org/prop-13/history/.

is, an influential model of public higher education combining broad access and high academic quality, into jeopardy.[45]

As a result of Brown's fiscal conservatism and the loss of tax revenue needed for public education brought on by Proposition 13, the implementation of affirmative action sat in limbo regarding faculty hiring and student admission. In fact, Chancellor Dumke had to delay rolling out a new systemwide Faculty Affirmative Action Development Program, which Herb Carter had begun developing before his promotion to Assistant Executive Vice Chancellor for the CSU. After the passage of Proposition 13, Brown attended the November 1978 trustees' meeting, where he was met with a chilly reception from the chancellor and trustees. The Finance Committee even passed a resolution that condemned Brown's budget cuts. Claudia Hampton, still a member of the Educational Policy Committee, openly expressed her concerns that these cuts would do irreparable damage to affirmative action implementation in the system.

At first glance, trustees' anger with Governor Brown over the proposed budget cuts seemed misplaced, given the impact of Proposition 13. However, given Brown's previous denial of CSU trustee budget requests for affirmative action and other campus programs, including a proposal to slash the CSU budget by 69 million dollars in anticipation of the passage of Proposition 13, frosty relations between the governor and the trustees were to be expected. Members of the California legislature found themselves drawn into the middle of these tense relations by approving $500,000 in stop-gap funding to help the CSU initiate a faculty development program for women and ethnic minorities in May 1978. These funds were used to fund pilot faculty affirmative action programs at only two of the system's then-twenty campuses: Dominguez Hills and Fresno. The legislature felt compelled to intervene to ensure that Assembly Concurrent Resolution (ACR) 151 (1974) remained on track. Nonetheless, the trustees continued making affirmative action funding requests, which Brown severely cut.

By early 1979, relations between the governor and the various sectors of public higher education had soured even further after the State Finance Office, which advised the governor in drafting the state budget, recommended cutting affirmative action as non-essential programming. After years of internal debating, drafting policies, and making public declarations of support for affirmative action, Chancellor Dumke and the CSU trustees reached an impasse with Governor Brown over funding for affirmative action and other essential campus services. Governor Brown challenged the CSU to identify system priorities for budget reductions. A shrewd politician,

---

45 John Aubry Douglass, *The California Idea and American Higher Education: 1850 to the 1960 Master Plan.* (Palo Alto, Stanford University Press, 2007).

Brown knew that by demanding that the CSU identify which programs, services, and staff could be eliminated, public anger would be directed toward the Chancellor and individual campus leaders instead of the governor. Chancellor Dumke responded to Brown's challenge: "Student access was a long-standing priority, but now financial aid, low fees, and special assistance programs have assured near complete equality of educational opportunity."[46] Dumke's comment was intended to remind the public that student access could not be achieved without proper funding and Brown's refusal to fund affirmative action would hinder the state's progress in achieving its goal of equal educational opportunity for all Californians. Dumke recognized that Brown's challenge was nothing more than a political stunt. Treading lightly, lest he get drawn into a nasty public feud with a popular governor, Dumke's comments, instead, focused on the benefits of affirmative action in achieving the access and retention goals set forth by the legislature with the release of the 1973 Master Plan and passage of ACR 151. If Governor Brown wanted to cut affirmative action or any other essential services within the CSU, he would have to do so without the CSU's participation and deal with the political fallout on his own.

Over the next two years, after Hampton was appointed board chair in 1979, the board faced numerous challenges, including an increased demand for minority student access in the state's large urban centers, juxtaposed with a significant state budget crisis that would impact the system's progress on its student and faculty affirmative action goals. Hampton's experience as a school administrator, classroom teacher, and negotiator between various constituent groups within LAUSD was brought to bear when she assumed the role of board chair. From a year of silent assessment and observation to board chair in five short years, Hampton's rise to one of the most influential trustees in board history went well beyond her being the first Black woman trustee. Her race and gender could have worked against her, but she deftly turned her disadvantages into advantages, using sly civility as her weapon of choice. In making the transition into board leadership, Hampton would need to apply all of her skills at strategy and negotiation to remain effective, in light of new challenges facing the CSU system.

46   Glenn Dumke, Chancellor's Report. May 1979. CSU Board of Trustees Minutes of the Meeting of the Board of Trustees, Board of Trustees of the California State University Collection. Courtesy of the California State University Archives. California State University Dominguez Hills.

Chapter Three

The Conciliator Makes Dinner

Beyond any federal and state mandates, it would take the cultivation of personal relationships with the board's white trustees by the "black woman on board" for the CSU trustees to begin to embrace affirmative action, both in principle and in practice. Within the California State University system, Mabel Kinney was the first woman appointed to the CSU trustee board in 1960. It would take another fourteen years before the board would have its first non-white woman trustee, with the appointment of Dr. Claudia Hampton. As the first Black woman board member, Hampton's appointment might have functioned as an indicator of racial equality and progress. Yet at the time Hampton was installed as a member of the board in 1974, hostile racial attitudes toward people of color were still deeply entrenched in California as in other parts of the country. Thus it should come as no surprise that Hampton's appointment to the CSU Board of Trustees was met with shock for some and open hostility from others. Claudia Hampton had to approach her work using finesse, subtlety, and shrewd thinking to counter this hostility and be effective in her role as trustee. This chapter focuses on how she enacted sly civility through a variety of strategies and tactics to protect affirmative action and push back against those forces that worked to obstruct, limit, or eliminate programs designed to increase access and equity for women and people of color within the California State University system.

In recounting the first few years of her appointment, Hampton told the story of an incident where fellow trustee board member, Wendell Witter, a managing partner of Dean Witter and Company, used a racist term during a disagreement with Hampton about affirmative action policy implementation. Hampton recalled, "Wendell Witter—He was the one who made the comment in a board meeting "I don't understand this. There's a problem. There's a n----- in the woodpile."[1] The specific phrase Witter used, "n----- in

---

1   Claudia Hampton (California State University Trustee), interviewed by Sarah Sharp (Bancroft Library Regional History Office), Los Angeles, California, 1984, transcript, California State University Trustee Archives, Carson, CA., 11.

the woodpile," was a figure of speech used in the United States dating back to the 19th century referring to the concealment of slaves under piles of firewood or other hiding places. Newman Ivey White describes how the phrase eventually meant that something was suspicious or wrong.[2] Regardless of the etymology of this particular phrase, Hampton and several of her white colleagues on the board took great offense to Witter's comments, particularly as the use of the term "n----r" was offensive no matter the context, time period, or intent of the speaker, and especially given that Witter specifically directed those comments toward a Black person. Hampton opted in that moment to deal with the matter privately with Witter, which ultimately helped her court favor with the staunchly conservative white male board members. She said of the interaction, "Wendell had no idea what he said which tells you . . . which gives you some notion of what I was dealing with. I told the chair that the matter had to be dealt with but in order to not disrupt the meeting, I would deal with that matter with Mr. Witter in a face to face situation immediately following this meeting. And it was then that Wendell Witter wanted to know "what did I do?" And they [other members of the board] were so appreciative that I didn't walk the table right there. And they were willing to help me beat him to pieces with leather belts."[3]

By not demanding a public censure of Witter for his deeply offensive comments, Hampton signaled to her white male board counterparts that she was a political moderate in these situations, indicating that they could discuss racial issues with her in the future. Hampton's years of experience as the Director of the Schools and Community Relations Unit for Los Angeles Unified School District undoubtedly came into play as she dealt with racist comments and other forms of discrimination while serving on the CSU Board of Trustees. Responsible for serving as a liaison between Black and Latino parents and Los Angeles schools during court mandated desegregation orders in 1970, Hampton's job as director was to identify and triage potential racial public relations problems for the school district. She became adept at addressing the concerns of different groups of people who were often deeply invested and passionate on both sides of the school busing and school desegregation issue. That experience served Hampton well as she faced a new set of challenges as the first Black woman on a board dominated by conservative, white men.

The manner in which Hampton chose to address Witter's comments was practiced and measured, giving us an early look at how she would handle herself as the "affirmative action trustee." Hampton was acutely aware of

---

2   Newman I. White "The White Man in the Woodpile. Some Influences on Negro Secular Folk-Songs." *American Speech* 4, no. 3 (1929): 207–15.

3   Hampton, interview, 1984.

her position as an African American and as a woman as central reasons for her appointment to the board. Hampton candidly talks about how she was initially perceived on the board when she says:

> I am identified, I know, as the affirmative action trustee. It is expected and I never fail to thoroughly march through any affirmative action measures to take a very strong stance and to guard very carefully to not only push for implementation of our own very good affirmative action program on paper. I'm just the guard at the gate of those matters. I think its proper and necessary. While I may be viewed in most matters as a moderate, I think by my peers and constituencies on affirmative action, I am viewed as a strong advocate. How could I be anything else?[4]

This quote helps us understand how others saw Hampton and gives us insight into her priorities for her board service, ensuring that affirmative action would be carefully considered. Instead of abdicating the responsibility to advocate for Black and other underrepresented groups within the system, Hampton wholeheartedly embraced this role, doing what was necessary to ensure that the rest of her board colleagues would treat affirmative action as an institutional priority in the same way she did. However, before becoming the "affirmative action" trustee, Hampton underwent a vetting process that was unlike that of any of her predecessors, foreshadowing some of the racial politics she would need to navigate as a trustee.

Vetting the Affirmative Action Trustee

While the CSU trustees were debating whether to implement federal guide-lines on nondiscrimination, Claudia Hampton was introduced to the person who would become instrumental in her appointment to the board.

Unlike most trustees, who were appointed because of their personal con-nection or business relationship with the governor, Claudia Hampton's appointment to the board was once shrouded in mystery, as she was neither a friend of Ronald Reagan nor a member of the Republican Party. Hampton was a staunch Democrat who helped establish a Black-women-led political action committee dedicated to electing Black people to local and state posi-tions. Instead, Hampton explains that her appointment came about from what she terms "a very fortunate accident" and a bit of ingenuity on the part of Virna Canson, regional director of the West Coast Office of the NAACP, that was highlighted in the introduction.[5] Hampton says of her appoint-ment, "I can tell you very quickly how I became a trustee. People are usually

---

4   Hampton, interview, 1984.
5   Hampton, Interview, 1984.

a bit puzzled. Appointed by Reagan, reappointed by Jerry Brown, now working under Deukmejian. I always give a bland but modest reply, 'Well, I try to work hard.' But I knew Alex Sherriffs first and there again was a very fortunate accident in my life."[6]

The person Hampton refers to in the above quote is Dr. Alex Sherriffs, who served as Education Secretary to Ronald Reagan when he was governor of California from 1969 to 1974. Sherriffs was later named Vice Chancellor for Academic Affairs for the CSU system in 1973, months before Reagan appointed Claudia Hampton to the CSU Board of Trustees. During Sherriffs' tenure as education secretary, two of the most pressing concerns in education in California and across the nation were desegregation and busing in public schools. Unlike states in the U.S. South, which had a formal and informal policy of Jim Crow segregation in schools, public facilities, and transportation, California's patterns of residential segregation had an important impact on school desegregation. Housing decisions were and continue to be largely based on perceptions of school quality, which is often closely related to the racial demographics of the school and community. White flight to the suburbs in the 1960s hastened this racial segregation. While the 1954 *Brown v. Board of Education* decision may have ended racial segregation in schools, it did not end racial segregation in housing in California. As a result, schools in California remained racially separate and academically and fiscally unequal.

Civil rights groups like the NAACP began filing lawsuits against school districts across the state that were said to have maintained racially segregated schools. By the early 1970s, cities like Los Angeles and San Francisco were ordered by federal district courts to adopt consent decrees calling for the elimination of racial and ethnic segregation in district schools, programs, or classrooms. It was Sherriffs' responsibility to keep abreast of these legal developments related to busing and school desegregation so he could advise the governor. One way that Sherriffs stayed informed on these cases was to invite representatives from organizations involved in the school desegregation fight to his office to share their concerns. In late 1973, one of the recipients of Sherriffs' invitation was Virna Mae Canson, West Coast Region Director of the NAACP.

Always thinking strategically, Virna Canson decided that instead of attending this meeting alone in Sacramento she would assemble a group of NAACP chapter presidents to attend with her and surprise Sherriffs with their numbers. Claudia Hampton recalls the meeting, "For this little briefing, she marches in about, all innocent, she called down here [to the Los Angeles NAACP Chapter Office] and asked the president of local branches to join her. Our president, unfortunately for him couldn't go, so he asked me if I

---

6   Hampton, interview, 1984.

would run up there with this group. Okay, it's about education. That's why he asked me."[7] Along with Canson and Hampton were eight or nine other local NAACP presidents or their proxies in attendance. The primary reason for the meeting was to discuss busing and desegregation, educational issues of great importance to African Americans in California. Virna Canson stated, "What we were trying to convey were some dimensions in education. I don't know that we could have ever convinced Alex to go out and be a rabid advocate for busing, but so much gets missed in terms of why the NAACP is always out there pushing for integrated education."[8] While an interview conducted with Alex Sherriffs in 1978 does not cover this meeting with Canson and the NAACP presidents, both Hampton and Canson's interviews tell a similar story of how Sherriffs extended his meeting from the scheduled twenty minutes to a full hour because he was deeply engrossed in the conversation, particularly pertaining to race relations. Furthermore, Canson recalls how Sherriffs was a new convert to conservative ideas and was interested in getting the group's opinion on more conservative thinkers' views on race and affirmative action. She notes, "He [Alex Sherriffs] would need to describe what it meant to him. He had a lot of ideas that he was working through. Our backgrounds and day-to-day experiences were quite different from Alex. For example, Alex was quite enamored with a book by Thomas Sowell, who is a black ultra conservative, now at the Hoover Institution at Stanford. Alex bought the book in quantity and distributed it widely among legislators, State Board of Education members, and others. We thought the book was bad."[9] But being so taken with the group's discussion Sherriffs asked if the group could continue meeting occasionally, with researchers referring to the group as a NAACP informal advisory group.[10] Eventually the group of ten was whittled down to just a few people, including Granville Jackson, president of the San Francisco NAACP chapter, and Dr. Claudia Hampton, member of the Los Angeles NAACP chapter.

Over the course of the next year, Sherriffs met with this group "at airports, just anywhere we could find a little space for two or three hours and he [Sherriffs and a member of his staff] would go back to Sacramento."[11]

---

7   Hampton, interview, 1984.
8   Virna Canson, "Waging the War on Poverty and Discrimination in California through the NAACP, 1953–1974," Interviewed by Sarah Sharp, Regional Oral History Office, The Bancroft Library, University of California Berkeley, December 1984, 2.
9   Canson interview, 1984, 3.
10   Canson interview, 1984, 1.
11   Hampton, interview, 1984

Eventually, Reagan asked Sherriffs about these informal meetings that were taking him out of the office and up and down the state a few times per month. After Reagan's query, Sherriffs arranged a meeting for the governor to meet with his "informal advisory group" which had been further whittled down to just Hampton. When asked by Sarah Sharp the nature of the things discussed during this meeting, Hampton responded, "We ranged further than that [education issues]. Cultural things. The differences between people. Just whatever came up. He was very interested in issues we would describe as black issues. He really was. He would bring in Melvin Bradley, [an African American aide to Governor Reagan on community affairs] whom he took to Washington. We had a series of those [meetings]."[12]

Hampton did not expect anything specific from these meetings with Governor Reagan. She and Sherriffs continued meeting sporadically with Reagan. Hampton and Sherriffs even developed a habit of exchanging Christmas cards annually, becoming friends through this informal advisory group. In 1973, Alex Sherriffs was named Vice Chancellor of Academic Affairs of the California State College system in what Hampton describes as an appointment arranged by Reagan. Hampton was surprised to learn that a few months later, in April 1974, Reagan had named her to one of two California State College Board of Trustees appointments that year. She says of the appointment, "Alex and I never discussed this openly, but my perception is that he wanted, by this time we had become good friends, he wanted on that board of trustees, as Ronald Reagan was leaving, a friendly face. Because the board would start in transition immediately after, and the governor had the opportunity to make two appointments. So, my understanding is that Alex asked the governor to appoint me. The governor was willing to do that. And nobody bothered to tell me about this until it was done. I was startled at that point."[13]

It is important to keep in mind that, while Hampton's appointment to the Board of Trustees may have startled or surprised her, it also surprised the CSC Chancellor at the time, Glenn Dumke, current members of the board and many of Reagan's biggest campaign supporters and donors. A bit of controversy was created with Hampton's appointment because not only was she the second African American trustee ever appointed, but Reagan had also appointed her to a longer term than Yvonne Larsen, a white San

---

12   Hampton, interview, 1984. Melvin Bradley, an African American former deputy sheriff with the Los Angeles Sheriffs Department, served as Reagan's assistant for community affairs from 1973 to 1975. When Reagan was elected president of the United States, he was appointed Special Policy Advisor for the Office of Policy Development and was later appointed to the Office of Public Liaison.

13   Hampton interview, 1984.

Diego-based civic leader and philanthropist whose husband, W. Daniel Larsen, was also a Reagan donor and appointee to the Contractor's State License Board in 1973. Hampton said of the controversy, "But somehow and I can't get that quite clear in my mind, San Diego was so upset. There was an eight-year appointment and one year the completion of somebody's term and of course they wanted the eight-year term. He didn't. He gave me the eight-year term and Yvonne Larsen the one-year term. San Diego was very upset about that."[14] Indeed, the negative reaction of many serving in various positions of power in San Diego County, particularly those affiliated with San Diego State College, to the eight-year appointment of Hampton over Larsen should have not been all that surprising since Claudia Hampton was a lifelong Democrat and an active member of the NAACP, which Reagan often viewed as hostile to his administration. Hampton also never gave any money supporting Reagan's campaign, nor his re-election bid for governor. But in listening to the audio recordings of Hampton's interview, you get the sense that without saying the words, she clearly understood that, in some circles, her presence on the board as a black woman was shocking for some and unwelcomed by others. The timing of Sherriffs' request for Reagan to appoint Claudia Hampton as a Cal State trustee was not a coincidence. It came precisely when various constituency groups within the CSC system were allowed to voice their support or opposition to affirmative action policy. Hampton would become that "friendly face" among the trustees who could help Sheriffs' shepherd along affirmative action policies and programs to help ensure their implementation. As nondiscrimination and affirmative action became codified policies within the CSC, Claudia Hampton's role as the affirmative action trustee took on greater importance given the early and consistent challenges and obstacles facing the actual implementation of these policies for several years to come. To that end, Hampton deployed sly civility as a form of indirect defiance to challenge the board's old norms, which largely ignored issues dealing with race and gender. Hampton knew that she had to gain access to influence and power on the board before she could work to change the board culture from within and ultimately shape policy that would extend educational and employment opportunities to underrepresented groups. To gain the requisite influence to effect change on the board, Hampton relied heavily on her personal attributes, including charm and persuasion as well as her leadership skills to bring her reluctant colleagues to her side when dealing with race, gender, and identity. The following is an explication of Hampton's five primary strategies and various tactics to achieve power and influence that she could use later.

---

14   Hampton interview, 1984.

Strategy: Quiet Observation and Extensive Preparation

Hampton quietly observed and studied the institutional culture of the board to identify gaps where she could be most effective in advancing access opportunities for underrepresented groups in the CSC.

Claudia Hampton's appointment to the board of trustees as the affirmative action trustee was of great importance when one considers how little the trustees seemed invested in ensuring that the affirmative action program they drafted could be successfully implemented across the system. Hampton eventually became known as a strong champion of affirmative action on the board, though she rarely spoke during her first year. A review of trustee records from March 1974 to July 1975 shows that Hampton only spoke occasionally, mostly as the chair of the Committee on Organization and Rules to relay the procedures for committee assignments for newly appointed trustees. As time went on and Hampton became more comfortable about the expectations for the work of the trustees, she became more active. But during this first year, Hampton used this time not only to familiarize herself with the procedures and protocols of how board business was conducted but also to observe the board's culture, paying close attention to where she could contribute and be most effective. Hampton said, "I soon realized, with the exception of Winnie Lancaster, there were few members on that board that understood real education issues. It was not that they were anti-education, not that they were antagonistic. It was just that educational issues were not their major concern. Their interest was in campus planning, architecture, and legislation. So, I saw there was a gap."[15] With the men on the board seemingly uninterested in educational policy issues, Hampton was able to carve out a niche for herself by identifying this gap where she could become an influential power player in what she describes as the "pragmatic part of boardsmanship."[16] Hampton was very adept at negotiating with people who often had seemingly divergent points of view on various issues. This experience came in handy as she moved into her new role as the resident expert on education for the board and when she chaired her first committee, the presidential selection committee for the Dominguez Hills campus.

Relying on her extensive preparation and research skills into the background of her fellow board colleagues, Hampton knew that she would need to compromise with trustee Charles Luckman, the influential chair of the Campus Planning, Building, and Grounds Committee, in order get the person she wanted selected as president at CSU Dominguez Hills. Her efforts

---

15   Hampton interview, 1984.
16   Hampton interview, 1984.

to influence the committee to select Donald Gerth as president of Cal State Dominguez Hills in 1976 is one example of how she played the game of "boardsmanship." Hampton had a very strong preference for Gerth, in which she was willing to trade some chits with Luckman to get her candidate the position. She detailed her strategy for getting Gerth appointed to the presidential post at Dominguez Hills in her 1984 interview stating, "Many of the board members didn't have that much interest or strong preference for the candidates at Dominguez Hills. It was kind of like the old boys' club. They said, "Okay, Claudia says "Gerth, so we'll go for Gerth." She goes on to explain: "I picked up some chits because I voted on how high the mound (for an art installation at Cal State Northridge) should be to agree with Luckman, somebody who wants it to be six feet instead of ten feet. So I have been lobbied and I had some outstanding chits and I picked them up."[17] Her willingness to compromise and be flexible with her colleagues, who took little interest in what happened at the campus with the largest African American student population, enabled Hampton to advocate on that campus's behalf. Dominguez Hills became Hampton's favorite campus, because it was the poorest in the system and had the most students of color, so she was invested in nurturing the campus to the extent she could, according to Herb Carter. Lobbying to have Donald Gerth serve as its president in 1976 was part of Hampton's plan to support "her campus."

Once dubbed "The HBCU of the West," Cal State Dominguez Hills is in Carson, California, near the cities of Compton, Gardena, Watts, and Long Beach, which had, and continues to have, significantly large African American and Latino populations. The college was originally named South Bay State College. In the early 1960s, the trustees sought to move the campus from the rented space that the college occupied in the affluent residential area of Palos Verdes Peninsula to a larger site to accommodate its rapidly growing student population. However, the real estate in Palos Verdes was too cost prohibitive, so the trustees began accepting bids for locations throughout the South Bay area of Los Angeles County. By 1964, three cities were competing for the contract: San Pedro, Torrance, and Dominguez Hills (which would later become incorporated into the City of Carson).

During the bidding process, the Watts Riots erupted on August 11, 1965, lasting for five days, leaving thirty-four (34) people dead and over 40 million dollars in property damage. One of the many causes of the riots was the lack of adequate educational opportunities for African American and other racial minority groups in Los Angeles. Groups like the Council of Black Administrators had been making regular complaints about the low number of schools in areas of the city with a sizeable number of Black residents.

---

17   Hampton interview, 1984.

Popular legend says that Governor Pat Brown had favored the Dominguez Hills site directly in response to the riots, because Brown heard directly from Black politicians, teachers, and parents about the need for a campus near the area's growing Black population. Evidence shows that the relocation of the campus at Dominguez Hills was primarily a fiscal decision rather an accommodation to Black demands for greater educational access.[18] Nevertheless, the move helped establish Governor Brown as a champion of social policies that favored the interests of the Black and Asian American communities living in or near that locale. Student enrollment increased dramatically once the Dominguez Hills site opened in August 1966 with an entering class of one hundred and twenty-five. By 1970, enrollment jumped to 2652. When Claudia Hampton was appointed trustee in 1974, Cal State Dominguez Hills was regarded as a "Black school" with a Black student population of over sixty percent for several decades even though the administration, faculty, and staff were overwhelmingly white. She took a very special interest in what was happening on that campus precisely because of its large Black student population.

According to Donald Gerth, once Hampton became aware about the growing racial tensions between African Americans and Asian Americans in the city of Carson. Hampton felt comfortable in sharing her concerns about the potential racial conflicts at the CSU Dominguez Hills campus with Donald Gerth, because she had developed a close friendship with him shortly after she was named to the board. The two first met in 1974 during Hampton's visit to CSU Chico, where Gerth had served as campus president since 1964. Impressed that a trustee would make it a priority to visit each campus, Gerth and his wife Beverly invited Hampton to their home for dinner that evening. Gerth says that he and Hampton "ended up having not only really a very pleasant time, but a very, very long conversation about the California State University. And we sat up until very late talking

---

18 For a detailed history of the founding of the CSU Dominguez Hills campus including a discussion of the political battle over the permanent location of the Carson campus, see Judson Grenier, *The Rainbow Years, 1960–1985: The First Quarter Century of California State University Dominguez Hills* (Carson: California State University Dominguez Hills Foundation, 1987). According to Grenier, at the close of the July 1965 board meeting, Brown's director of finance Hale Champion was lobbying for the selection of the Dominguez Hills site because the other two sites, at Friendship Park in San Pedro and a landfill in Torrance, would drive up construction costs because of the hilly terrain in San Pedro and the environmental degradation in Torrance. Champion had already refused to increase the budget allocation for this purchase so, in essence, Dominguez Hills would have likely been the selection with or without the Watts Riots.

and became friends. And we stayed in touch. We were very, very close."
From that initial encounter, they discovered both grew up in Chicago and
had attended Morgan Park High School, one of Chicago's few integrated
high schools in the late 1940s/early 1950s. Their shared Midwestern background helped to solidify their friendship and over time they discovered, "a
shared respect for institutions and for doing business in an orderly way."[19]
So Hampton lobbied hard for Donald Gerth's selection as the Dominguez
Hills campus president because, as Gerth recalled, "Claudia said to me, you
know, that if it's a black appointee or an Asian appointee, it simply would
create a problem with the other constituencies. The only choice is that has
to be a white, Caucasian appointee, and she came down like a ton of bricks
on that issue."[20]

Carson was incorporated as an independent city in 1968 due to heavy
lobbying by a coalition of local business owners and community activists.
Many Carson activists were appointed as Carson's first city council members, including Japanese American community activist Sak Yamamoto and
African American business owner Gilbert Smith. Both men would also eventually serve multiple terms as mayor of Carson. However, a dispute over a
trash hauling contract that Yamamoto agreed to as city councilman during
Smith's second term as mayor created a permanent rift between Yamamoto
and Smith, where the battlelines in the dispute were drawn along racial lines
that continue to impact politics in the city to this day.[21]

As a result of this rift, Hampton grew concerned with how the sizeable
Black student population at CSU Dominguez Hills might be impacted when
the Toyota Motor Company announced plans to establish their first U.S.-
based corporate headquarters in neighboring Gardena in the mid-1970s.
During his on-campus interview for the presidential post, Donald Gerth
even recalled "Bev (Gerth's wife) and I were invited to some kind of a function, and I met Shoichiro Toyada. He was the son of the founder of the
company, and he was the principal owner. I was sort of astonished. I didn't
know there was such a person."[22] After that meeting with Toyada, Gerth
says he began to understand why Hampton saw him as a safe, neutral choice
between African Americans who considered Dominguez Hills to be "their
campus," and Asian Americans whose political influence and population

19   Gerth interview, 2018.
20   Gerth interview, 2018.
21   Sam Gnerre, "Sam Yakamoto: Former Carson Mayor and Unlikely Film
     Star," *South Bay History* (a Daily Breeze newspaper history blog). Accessed
     June 1, 2023, http://blogs.dailybreeze.com/history/2014/09/20/
     sak-yamamoto-former-carson-mayor-and-unlikely-film-star/.
22   Gerth, interview.

was steadily increasing in Carson and the surrounding communities. By the time Toyota set up its headquarters in Gardena, the political pendulum had shifted in favor of Asian Americans. Sak Yamamoto was elected mayor of Carson for two consecutive terms starting in 1977. As far as the other ethnic constituent groups were concerned, Gerth says:"The white people who lived along Manhattan Beach and Torrance and all those people on the peninsula didn't give a hoot about Dominguez Hills. They didn't want to have anything to do with it. I did not mention the Hispanic or Mexican community because of the standpoint of Dominguez Hills in 1976, it didn't exist. That happened over time later."[23]

Hampton's lobbying for Donald Gerth as the next president for Dominguez Hills was motivated largely by what she perceived as his ability to work well with Black students and the Black community in the surrounding areas near campus, while simultaneously being able to placate and avoid raising the ire of the growing Asian American community. After suggesting to Hampton that the next president of Dominguez Hills should be a Black person, Gerth reported that Hampton balked, saying: "Claudia was not subtle. She was very blunt. It's got to be a white president from her standpoint and there's no two ways about it. . . . My impression at the time was that Claudia stacked the deck [in Gerth's favor]."[24] It might seem curious, if not downright odd, to the casual observer why Hampton would pass up an opportunity to appoint only the second Black CSC campus president in the system's history. However, Hampton's favoritism for the Dominguez Hills had more to do with the campus's predominantly Black student body than anything else. To the extent that she could exert her influence to ensure consistent access for Black students, Hampton was willing to forego having a Black person appointed as the CSC Dominguez Hills president if it meant that Black students did not get caught in a fight between two ethnic/racial groups vying for political control of the city.

Hampton's effectiveness in picking up chits for future votes on affirmative action policy and programs was largely due to her preparation for important board votes. Part of her preparation involved bouncing ideas off Herb Carter, the other African American serving at the Chancellor's Office, who could provide her with an "outsider–within" perspective on upcoming board decisions. As Herb Carter noted in his 2017 interview, "Claudia had risen to be a leader on the board. . . . She became kind of the confidante of both wings of the board. She was accepted and loved by everybody. And when she was confronting issues, she would call me."[25]

---

23   Gerth, interview.
24   Gerth, interview.
25   Carter, interview.

The amount of attention and care that Hamp ton put into preparation for board meetings is indicative of her commitment to her work as the affirmative action trustee and her foresight to anticipate possible obstacles or roadblocks in her path. With her extensive experience in fielding questions and making persuasive arguments to help influence policy changes in her work with Los Angeles Unified School District, she brought that expertise to bear as a CSU trustee. Based on the assessment of her contemporaries like Donald Gerth and Herb Carter, Hampton was adept and skillful in bringing opposing groups to her side, which can be largely attributed to the amount of preparation she engaged in before it was time to vote.

Carter also recalled that Hampton would be strategic and careful conducting herself in meetings, especially when chairing a committee. He said, "When she came to the meetings, even when she was the chair of a committee, she would be very careful about how she called on board members to talk. She would always get the people who were for whatever we were trying to accomplish in the spotlight first and then other people would have to attack their colleagues on the board and get some momentum to overcome what had been put in place by the more liberal voices on the board."[26] When asked his assessment of Hampton's ability to be strategic, Gerth said, "You would not take Claudia on in a board meeting. You just wouldn't. She's one of the relatively small number of really effective trustees, even in the dynamics of board meetings. I never missed a board meeting from 1976 to 2003. I just made it my business always to be there. I don't I ever recall a president really fighting with her in the board meeting. You wouldn't even do that with Claudia. And they took on other board members."[27] Combining her preparation before an important vote and the way she conducted herself in meetings gave Hampton the strategic advantage and, very often, the outcome she was seeking.

Strategy: Downplay Identity/Strategically Play to the Norm

Hampton strategically disarmed the threat posed by her race by playing to the gender norm using sly civility and respectability as resistance tools.

In the early years of her appointment, Claudia Hampton used her charm and wits to influence her colleagues to side with her position when it came to selecting presidents or voting on resolutions because, for the first few years, Hampton was closed out of the "telephone network." She says, "It was

---

26   Carter, interview.
27   Gerth, interview.

several years before I became part of the 'telephone network.' For several years, three or four, I didn't hear from anybody from July to September."[28] The telephone network was an informal system where trustees would discuss upcoming votes before board meetings, using this informal time to "count votes" before the next meeting. The telephone network utilized phone calls and in-person meetings to discuss board business outside of normal board meeting times. Since Hampton did not know anyone on the board prior to her appointment, she was not granted access to this network for several years and often had to make her case during board meetings that were so structured that it was often difficult to discuss a particular issue at length.

After observing the meeting structure and how her fellow trustees conducted themselves during meetings, she decided she needed to find a way to become more of a participant rather than a mere observer. "I daresay the first board meetings I went to I never opened my mouth. But eventually I said, well I'm here for eight years, I must be here for a reason. Somebody thought I should be here. And I've gotta really get into this thing and participate."[29]

Hampton figured out quickly that she needed to trade votes to gain some favor with trustees with whom she often disagreed politically to gain access to the telephone network. For example, Charles Luckman, the trustee with whom Hampton traded chits to get the votes needed for Donald Gerth to become president of CSC Dominguez Hills, had considerable influence on the board. A Pat Brown appointee who was decidedly conservative in his politics, Luckman derived much of his power on the board due his success as a businessman and architect responsible for designing some of the nation's most iconic structures, including Madison Square Garden in New York City and The Prudential Tower in Boston. He was one of the original trustees appointed in 1960, meaning those appointed after him often deferred to his knowledge of the system's inner workings. Luckman had also served on the board for twenty-two years, longer than any other trustee to date, so Hampton knew it was vital to try to gain Luckman's favor because he was influential, well liked, and respected. Gerth said, "Claudia was able to work with all these people," when speaking about Hampton's relationships with powerful trustees like Luckman, governors, and chancellors.[30]

Hampton's success in convincing her fellow trustees that she was a political moderate, even though she vigorously championed affirmative action, helped her eventually gain access to this network, which was generally reserved for more experienced white male members of the board. After she

---

28   Hampton, interview.
29   Hampton, interview.
30   Gerth, interview.

was accepted into this informal network, Hampton's influence and power on the board grew considerably. For example, Hampton could easily gain support for affirmative action because she had already discussed her position and was able to change someone's mind during the telephone network process.

Once Hampton was accepted into the fold, the in-person "telephone network" meetings often took place at Hampton's home in Los Angeles, where she became hostess, preparing a meal and entertaining a select group of trustees and campus presidents. Herb Carter says that days before hosting the telephone network meetings, he and Hampton would meet at her house to plan and strategize before she made dinner for her white trustee colleagues, "We'd sit there and drink wine. Smoke and drink. That's how she kind of ran stuff in the board."[31] Hampton continued hosting the telephone network for several years after she was appointed board chair. Donald Gerth recalls that sometime in the mid-1980s: "I can remember going to Claudia's house. Well, I remember one time I brought about three or four presidents with Jim Cleary, Ellis McCune, and a couple of others to her house, where we talked about settling some disputes when Ann Reynolds was chancellor."[32] Playing hostess was one sure-fire way that Hampton could participate as a full member of the network while playing to the gender norm of the day.

Nothing in the historical record indicates that Hampton was asked to host these meetings by her white male peers. Instead, Hampton and other Black women like her, who had to work with white men to secure opportunities and resources for their communities, often volunteered and placed themselves in situations where they could influence their peers in a less-formal work setting. As an example, Virna Canson recalls that on two separate occasions she and Claudia Hampton hosted parties in honor of Alex Sheriffs when he left the Reagan administration before joining the CSC Chancellor's Office, "We had a party for Alex at my house. My husband cooked steaks and stuff. We just had a great time. There was a later party, which Claudia gave. It was very interesting. There is a science to that."[33] Here, Canson is referring to the science of informal social networking with someone for whom you might not have much in common with politically, but you can have a good time together socially. Herb Carter even recalled Hampton going out for beers and cigarettes with individual trustees after board meetings. This type of hosting and socializing gave Black women a unique opportunity to potentially develop lasting friendships with their white peers, which could help influence their votes on issues of importance to these women.

---

31   Carter, interview.
32   Gerth, interview.
33   Canson, interview.

Thus it was a stroke of genius for Hampton to engage in this sort of sly civility behavior, because she could downplay the threat posed by her race, since she was not challenging the status quo regarding gender. Hampton was likely to have advanced much further in her role as trustee as a Black woman than if a Black man had served, because her gender posed little to no threat to the majority white male board. Serving as a hostess in this regard allowed Hampton to play the long game of "boardsmanship" because she could disarm some of the racial hostility she might have encountered, had she also presented herself as a staunch feminist. This point is made clear by Hampton's assessment of how board members regarded other women who came after her. She noted that despite being the affirmative action trustee she was not regarded as narrow-minded in that respect, like some of her white female counterparts. She says:

> We've had two other women. Both were viewed as having tunnel vision. In one case, I think it is more accurate than the other case. One of the things they say to me is that I'm all over the territory. But I defend affirmative action. And there are other very strong supporters of affirmative action on the board. But some of them just seem to have an interest in women's issues in certain aspects of affirmative action. I try to be attentive to anything having to do with affirmative action. But I never to my knowledge have been criticized for being a one-issue trustee.[34]

This assessment of the other women on the board is revealing, because it shows how Hampton's efforts at using charm, wit, and even hosting fellow trustees at her home gave her more political and social capital to defend the issues she cared for most deeply. At the same time, it also demonstrates the unwillingness of her white male colleagues to take seriously the issue of gender discrimination when addressed by white women trustees. Note the irony that a Black woman had more influence regarding board decisions than her white female counterparts because she played to the gender norm instead of seeking to disrupt it.

It is also important to note that Hampton had to earn access to the telephone network, which explains why she had to spend time building capital, as she had realized early that she could not address both race and gender simultaneously until she had enough power and influence to do so. Even before Hampton could enter into her own type of power on the board, the reality was that, typically, women of color are required to choose one identity over the other or risk not being taken seriously. Legal scholar Kimberle Crenshaw describes this phenomenon as political intersectionality which "highlights the fact that women of color are situated within at least two subordinated groups that frequently pursue conflicting political agendas.

---

34   Hampton, interview.

The need to split one's political energies between two sometimes opposing groups is a dimension of intersectional disempowerment that men of color and white women seldom confront."[35]

Black women like Hampton must therefore calculate which identities they will emphasize and prioritize in order to be effective in a white male-dominated arena such as corporate or university boards. Even when Black women are victims of racial and gender discrimination, the United States Supreme Court has a record of forcing these women to pick an "injury"—that is, one cannot seek redress for racial and gender discrimination simultaneously. The landmark Supreme Court decision in *Vinson v. Meritor Savings Bank* (1986) which recognized sexual harassment as a violation of Title VII of the Civil Rights Act of 1964, provides the clearest example of the court's failure to recognize how both race and gender shape Black and other women of color's experiences with discrimination. Mechelle Vinson, a black woman, had been subjected to three years of recurring sexual harassment by her supervisor, Sidney Taylor, when she worked as a bank teller at Capitol City Federal Savings and Loan (which later changed its name to Meritor Savings Bank) in Washington, D.C. In 1978, Vinson was fired from her job for excessive use of sick leave, which Vinson testified was taken because of the physical and psychological trauma she endured by being forced to have sex with Taylor at work, including his touching her in public, exposing himself to her, and forcibly raping her multiple times. Vinson had attempted to report Taylor's harassment to the company officials early on when the harassment began. However, Vinson was told that she could only file a complaint based on race though they advised her that it would be difficult for her to get a ruling in her favor, since Taylor had never been cited for racial discrimination before. After she was fired and Vinson sought legal help, several lower courts ruled against her, stating that she could not prove she was a victim of racial discrimination as defined by Title VII. Even when the case finally made it to the Supreme Court and the justices agreed that she was subject to a "hostile work environment," she had to decide whether she would pursue the case based on race or gender; not both. Since race was clearly defined as a protected class in Title VII, Vinson and her legal team sought redress for gender discrimination. In a 9-0 decision, the case made sexual harassment in the workplace an illegal form of discrimination for the first time. Not only did this landmark case help to define sexual harassment for the first time, it also highlighted the need of the legal profession to grapple with its shortsightedness regarding Black women's experiences as women and as people of

---

35 Kimberle Crenshaw, "Mapping the Margins: Intersectionality, Identity Politics, and Violence against Women of Color" *Stanford Law Review* 43, no. 6 (1991): 1241–99.

color. Thus Crenshaw's work on intersectionality and Wing's work on critical race feminism provides an important corrective to this oversight.[36]

Unfortunately, Black women and other women of color continue to encounter intersectional oppression in the workplace, in social justice organizations to which they belong, and even in their choice of politicians to represent them. Despite the number of academic, political, and social organizations which address these intersections having grown substantially in recent years, most of the places where these women must work and try to make change still do not fully recognize or understand what it means to embody multiple intersecting identities. Therefore Hampton's choice to "play to the gender norm" in her early years on the board to avoid or disarm potential racial tensions due to her race clearly demonstrates how she utilized a sly-civility approach to great effect, despite many of her contemporaries on the board and among the Chancellor's Office staff voicing misgivings about affirmative action.

Strategy: Accepting Her Responsibility as the Affirmative Action Trustee

Hampton served as the primary champion for the interests of people of color, leveraging her position as a trustee to advocate for greater access and resources for underrepresented faculty, staff, and students within the CSU.

Being the first African American woman trustee meant that Hampton encountered a special set of responsibilities that her white and male colleagues on the board did not have to face. Hampton initially had to contend with her white male colleagues' surprise at her appointment. She recalled, "They admitted this to me later when we got to be real friends. I got to be very good friends with some of those men, although we often disagreed. We stipulated on certain issues we were not going to agree. But they were absolutely dumbfounded and asked, "What was Ronnie (Ronald Reagan) thinking?"[37] Undergirding this questioning of Reagan's appointment of Hampton to the board was undoubtedly a belief in the presumed incompetence that African American women and other people of color often face within American higher education. In the ground-breaking compilation of essays on race and gender in academia, *Presumed Incompetent: The Intersections of Race and Class for Women in Academia*, the editors say:

> On the one hand, the university champions meritocracy, encourages free expression and the search for truth, and prizes the creation of neutral and

---

36   Adrien K. Wing, ed., *Critical Race Feminism: A Reader.* 2nd ed. (New York: New York University Press), 2003.

37   Hampton, interview.

objective knowledge for the betterment of society—values that are supposed to make race and gender identities irrelevant. On the other hand, women of color too frequently find themselves "presumed incompetent" as scholars, teachers, and participants in academic governance.[38]

In fact, Hampton explained that despite being recommended by Reagan for the trustee appointment, she still needed the endorsement of a white male trustee to smooth things over with the rest of the board members. Hampton's race and gender was shared with the board before she was even introduced to the group and thus in a preemptive move Hampton said, "I'll never forget Roy (Brophy). I understand because of his relationship with Alex Sheriffs that he went to the governor's office to be supportive of my candidacy. I understand that he was very effective in that regard even though he had never seen me."[39] So despite having earned a doctorate in education along with having several decades of experience as a school teacher and school administrator, which in itself would make Hampton more qualified to serve on the board than most of her white counterparts, she needed a white man to endorse her candidacy, because her lesser-qualified white colleagues would question her because of her race and gender. No other trustee, not even the white women who served on the board prior to Hampton's appointment experienced this level of scrutiny—which is indicative of the racial climate of the day but also the racist assumptions about black women's qualification to serve in university governance and oversight roles. While Hampton had an early champion in Roy Brophy, the trustee who proceeded her in serving as board chair, it would take her a number of years to develop collegial and cordial relations with other board members. For one thing, Hampton stated that because the board meetings were so structured and she did not feel comfortable in asserting herself until she felt fully comfortable, she rarely spoke during her first year. Additionally, since she had no contacts on the board, Hampton had to rely on Chancellor Dumke and Vice Chancellor for Academic Affairs Alex Sherriffs to help her get oriented to her role and duties on the board. Dumke would frequently call Hampton to discuss board protocol, providing her with an informal orientation to board participation. Though they did not agree on much ideologically, Hampton says she had an excellent relationship with Dumke. Eventually, she got along with the "real die hard, honest to goodness, right to the wall white male conservatives. But I got along with them fine . . . I really did."[40] This ability

---

38   Angela P. Harris and Carmen G. Gonzalez, "Introduction" *Presumed Incompetent: The Intersections of Race and Class for Women in Academia*, eds. Gabriella Gutierrez y Muhs, Yolanda Flores Niemann, Carmen G. Gonzalez, and Angela P. Harris (Utah State University Press, 2012, first ed.), 1.

39   Hampton interview, 1984.

40   Hampton interview, 1984.

to establish and maintain friendly relations with people she disagreed with ideologically enabled Hampton to remain an effective negotiator for issues and programs of the greatest importance to her. Nevertheless, in her earliest days on the board, Hampton still had to confront the realities of racism and resistance to the principle of affirmative action. Trustee Witter's comment about "a n----- in the woodpile" was one such example of the racism that Hampton faced.

While Hampton faced questions about her competency from her white colleagues on the board and around the system, she also had expectations placed upon her by the Black community. She embraced her responsibility as the affirmative action trustee, but she sometimes made pragmatic and politically expedient decisions that were not always in lockstep with other African Americans on board or in the California Legislature. Her vote in opposition to collective bargaining, for example, though based on her belief that the affirmative action provisions of the proposed resolution needed to be strengthened, meant that she was voting against fellow African Americans like Lieutenant Governor Mervyn Dymally, whom she often sided with on affirmative action related matters. Hampton made decidedly pro-Black decisions with a strong emphasis on advocating for students from lower socioeconomic backgrounds. Her experience working with low-income Black students and parents in the LAUSD while serving as the Director of Schools and Community Relations spawned this interest.

Being the first Black woman trustee meant that Hampton was expected to advocate for the interests of all other non-white people and women, regardless of the issue. Hampton's "charm offensive" early into and throughout her tenure on the board helped her cultivate her reputation as "their trustee" among the white members of the board, enabling her to both formally and informally advocate for racial and ethnic minorities across the board. One such example is where Hampton expressed concern about the lack of non-white staff at the Chancellor's Office. She said "I walked into the premises, and I didn't see any minorities in any position. The legal office for example. Ten white male lawyers. So, I discussed that with some of my colleagues, knowing full well that it was not a matter of particular interest to them. So I couldn't handle it through the board."[41] Instead, Hampton explains, she had to approach the Chancellor's Office staffing issues delicately, using a politically strategic approach by taking her concerns directly to Chancellor Dumke. She said, "I handled it individually and by going to Glenn Dumke. A Chancellor is always aware of the need for that vote. Particularly when Glenn was getting a whole new Jerry Brown board, he needed bridges. So I'm saying when the political aspects came into play, he would operate and give me

---

41   Hampton interview, 1984.

something that I asked for in order to keep me in that bridge position."[42] Serving as the bridge between the Reagan board and the incoming Brown board gave Hampton an unusual amount of leverage between two ideologically opposed sides and also helped Dumke, a seemingly reluctant supporter of affirmative action, over to Hampton's side.

Strategy: Build Relationships to Gain Access and Influence

Hampton cultivated personal relationships with fellow board members, campus presidents and even students, which came in handy when seeking support for the policies and programs she championed.

In his 2010 epic tome chronicling the history of the California State University system, Donald Gerth explained: "On every campus, faculty, student leaders, presidents and other administrators inevitably developed the idea that one or two trustees were "their" trustees. Claudia Hampton was considered "our trustee" on all of the campuses."[43] Gerth did not specify exactly what made Hampton "their trustee" in this particular book. Later, in a 2017 interview, he said that Claudia Hampton was one of the most "significant trustees in the whole history of our system."[44] In Gerth's opinion, Hampton's twenty-year length of service on the board was at least partially indicative of her effectiveness as a trustee. Still, even her long tenure does not tell the complete story, nor does it help us understand why Hampton was so beloved on so many CSU campuses. Most college or university trustees go unnoticed unless a major conflict or controversial policy decision garners the attention of the campuses. Claudia Hampton was the exception.

Despite being the second African American trustee and only the fifth woman on the board until her appointment in 1974, Claudia Hampton was unlike any other trustee, according to Gerth, who recalled that, "in her [Claudia Hampton] early days on the board as a new member made it a point to visit all the campuses."[45] While there might have been an occasion for a trustee to visit a campus in the system for a special event, such as a groundbreaking ceremony, more often than not trustees maintained both a physical and professional distance from the campuses and members of the campus community. Hampton's hands-on approach to trustee service was novel. Yet by visiting each campus and talking to the various campus constituents, Hampton had endeared herself to campus leaders like Gerth, who saw

---

42 Hampton interview, 1984.

43 Donald R. Gerth, *The People's University: A History of the California State University*, (Sacramento, CA: Institute of Governmental Studies Press, 2010).

44 Gerth Interview, 2018.

45 Gerth Interview, 2018.

her visitations as indicative of her commitment to get to know the campuses' needs to ensure the system's success. During her tenure as board chair, Hampton also gave student leaders opportunities to address the board to weigh in on proposed tuition increases and admission requirement changes. Hampton's overtures to campus officials and student leaders were important steps in bridging the gap between board and the campuses directly impacted by board decisions. Nevertheless, it is also critically important to consider the role that race and gender had in shaping the relationships between Hampton and the constituents she was entrusted to oversee as a trustee.

According to Donald Gerth, many of the white board members deferred to Claudia Hampton, particularly because her role as the Director of School and Community Relations for Los Angeles Unified School District. He declared that "She had a significant influence on the board, particular among some of the board members on issues having to do with race, ethnicity and so on, because the board was composed almost totally of fairly affluent and in some cases, very rich, very wealthy white folks who would never really come to grips with ethnicity. And this was a topic about which Claudia was strong, given the role she played with L.A. Unified School District."[46] Former CSU Affirmative Action Officer and former Executive Assistant Vice Chancellor, Herb Carter, described the CSU system as a ". . . racist institution. And the board of trustees reflected that. You know, that was no big secret. Maybe one or two people on the board were reasonable people but for the most part, they didn't want us to talk about minorities."[47] The conservative white board members' refusal to engage in serious discussions about race and diversity issues meant that it would take several years of Hampton cajoling, bargaining, and even making dinner for white male campus presidents and trustees for her to finally begin seeing her years of lobbying paying off. But as Carter points out, Hampton's success in getting the board to pay attention to minority issues also came about because of Hampton's friendship with trustee Roy Brophy. "Roy Brophy was the leader of that block (of Republican trustees). He was a conservative Republican but the most sensible of that group. And he would try to nudge them (into supporting minority issues)."[48] The unlikely friendship between a white conservative Republican and a black moderate Democrat led to what Carter describes as "a kind of settling down of the Republican appointees," where Hampton could at last gain some traction on the discussion of affirmative action.[49]

---

46   Gerth interview, 2018.
47   Carter interview, 2017.
48   Carter interview, 2017.
49   Carter interview, 2017.

Aside from strategizing her votes, hosting dinner, and visiting campuses around the system, Hampton also took the time to get to know each trustee personally by learning about their backgrounds, sending holiday cards to each trustee, and asking about their families. She described her relations with some of her conservative white male peers as close friendships, "Ideologically, we didn't agree about a lot of things. But we got along really well. That was one of the reasons I made it as well as I did. Bob Bever and I . . . and we still are when we see each other, we act like long lost friends. Brophy. I'm going to have dinner with Brophy tonight. I gotta keep him in check (laughs). Dean Lesher. I found him delightful, and we agreed when we could and disagreed without passion when we couldn't. . . ."[50] This informal networking with board colleagues, even those with vastly different political outlooks, helped to solidify Hampton as one of the most beloved members of the board and contributed greatly to her effectiveness in advocating for under-represented groups as "she was always concerned about people who didn't have much money."[51]

Since university boards across the country did not begin diversifying their membership until the 1980s, it was commonplace that the input and opinions of people of color and women were largely ignored when university policies were being proposed, deliberated, and voted upon. To be effective as a university trustee in the late 1970s, while being neither white nor male, meant one had to become skillful at bringing mostly white male board members to one's side. Claudia Hampton was an effective political bargainer utilizing sly civility as her approach with strategic preparation as the tool to resist selling out while simultaneously working to change the system from within.

Strategy: Practice Instrumental Leadership

Hampton practiced instrumental leadership in her role on the board, where her typical opponents on affirmative action would defer to her because of her style, the personal relationships she built, and her moderate political stance on most matters.

Hampton made a space at the table for herself by identifying the gaps on committees, cultivating friendships, and accepting her role as the affirmative action trustee who would advocate for under-represented groups of students, faculty, and staff whose concerns might not receive any consideration, let alone decisive action, had she not stepped up as she did. She also understood that, as a Black woman, she was the embodiment of those groups that the largely conservative, white male board ignored, or hoped would go away somehow. So she confronted her colleagues' lack of interest

---

50   Hampton interview, 1984.
51   Carter interview, 2017.

in minority concerns using a style that was neither bombastic nor aggressive. She brought people along with her by networking and interacting with them, allowing her to use personal persuasion to bring them to her side. Organizational behavioral scholar Jean Lipman Blumen refers to this maximization of personal interactions as an "instrumental" style of leadership.[52] Hampton, therefore, becomes the implement or instrument to influence the voting behavior of her board colleagues where those personal relationships become as important as the actual merits of the proposed policy or board action. By no means does Hampton forego her blackness to help cultivate these relationships, but she had an uncanny knack for making her white male colleagues put aside her racial identity by performing a type of respectable Black womanhood, which distracted her white male peers from her actual goal of extending opportunities for Black and other underrepresented groups. Historian Sonya Ramsey argues for a reconceptualization of respectability politics as "charismatic advocacy" in the case of Black women like Bertha Maxwell-Roddy and Claudia Hampton, contemporaries engaged in educational activism in the post-desegregation era. Ramsey says, "Adept at negotiating with everyone from educational administrators to non-profit board directors, to city and corporate leaders, Maxwell-Roddy did so to secure tangible benefits for Blacks and others after the public marches dissipated and the behind-the-scenes work to ensure that the activists' demands be met continued."[53] In similar ways to Bertha Maxwell-Roddy, Hampton's white male peers spoke of a deep affection and respect for Claudia Hampton, giving her enormous access to power and influence. Over time, as Hampton built up her political capital, her style shifted from instrumental to relational. She became more collaborative and contributory, and a mentor to board colleagues and Chancellor's Office staff. Even on the issue of affirmative action, Hampton never adopted what is often considered a masculine style of leadership that was direct or competitive.

Other women on the board, namely Trustee Mary Jean Pew, gained a reputation for being difficult to work with and overbearing with her male peers. When asked about the board's relationship with other women on the board in contrast to Hampton, Herb Carter described Dr. Mary Jean Pew, Jerry Brown's first appointee, as "an extraordinarily difficult person. We tolerated her. She could not be the leader of the board because she could be an obstructionist, even though she was the leader of the liberal bloc."[54] Without naming a specific person, Hampton implied that other women on

52   Jean Lipman Blumen, *Connective Leadership: Managing in a Changing World*, 1st ed. (Oxford: Oxford University Press, 2000).

53   Sonya Ramsey, *Bertha Maxwell-Roddy: A Modern-Day Race Woman and the Power of Black Leadership* (Gainesville: University Press of Florida, 2022).

54   Carter interview, 2017.

the board gained a reputation as single-issue trustees focused almost exclusively on women's issues, "We had one trustee who was perceived as a being a one-issue trustee and very narrow-minded . . . this is not my judgment. This is a general judgment."[55] While Hampton and Carter's characterizations of the white women on the board do not speak to the sexism they might have endured, the inability of these women to extend their sphere of influence speaks to their positionality as white women who assumed that simply being nominated to the board was enough to enact change within the CSU regarding issues of gender/gender equity. The white women who served as trustees during Hampton's tenure relied on the righteousness of their cause against gender discrimination and inequality, rather than working to build coalitions with men to create policies that would help eliminate sex discrimination and gender bias throughout the system.

Claudia Hampton, on the other hand, was all too aware of how her identity as a Black woman could limit her ability to get things accomplished, so she enacted sly civility as a counterstrategy against the deeply embedded racist and sexist culture of the board. However, Hampton's success in amassing power and influence on the board belies the reality that she was also a victim of the "curse of competence" where women of color often experience significant cultural-identity taxation. Cultural identity taxation is a specific type of burden placed on women of color in the academy to serve as both ethnic and gender representatives on university committees as a result of white women and men of all races abdicating their responsibility to be partners with women of color in advocating, implementing, and promoting equity.[56] Hampton might have accepted her role as the board's affirmative action trustee, but the silence from her white colleagues, especially in her earliest days on the board, spoke volumes about their lack of interest in promoting racial equity throughout the system. Instead of publicly declaring their opposition to affirmative action or other diversity initiatives, most of the trustees used white silence as a weapon that would work to maintain the status quo, which was just as damaging to the goal of expanding access to all. Even after Jerry Brown appointed more liberal trustees in the late 1970s, the board came to rely on Hampton as their default diversity representative. The sheer volume of committees Hampton served on and chaired also highlighted the ways in which Black women are often used as "pack mules" in predominantly white and male spaces. Nevertheless, Claudia Hampton was able to use this service to increase her access to power and influence on the board, which was needed to make positive change within the CSU.

---

55   Hampton interview, 1984.

56   Donna J. Nicol and Jennifer A. Yee "Reclaiming Our Time: Women of Color Faculty and Radical Self-Care in the Academy," *Feminist Teacher: A Journal of the Practices, Theories and Scholarship of Feminist Teaching*, 27 no. 2–3 (2017): 133–156.

Figure 1. Claudia Hampton, early career portrait. Date Unknown. California State University Archives Digitization Project. California State University Office of Public Affairs. Reproduced with permission from CSU System Archives.

Figure 2. Trustee Claudia Hampton, Trustee Roy Brophy, and Chancellor Glenn Dumke during board meeting. 1980. California State University Archives Digitization Project. California State University Office of Public Affairs. Reproduced with permission from CSU System Archives.

Figure 3. CSU Chancellor and Trustees visiting CSU Dominguez Hills. 1977. (Left to Right, CSU Chancellor Glenn Dumke, Board Chair Roy Brophy, CSUDH Student Body President Brenda Gonzalez, CSUDH President Donald Gerth and Board Vice Chair Claudia Hampton). California State University Hills Photograph Collection. Reproduced with permission from CSUDH Gerth Archives and Special Collections.

Figure 4. Chancellor Glenn Dumke and CSU Board Chair Claudia Hampton. 1981. California State University Archives Digitization Project. California State University Office of Public Affairs. Reproduced with permission from CSU System Archives.

Figure 5. Mayor Katy Geissert of Torrance presenting to Claudia Hampton a Silver Anniversary Award for outstanding service at CSU Dominguez Hills. 1986. California State University Archives Digitization Project. California State University Office of Public Affairs. Reproduced with permission from CSU System Archives.

Figure 6. Executive Vice Chancellor Herbert Carter
sitting and Chancellor W. Ann Reynolds standing.
1989. California State University Archives Digitization
Project. California State University Office of Public
Affairs. Reproduced with permission from CSU
System Archives.

Figure 7. California State University Executives. Date Unknown. (Left to Right, Trustee Claudia Hampton, Cal Poly Pomona President Hugh La Bounty, CSU Chancellor W. Ann Reynolds, and unidentified woman.) California State University Archives Digitization. California State University Office of Public Affairs. Reproduced with permission from CSU System Archives.

Figure 8. Trustee Claudia Hampton at podium with Trustee William Campbell in the background at a banquet to honor the inaugural Hampton Scholarship Recipients. 1994. California State University Archives Digitization Project. California State University Office of Public Affairs. Reproduced with permission from CSU System Archives.

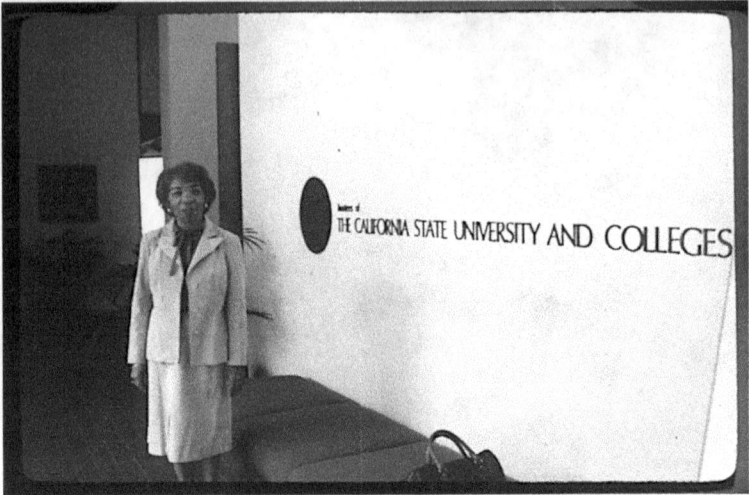

Figure 9. Board Chair Claudia Hampton at the CSU Chancellor's Office in Long Beach. 1981. California State University Archives Digitization Project. California State University Office of Public Affairs. Reproduced with permission from CSU System Archives.

Chapter Four

A Hammer in a Velvet Glove

Following years of slowly and methodically building rapport with her board colleagues, Claudia Hampton was able to translate the social capital she had cultivated into increased soft power that she used in circumventing process obstacles, influencing and shaping policy, and effectively changing the organizational culture of the CSU Board of Trustees from within. This chapter details how Claudia Hampton used the power and influence that she had skillfully acquired in her earliest days on the board, including downplaying her race and playing to the gender norm of the day, to assist the CSU system in the implementation and expansion of its affirmative action program for students, faculty, and staff.

On May 23, 1979, in his final speech as the chair of the California State University Board of Trustees, Roy T. Brophy, a stocky-built white man who made millions in construction in Northern California, stood before the audience gathered at the CSU Board offices in Los Angeles and closed his address with this: "A woman I have known and respected and loved for many years is our new chair. She will be known as the first black and the first woman chair of this or any other major university board of trustees. But she is more than that—she is a person with special sensitivity, special abilities, and special gifts; I am sure we will gain something in sharing them with her in the now future, Chair Dr. Claudia Hampton."[1] Brophy's somewhat clumsy attempt to mark the historic nature of the election of Dr. Claudia Hampton as just the second African American trustee and the first woman board chair for the California State University Board of Trustees takes on even greater importance when some months later on July 18, 1979, Dr. Hampton stood before the members of board to give her first address as chair. Hampton thanked her peers for the opportunity to serve as their leader and laid out her broad

---

1   Roy Brophy, Report of Chair Roy T. Brophy, May 23, 1979. CSU Board of Trustees Minutes of the Meeting of the Board of Trustees, Board of Trustees of the California State University Collection. Courtesy of the California State University Archives. California State University Dominguez Hills.

vision for the board during her term in office, never mentioning that she was the embodiment of history in the making. Hampton's silence on the significance of her race and gender in her appointment was characteristic of how she handled herself as a trustee and later as board chair when dealing with race and gender matters within the CSU system.

Hampton was acutely aware of how her racial and gender identity was perceived as an unwanted intrusion into what was essentially an old boy's club in the nation's largest public university system. The CSU Board and Chancellor had a notorious reputation for being openly hostile to change, following their handling of the late 1960s student protests demanding ethnic studies curriculum, additional funding for affirmative action and Equal Opportunity Programs, and increased admission of Black and other non-white students. While oversight is the primary role and function of a university board, Claudia Hampton understood that her work on the board required her to provide more than basic oversight of system budgets, policies, and programs. She had to be able to influence the conservative white members of the board to support initiatives that would extend access and opportunities to women and people of color within the California State Universities, using sly civility as an approach that fellow trustee Roy Brophy referred to as her "special sensitivity, special abilities and special gifts." Similar to those operating in the political arena where the ability to influence and persuade is paramount to electoral success, university trustees must also use their influence to bring their colleagues on the other side to their viewpoint, to secure votes on certain policy and programming proposals.

Furthermore, effective trustee leadership is often measured by the performance of the board chair in keeping the board on top of its oversight duties and advisory role and meeting the board chair's stated goals laid out in their initial address. Board chairs develop their goals in conjunction with the Chancellor's Office, whose job it is to inform the board of pending and upcoming system-wide program priorities, policy consultations with the California Legislature, and budget and personnel matters needing board approval. Claudia Hampton kept her board chair goals intentionally vague. While Hampton had the "special gift" to bring people of opposing political viewpoints together, she also had "special sensitivity" as to how she would engage and broach the discussion about affirmative action with fellow trustees who were often ignorant or refused to see the importance of race and gender in setting university policies. This sensitivity was especially important as Hampton was appointed board chair just as the composition of the board changed quite dramatically with the election of Edmund Gerald "Jerry" Brown Jr. as the new governor of California in 1976. In direct contrast to his father, Edmund Gerald "Pat" Brown, Sr. and Brown Jr's immediate predecessor, Ronald Reagan, Jerry Brown made several ethnically and politically diverse appointments, naming trustees whose ideological stances were in sharp contrast to their more conservative, mostly white and mostly male peers on the board. As the new board chair, Claudia Hampton kept the opposing sides on task to minimize political in-fighting, which could lead to a stalemate. Former CSU Executive Assistant Chancellor Herb Carter once described Hampton as the "the conciliator between various members of the board—the Roy Brophy wing and the Dean Lesher wing"—with Lesher representing the more conservative of the two pre-Brown wings.[2]

According to Carter, becoming chair at this time was difficult for anyone to maneuver. Yet Hampton became the confidante of now three wings, with the addition of the liberal bloc appointed by Jerry Brown, as she was accepted and loved by all three groups due to her "special abilities" in the use of charm and developing close personal relationships with fellow trustees before trying to persuade them to take a particular stance on an issue. Donald Gerth, former president of the CSU Dominguez Hills and Sacramento campuses, said that Hampton's meteoric rise to board chair was due to her talent at relationship building, "She worked with people so well, she became chair rather quickly. Somebody else was programmed to be chair, Eli Broad. But she quickly was respected by the entire board of membership and became chair and exercised enormous influence, not only as chair, for obvious reasons, but after she left the chair's role."[3]

Using personal relationships to build social capital with the mostly all-white male board went beyond simply making idle chit-chat with fellow board members for Hampton. Becoming hostess to the "telephone" network and carving out a space for herself at the table, as detailed in chapter 3, enabled Hampton to get to know her colleagues on an interpersonal level and then influence and sway votes of her peers in her favor. Even after being elected board chair, she continued serving meals to fellow board members. Hampton described the actions she took as trustee and later as board chair as "playing the game of "boardsmanship." In a 1984 interview, Hampton explained how the game was played, "Well, you have to know enough about boardmanship to know how some decisions are made. What happens politically is what always happens in the board meeting particularly between the more experienced board members. There is generally considerable conversation prior to board meetings between trustees. You know you could trade

---

2   Herbert Carter, "Interview of Herbert Carter," Interviewed by Donna J. Nicol. Personal Communication, March 9, 2018.

3   Donald Gerth, "Interview of Donald Gerth," Interviewed by Donna J. Nicol. Personal Communication, November 7, 2017.

your votes to see how things line up on an issue. You've changed somebody's mind on something."[4]

Hampton's skill at boardsmanship using a soft touch with her board colleagues did not mean she was not a relentless fighter, however. W. Ann Reynolds, the CSU's first woman chancellor, described Hampton as "a hammer in a velvet glove who would stay after stuff and could get there by persuasion."[5] Echoing Reynolds' assessment of Hampton's effectiveness through a softer touch, Donald Gerth maintained that "she [Hampton] knew how to work with people and bring them along," as opposed to other powerful trustees such as Louis Heilbron, the founding chair of the board, who was "enormously powerful but in a blunt kind of way."[6] Hampton's style of board service was grounded in a "political bargainer" approach to Black equality and social advancement. Black political science professor and activist Charles Hamilton, in his explication of the four categories of Black Power, describes the political bargainer as "someone who conforms to the established political process because he or she can work within the two-party system" with the major goal of "equalizing opportunities to goods and services."[7] African Americans elected to political office often have to function as political bargainers to be effective amongst their white peers, even at the risk of being labelled "sellouts" by the black community. Such was the case with people like Shirley Chisholm, who defiantly responded to those in the black community who believed that violence was the only way to effect change, "'I'm fighting,' I tell them. 'I know I'm here in Congress, part of the establishment, but you can see I haven't started to conform. I haven't sold out. I'm fighting within the system. There is no other place to fight if you only understood it. There's no other way for us to survive because we really don't have anything.'"[8] Though the political arena is different than academia, a similar institutional culture exists between the two, which favors white men exercising power, to the exclusion of women and people of color, even if a proposed policy or program most impacts the latter groups.

---

4   Claudia H. Hampton, "Claudia H. Hampton interview," Interviewed by Sarah Sharp (2 audiocassettes), Regional Oral History Office, The Bancroft Library, University of California Berkeley, July 1984.

5   W. Ann Reynolds, "Interview of Dr. W. Ann Reynolds," Interviewed by Donna J. Nicol. Personal Communication, July 12, 2018.

6   Gerth, interview.

7   Charles V. Hamilton, "An Advocate for Black Power Defines It," in *The Rhetoric of Black Power*, ed. Robert Scott and Wayne Brockriege, (New York: Harper & Row, 1969), 179.

8   Shirley Chisholm, *Unbought and Unbossed* (Boston: Houghton Mifflin, 1970), 157.

Hampton played the game of "boardsmanship" to great effect such that her "special sensitivity" to the reluctance of her white male peers in addressing race and gender matters in the university enabled her to secure their support to both protect and expand affirmative action programs to assist women and people of color in all levels within the CSU system. Though Hampton never described herself in this way, she displayed a high level of social intelligence using respectability and sly civility, which allowed her to design a number of strategies and tactics for overcoming roadblocks in her path. The following explains how Hampton took the hard-earned soft power, or social capital, she gained during her first five years and translated it into substantive change within the system through her tenure as board chair, until her death.

Strategy: Playing the Long Game

To "play the long game," Hampton carefully selected her interventions and strategically cast votes that were sometimes unpopular in the short-term but would reap benefits over time.

By the mid-1970s, the battle over racial quotas in university admission was just heating up when Allan Bakke, a white applicant who was denied admission to the University of California at Davis in 1974, sued the university, seeking an order to admit him to the medical school. Bakke maintained that the university's special admission program for minority applicants violated the U.S. and California constitutions and Title VI of the Civil Rights Act of 1964, denying him an admissions spot. For the next several years, this case made it through the court system, with the lower courts ruling in favor of Bakke. The university lost its petition for a rehearing and filed an appeal with the United States Supreme Court, which agreed to take the case in October 1977. University officials at all the state colleges and universities paid close attention to the outcome of this case, as it would have a serious and long-lasting impact on affirmative action enforcement within the system. There were even discussions among the representatives for the California Postsecondary Education Commission (CPEC), California's planning and coordinating board for higher education, expressing concerns about the effect of the Bakke decision on various special admission programs targeting mostly ethnic and racial minority students. Ahead of the Supreme Court ruling in Bakke, CPEC representatives reviewed the state's progress in recruiting, admitting, and graduating African American and Mexican American students, and found that those two groups were still underrepresented in all segments of California public higher education. The data for these progress reports were provided by CPEC representatives from the University of California, California State University, California Community Colleges and independent colleges and universities to comply with ACR 151 (1974), the California state law mandating that public higher education institutions' student composition reflect the economic, ethnic, gender, and racial diversity of California high school graduates by 1980. The CPEC was responsible for collecting affirmative action plans from each institution in the Commission and reconciling them to create a comprehensive state plan to increase minority participation in higher education. Representatives from the Commission were encouraged to return to their respective institutions to discuss how the Bakke ruling might impact the affirmative action plans being developed. Claudia Hampton was appointed as the CSU representative to the CPEC by board chair Roy Brophy in 1977. Then Chancellor Dumke announced a series of information sessions presented by an ad-hoc affirmative action taskforce focusing on women and minorities by the board's Faculty and Staff Affairs Committee. The first of such information sessions would focus on the needs of Mexican American students.

Since Claudia Hampton served as chair of the Educational Policy Committee and served on the Faculty and Staff Affairs Committee simultaneously, she initiated a request for a joint information session about the educational needs of Mexican American students. During these information sessions, Mexican American educators and community activists discussed cultural and language barriers, lack of financial resources, and institutional red tape as the main challenges to increasing Mexican American student participation in higher education. Out of this meeting came a proposal, crafted by Hampton, to increase the number of bi-cultural and bilingual Mexican American teachers, especially in the Los Angeles area. The Los Angeles Times reported "Under the proposal, state colleges in the area (Los Angeles City Schools) would recruit Mexican American graduates of local high schools for enrollment in teacher-training programs that would prepare them for employment as city schoolteachers."[9] Hampton also included provisions to offer counseling and tutoring to Mexican American students "deemed promising by their high school instructors."[10] Since Hampton was still the Director of the Office of School-Community Relations with Los Angeles Unified School District and a had strong working relationship with the Los Angeles Unified School District Board of Education (hereafter "LA School Board"), she believed she could expedite the approval process and respond to Mexican American community demands for more programming to increase access into the state university system. Hampton said of the proposal, "The need is great. Now the ball is in their court (LA School

---

9   Chris Woodyard, "Latin Teacher Proposal Okd by College Trustees," *Los Angeles Times*, July 26, 1978, C1.

10   Woodyard, "Teacher Proposal," C1.

Board) and my assumption is that the Board of Education will join us."[11] Hampton's work to increase the number of teachers and academic support services for Mexican American students in Los Angeles-area schools would eventually pay big dividends when she faced accusations of undermining the leadership aspirations of Mexican Americans within the CSU system. Amid a scramble for resources to support system-wide affirmative action efforts, a new storm was brewing over the selection and appointment process of campus presidents which tested what attorney and sociologist, Nicholas C. Vaca, refers to as the "unspoken conflict between Latinos and Blacks" in the United States.[12]

In 1978, CSU Los Angeles president John E. Greenlee announced his plan to retire at the end of Spring term 1979 and a search for the campuses' top administrator was convened. Post-World War II demographic shifts prompted calls for a new president at CSU Los Angeles, who would reflect the racial and ethnic mix of the area surrounding the campus. The Los Angeles campus was established in 1947 during the state's postwar expansion of the public higher education system, which coincided with an influx of African Americans migrating from mostly Texas and Louisiana during the Second Great Migration. This group included several African American veterans who had served during the Second World War. Mexican Americans also added to the changing demography of the City of Angels.

During the 1940s, California's manufacturing boom and rapid growth in government, product distribution, and consumer-oriented activities, changed occupational patterns such that Mexican Americans' percentages in agriculture and unskilled labor positions began to decline in favor of skilled craft, clerical, and semi-skilled occupations.[13] Due to Los Angeles moving to a service-based and skilled trades economy, local and state officials began to lobby for the city's first public university. By the mid-1950s, the campus was moved to its current site about five miles east of Downtown Los Angeles in an area known as El Sereno. The area experienced major industrial growth in aircraft and munitions industries during the Second World War. Mexican American families moved into the area in large numbers to pursue these opportunities, once restrictive covenants were lifted in 1948 with the *Shelly v. Kraemer* decision. Despite living and working near the Los Angeles campus, the Mexican American student population remained relatively small for several years, hovering around four percent of the total student population

11   Woodyard, "Teacher Proposal," C1.

12   Nicholas C. Vaca, *Presumed Alliances: The Unspoken Conflict Between Latinos and Blacks and What It Means for America*, (New York: HarperCollins, 2004).

13   National Park Service. "A History of Mexican Americans in California: World War II and Its Aftermath." November 17, 2004.

when CSU Los Angeles established the nation's first Chicano Studies program in 1968. By 1978, the Mexican American student population rose to sixteen percent, which ignited calls from students and community activists for the selection of the system's first Chicano[14] university president at CSU Los Angeles.[15] African American civic leaders and students had also expressed their interest in seeing another African American university president named following the appointment of Dr. James G. Bond, who became the system's first African American campus president at Sacramento State College (now CSU Sacramento) in 1972.

During the early 1960s rollout of the California Master Plan, over seventy (70%) percent of enrollment in California's public higher education system shifted to the community colleges to control costs. This proposal in effect meant that most of the state's high school graduates would begin their educational journey at a community college. If they met the transfer requirements, those students could continue working toward a bachelor's degree at one of the California State College campuses or the University of California. Since Los Angeles was not prepared for the influx of newly arriving African Americans from the South in the late 1940s and continuing through the 1960s, these African American students often faced overcrowded schools, poorly trained teachers, and housing insecurity. As a result, African American students who wanted to attend college or university often got their start at one of the Los Angeles Community Colleges before transferring to CSU Los Angeles or CSU Dominguez Hills in numbers comparable to their Chicano counterparts. Pan African Studies was established at CSU Los Angeles as the nation's second Black Studies program in 1968 and formally recognized by the Academic Senate in 1969, concurrently with Chicano Studies. While African Americans mostly lived to the south of Downtown Los Angeles at distances upwards of fifteen to twenty miles away, CSU Los Angeles was viewed as a main destination campus for African American students. Court-ordered desegregation by way of busing during the early 1970s meant that African American students who might not have lived near or around the Los Angeles campus were now being bused to schools within the university's catchment area. Like their Chicano counterparts, African American community activists and local officials were also lobbying for the president's position

---

14   In the 1960s, the term "Chicano" was used by activists, scholars, and students to signify ethnic solidarity, pride in one's indigenous ancestry and to reject the assimilationist aspirations of older generations of Mexican American civic and political leaders. During the presidential search at CSU Los Angeles, Chicano student groups wanted the next president to be a person of Mexican descent, preferring someone who embraced a Chicano/a identity and worldview.

15   The CSU Los Angeles campus" student racial demographics were African American (14%), Asian American (15%) and Hispanics (16%) in 1978.

to be filled by an African American. Presumed to be natural allies because of their shared experiences with racism and poverty, Mexican Americans and African Americans within the CSU system were on a collision course over the presidency at L.A. State (the nickname used by locals).

The selection committee, appointed by immediate past board chair Roy Brophy, named Dr. James Rosser as the next president of CSU Los Angeles in 1979, sparking outrage among many in the Mexican American community. Collectively, "the six-member Chicano Caucus in a statement released in Sacramento said they had heard from "thousands" of Hispanics who voiced "dismay and shock" at the appointment of a "non-Hispanic outsider" where there were "qualified Hispanics."[16] Despite his background as a health education and microbiology scholar, experience as Acting Chancellor of the New Jersey Department of Higher Education, and extensive background as a research biologist for private industry, Rosser was considered an outsider because he was an African American. Chicano students, faculty and community activists wanted the position to go to Dr. Julian Nava, a professor of history at CSU Northridge, who was elected as the first Mexican American to serve on the LA School Board. Nava was elected for three consecutive terms from 1967 to 1979 and chaired the board through some of the most tumultuous periods in the city's history, including federal desegregation of Los Angeles Unified School District in 1972.

Both men were well qualified for the position. Rosser had extensive university administration and research experience. Nava knew the state college system well, having served as faculty at the CSU Northridge campus since 1957 (he would retire in 2000). He was very familiar with the inner workings of Los Angeles Unified School District, whose schools were the primary feeder into CSU Los Angeles. Nava presided over the school board during the 1968 "East LA Blowouts," when over 15,000 mostly Chicano students, faculty, and community members walked out of seven area East Los Angeles Schools. They were protesting inequality in the school system due to overcrowding, faculty and staff shortages, and an astronomical Chicano student drop-out rate of upwards of 58%.[17] Those East Los Angeles schools involved in the 1968 walkouts also happened to be located in the catchment area of the CSU Los Angeles campus, as the area in and around CSU Los Angeles was nearly 75% Latino by the early 1970s. Given the demographic makeup of the area around the CSU Los Angeles campus and Nava's extensive

---

16   Mario T. Garcia and Sal Castro, *Blowout! Sal Castro and the Chicano Struggle for Educational Justice* (Chapel Hill, N.C., The University of North Carolina Press, 2011).

17   Los Angeles Times, "Chicanos Protest Selection of Black to Head L.A. State" *Los Angeles Times*, May 27, 1979, B5.

background with the local school board and the CSU system, it would seem like a foregone conclusion that Julian Nava would be selected for the CSU Los Angeles presidency. Once Rosser was named, however, the condemnation from the Chicano community was swift.

Julian Nava believed Claudia Hampton's recusal from voting for the search committee's final selection was politically motivated because as he explains in his biography, *Julian Nava: My Mexican American Journey*, "rivalries between black and brown leadership caused friction over the few openings made available by institutions that were dominated by the white majority."[18] Nava further contends that "I lost the selection because one favorable vote failed to show up as promised. . . . About a week later, I spoke to Dr. Claudia Hampton, a black trustee who promised to vote for me. At the last minute she abstained, costing me one vital vote."[19] According to Nava, Hampton's reason for abstaining was pressure she received from one of his political enemies on the LAUSD school board, State Senator Diane Watson. Nava said, "Diane Watson threatened her if she supported me over a Black candidate. Blacks must stick together, Watson said, according to Hampton, and if a prominent Black educational administrator like Claudia supported a Mexican American over one of her own, she would have to pay dearly for it."[20] In Nava's assessment of Hampton's abstention, Hampton sought a way to avoid raising the ire of powerful Black officials like Watson by abstaining without outright going back on her promise to her friend. Nava's interpretation of these events suggests that Hampton approached CSU general counsel Mayer Chapman for advice on extricating herself out of a no-win situation. Such an assessment of Hampton's actions is speculative at best. Chapman never denied the advice he gave to Hampton. Some members of the Chicano Caucus called for the reduction of funding for the entire state university system led by State Senator Joseph B. Montoya (D-Los Angeles) who also called for the resignations of CSU Chancellor Glenn Dumke and CSU general counsel Mayer Chapman.[21] Montoya argued that Dumke was in the chancellor's position too long and Chapman gave trustee Claudia Hampton ". . . advice on conflict of interest at the meeting in which the president was selected that was "without foundation in law."[22] Montoya was referring to the advice given to Hampton to recuse

---

18   Julian Nava, *Julian Nava: My Mexican American Journey* (Houston: Arte Publico, 2002), 129–130.

19   Nava, *Julian Nava,*" 130.

20   Nava, *Julian Nava,*" 130–131.

21   Kenneth J. Fanucchi, "Latin Educators Hit Appointment of Cal State Chief," *Los Angeles Times,* June 7, 1979, SG2.

22   Fanucchi, "Latin Educators," SG2.

herself from the vote on the appointment of the CSU Los Angeles president because of Hampton's former working relationship with Nava when she worked for the Los Angeles Unified School District and Nava served on the LA school board. Chicano students, activists, civic leaders, and educators steadfastly believed that Hampton's recusal was politically motivated, costing Nava the presidency.

What is certain is, while Black and Brown groups were fighting amongst themselves about the presidency of CSU Los Angeles, the white majority on the selection committee and in the Chancellor's Office sat back and watched this play out with little or no repercussions. There was no accusation of betrayal or malfeasance against the white and Jewish members of the selection committee who constituted the majority. Nava and other Mexican American leaders reserved their harshest critiques for Hampton and Wilson Riles, the first Black State Superintendent of Public Instruction, who was an ex-officio, non-voting member of the CSU board of trustees.[23] Julian Nava said of this perceived betrayal, "After this event, I was very selective in supporting black causes. Black/brown coalitions pretty much evaporated. What Riles and Hampton did was no surprise, in some respects. White and Black Americans pretty much ignored Hispanics until black needs were met." Nava took the critique further when he accused Hampton and Riles of "behaving like gringos." But aside from a single comment in his autobiography about the "the Jewish member of the trustees also set aside her promise of support for me and voted for Rosser," Nava reserved his ire for African American leaders like Claudia Hampton. [24] However, other factors might have been at play to thwart Nava's selection as the CSU Los Angeles president.

According to CSU biographer Donald Gerth, an important factor working against Nava's bid for the CSU Los Angeles presidency was the political opportunism and strong-arm tactics of then-governor Jerry Brown. Gerth wrote, "It was no secret that the chancellor liked the candidacy of a faculty

---

23   Nava, *Julian Nava*, 131. Wilson Riles served as State Superintendent for Public Instruction from 1971 to 1983. He was the first African American elected official in California. He won in an upset victory against incumbent conservative Max Rafferty. As State Superintendent for Public Instruction, Riles also served as a voting member on the CSU Board of Trustees. During the presidential selection process at CSU Los Angeles, Riles was absent on the day when the board took the vote to confirm the selection committees" recommendation to hire Rosser over Nava. According to Nava's autobiography, "Rather than break his promise to vote for me by voting for another, Riles did not attend the meeting, even after he had said, "Julian, I owe you one." He was referring to the fact that I had been very instrumental in his election as the first black to statewide office."

24   Nava, *Julian Nava*, 132.

member from another CSU campus; that faculty member had no administrative experience, but he had substantial experience in the public policy arena."[25] In this case, Gerth was referring to Julian Nava. Additionally, Nava had the backing of Governor Jerry Brown. Unlike Chancellor Dumke, who did not make his preference known to the selection committee, according to Donald Gerth, who was serving as president of CSU Dominguez Hills at the time, "Governor Jerry Brown weighed in, putting pressure on the trustees whom he had appointed and who were also on the search committee, to recommend a specific candidate, Julian Nava, to the full board for appointment. The governor's reason for pressing for the appointment of Nava was simply political."[26] While Gerth doesn't fully elaborate as to why Brown's choice in Nava was "simply political," one can surmise that Nava's highly visible position as school board chair was a key part of Brown's calculations. Likewise, it would be a feather in Brown's cap to have the first Latino university president named during his administration as Brown also named the first Latino CSU trustee in 1976 with the appointment of UCLA Chicano Studies professor Dr. Juan Gomez-Quinones. The trustees on the CSU Los Angeles presidential selection committee, according to Donald Gerth, rebelled against Brown's pressure, and selected James Rosser instead.

The controversy over the presidency at CSU Los Angeles is illustrative of the unraveling of the black/brown coalitions which characterized the relationship between ethnic nationalist groups like the Black Panthers and Brown Berets, among others, in the late 1970s.[27] The leaders of these organizations, who preached inter-racial cooperation and anti-capitalist/anti-colonial political ideals, were often targeted by the FBI and local law enforcement agencies with many members facing incarceration or even assassination. Without these groups stressing unity amongst each other, it became customary for them to become adversarial, competing against each other for scarce educational resources with white politicians and school officials serving as the arbiter of who should be granted these precious few educational opportunities. By 1979, the days of "third world solidarity" were gone. In its place were African American and Mexican American groups, pursuing separate paths as the political space narrows, in the wake of white backlash against affirmative action with the Bakke decision in 1978.

---

25   Donald R. Gerth, *The People's University: A History of the California State University*, (Sacramento, CA: Institute of Governmental Studies Press, 2010), 421.

26   Gerth, "People's University," 421.

27   Jeffrey O. G. Ogbar, "Rainbow Radicalism: The Rise of Radical Ethnic Nationalism" in *The Black Power Movement: Rethinking the Civil Rights-Black Power Era*, ed. Peniel E. Joseph (New York: Routledge, 2006), 193–228.

Nava's framing of Hampton as a traitor who knifed him in the back ignored the new political realities of white conservative backlash and claims of "reverse racism" aimed specifically at affirmative action policy, programs, and hiring in public universities. Nava experienced racial coalition politics during his tenure on the LA School Board. He claims, "the coalition of various minority groups and white liberals dissolved to some extent because now each group sought its own interests."[28] He opted to retire from the LA School Board rather than play in the new system. The Bakke decision created the perfect opportunity for affirmative action opponents to use divide and conquer tactics to weaken Black-Brown coalitions. Nava's refusal to adapt to the realities of racial coalition politics may have been his undoing. However, he could not decisively say that Hampton intentionally torpedoed his chance to become the next CSU Los Angeles president. Claudia Hampton, on the other hand, was acutely aware of the structure of white racism, which not only pits minority groups against the other but demands groups make politically expedient choices for one's survival. While she advocated for Mexican American students throughout her career as a teacher to English language learners in East Los Angeles, in her work in desegregating Los Angeles public schools, and in her role as the chair of the Educational Policy Committee on the board, Hampton was also a pragmatist who did not hesitate to make an unpopular choice in the short-term to reap a bigger reward in the long-term.

Having brokered a deal between the CSU system and LA School Board to increase the number of Mexican American teachers before assuming the role of chair of the CSU Board of trustees, Hampton had already demonstrated her long-standing commitment in supporting Mexican American educational progress in the Los Angeles area. Therefore, for her role in recusing herself on the final vote for Rosser over Nava, Claudia Hampton did not appear to experience any significant backlash from the Hispanic community. Immediately following the announcement of Rosser as CSU Los Angeles' newest campus president, Hampton also acted quickly to invite a delegation of Mexican American representatives to make a presentation before the board regarding the challenges that Mexican Americans faced within the system. Her quick thinking helped to quell any potential bad publicity for the board. Among those invited was a CSU Los Angeles student group called the Students' Committee for Justice (SCJ) which was organized to protest the appointment of Rosser. In the days leading up to the presentation before the Board, the group organized a "tardeada," or community party, to strategize for their upcoming meeting with the board. One of the group's letters was sent directly to James Rosser imploring him to not accept

---

28   Nava, "Julian Nava," 124.

the position at CSU Los Angeles. The Students' Committee for Justice cited the demographics near and around CSU Los Angeles, which was predominantly Mexican American in the late 1970s, as one of their chief reasons why they felt Nava would be better suited to lead the Los Angeles campus. Part of the letter stated, "We urge you to not accept the position of president of C.S.U.L.A. This is a difficult request we are making because we are fully cognizant of your outstanding abilities as an individual. Yet we only hope you can extend your vision beyond individual horizons to the needs of the Hispanic community which by 1990 will be the majority of the population of Los Angeles."[29] Additionally, SCJ enlisted the help and support of Mexican American legal advocacy groups like the Mexican American Legal Defense and Education Fund (MALDEF) to help the students file a class-action suit against the Board of Trustees and sought both financial and planning assistance from the Committee of Chicano Rights, a Chicano human rights advocacy group based in San Diego, California, to prepare for SCJ's presentation before the CSU trustees.[30]

The presentation by the Mexican American delegation led to the development of a detailed system-wide report entitled "CSU Affirmative Action and the Mexican American." By the next board meeting, the board voted to approve three new affirmative action pilot programs targeting Hispanic students at the Dominguez Hills, Fresno, and San Jose campuses. During that same meeting, now Board Chair Hampton expressed serious concerns about the selection of campus presidents and appointed a four-member ad hoc committee to review the process. By March 1980, the committee submitted their recommendations to the Faculty and Staff Affairs Committee for full review, which reaffirmed that it was the board's responsibility to select presidents. Fundamentally at issue was the idea of "a rainbow principle" in which the trustees would engage in broad consultation with different constituents to avoid a schism with the campus community. Some trustees, and Chancellor Dumke, were concerned that campuses had too much sway early in the process to eliminate viable candidates. Hampton passed the chair's gavel to defend the newly proposed procedures. Her decision to review presidential selection procedures undoubtedly connected to fallout from the Black/Brown conflict over the CSU Los Angeles presidency. While the result of the ad-hoc committee's deliberation only clarified current practice regarding presidential selection, Claudia Hampton deftly outmaneuvered

29   Student Committee for Justice Letter to Dr. James Rosser, July 2, 1979. Herman Baca Papers. MSS 0649. Special Collections and Archives, UC San Diego.

30   Student Committee for Justice Letter and Donation Form to Committee of Chicano Rights, July 2, 1979. Herman Baca Papers. MSS 0649. Special Collections and Archives, UC San Diego.

her critics. She came away politically unscathed from the CSU Los Angeles controversy, because she quickly responded to calls for the system to be responsive to the unique needs of Mexican Americans. Hampton's invitation to the CSU Mexican American community to make a presentation in 1979 was the first time the board seriously considered Mexican American issues. Racial and ethnic groups were often lumped together under the label of "minority" and the unique characteristics of each group were ignored.

Hampton's invitation helped to change the board's approach to the special needs of the various ethnic/racial groups such that by October 1983, the issue of "Hispanic Under-Representation" would become a regular discussion point in board meetings with a special task force established by newly appointed CSU Chancellor W. Ann Reynolds. Following the Rosser appointment, Hampton's quick thinking to engage various members of the CSU Mexican American community also helped to stave off a class-action suit that the Student Committee for Justice had threatened. Julian Nava might not have gotten the presidency at CSU Los Angeles because of Hampton's recusal, but she worked to ensure that the challenges faced by Mexican Americans in the CSU finally received the attention these issues deserved.

Strategy: Strategically Applying Pressure with Allies of Color

To overcome white resistance to affirmative action, Hampton strategically applied pressure on the board as a united front with other colleagues of color.

Claudia Hampton's tenure as chair of the CSU BOT from 1979–1981 was also marked by state budget cuts, which had a ripple effect on affirmative action programs and student access to financial aid. With a national recession triggered by tightened monetary policy to fight inflation and an overall reduction in the state's EOP budget, the CSU system-wide student enrollment was down by more than 1,500 students at the end of 1979. To make matters worse, by 1980 anti-tax advocate Thomas Jarvis, author of Proposition 13 in 1978, was proposing a new iteration of his earlier anti-tax legislation, known as Jarvis II (or Proposition 9). This new legislation called for a 50% reduction of the personal income tax and business inventory tax in California. If passed, this new legislation would cut state revenue and the state college budget by an estimated 20–25%, just as the CSU was finalizing a $1 million request to Governor Brown to support the system's implementation of a legislature mandated student affirmative action plan in 1980. The possibility of another budgetary crisis sent the CSU into contingency planning mode. The Chancellor's Office and trustees' discussions focused on generating alternative sources of revenue by increasing student fees and further reducing affirmative action hiring for faculty and staff. Affirmative action budgets were preemptively cut, and the CSU had to devise lower cost means of preparing "disadvantaged" students for entry into the CSU to help the system meet its student affirmative action admission goals.

By partnering with local high schools using federal Talent Search and Upward Bound grants, select campuses rolled out the Program for High School Students, including campus-sponsored curricular and extra-curricular programs. For example, nine CSU campuses developed MESA (Math, Engineering and Science Achievement), MEP (Minority Engineering Program) and WISE (Women in Science and Engineering) programs, all of which were designed to augment the system's student affirmative action, EOP, and Office of Relations with Schools programs. Some campuses even enlisted student cultural groups to assist with off campus tutoring activities at nearby schools. Newly admitted CSU students who participated as high school students in one of these programs were eligible for a reduction or a complete waiver of application fees, instructional fees, and health facilities fees, but for those campuses that did not receive federal grant monies, the system was not forthcoming with any additional funding to support college readiness programs for "disadvantaged" students. As the budget crises worsened for the state, the system once again relied on these federal grant-funded programs to meet its student affirmative action obligations as required by state law (ACR-151).

Meanwhile, Chair Hampton and trustees Willie Stennis (the system's third African American trustee) and Gomez-Quinones openly questioned why the Governor and the State Legislature would target affirmative action programs for reduction or elimination even after Chancellor Dumke went on the record to say, "In all of our contacts, we have stressed the need to maintain quality, and—to the degree possible—to maintain open access for the students, including THE minorities, to whom both of our own initiative and legislative direction, we have been orienting our outreach programs."[31] The Black and Brown trustees on the board kept fighting and refusing to bend even in the face of the budgetary crisis, while their white counterparts continued to remain silent. Even after the defeat of Jarvis II, Governor Brown and the Legislature continued to either eliminate or severely cut the CSU's requests to return the affirmative action hiring budgets to baseline levels. In a report of affirmative action programs based on employment utilization of ethnic minorities and women in the CSU from 1975–1981, Trustee Stennis

---

31 Chancellor Dumke's Remarks on the 1981–1982 Budget. CSU Board of Trustees Minutes of the Meeting of the Board of Trustees, Board of Trustees of the California State University Collection. Courtesy of the California State University Archives. California State University Dominguez Hills.

pointed out some actual decreases in minority hiring and retention, particularly amongst the faculty ranks. Stennis expressed his great disappointment, given the Board's time and resources on affirmative action.

Between 1972 and 1980, for example, there was a decrease in the number of Black men and women in the faculty at all ranks. Hampton and Gomez-Quinones expressed frustration about the lack of policy regarding campus implementation of affirmative action. They both were concerned that while the Board approved affirmative action policy and challenged both the governor and legislature on proposed cuts to affirmative action budgets, there was no policy for holding campuses accountable for implementation. Instead, a lack of competitive salaries and poor tracking software/hardware contributed to the CSU not having diverse faculty hiring pools for what board members called "affirmative action faculty." Immediately following the presentation of this report and the commentary offered by chair Hampton, and trustees Stennis and Gomez-Quinones, Chancellor Dumke issued Executive Order 340 in 1981, giving campuses specific guidance for the recruitment of under-represented faculty groups. Such guidance could have helped to prevent the considerable drop in faculty members of color that the CSU experienced in the late 1970s/early 1980s but had these three trustees of color not been present and vocal on this issue, neither the Chancellor's Office staff nor the white members of the board would have felt compelled to act with regard to the troubling data contained in this report. This was a major policy victory for Hampton and the other trustees of color, because it was through their agitation that Chancellor Dumke finally took decisive action on enforcing affirmative action throughout the system.

The issuance of Executive Order 340, albeit a welcomed change in policy, did not stop Hampton from expressing her concern that the board was once again busy trying to limit and narrow the scope of affirmative action policy. Hampton said she was frustrated by "the continued emphasis on framing policy, rather than upon action."[32] Robert Tyndall, Acting Vice Chancellor for Faculty and Staff Affairs for the CSU, attempted to correct Hampton by asserting that "the procedures had translated into action and the CSU has made considerable progress."[33] Newly appointed CSU Affirmative Action

---

32 Chair Hampton's Report July 1980. CSU Board of Trustees Minutes of the Meeting of the Board of Trustees, Board of Trustees of the California State University Collection. Courtesy of the California State University Archives. California State University Dominguez Hills.

33 Policy on Non-Discrimination and Affirmative Action in Employment Report July 8, 1980. CSU Board of Trustees Minutes of the Meeting of the Board of Trustees, Board of Trustees of the California State University Collection. Courtesy of the California State University Archives. California State University Dominguez Hills.

Officer Jeffrey Stetson countered Tyndall and sided with Hampton when he said "Federal regulations emphasize procedures and reporting at the expense of action."[34] Stetson advocated "more vigorous actions in the future from (campus) administrators so that affirmative action does not take second or third place."[35] Hampton and Stetson, both African Americans, found the CSU's lack of progress on affirmative action implementation troubling in 1980, but none of their white counterparts expressed any concern. In 1982, they were joined by two additional trustees of color, Willie Stennis and Juan Gomez-Quinones, in keeping up the pressure on the system and resisting the silence from their white counterparts on the board. Stetson admonished the board for "spending a great deal of time with procedural and technical issues when more time needs to be spent discussing how campus leadership can investigate ways to have a more successful affirmative action program."[36] He went on to ". . . stress that affirmative action needs to be integrated into the philosophy and purposes of the CSU; not just an extra mandate."[37] Stetson's last point gets to the heart of the matter regarding affirmative action—many campus leaders and Chancellor's Office staff did not believe in the over-arching goal of the CSU's affirmative action program, as demonstrated by their failure to take action to increase hiring and retention of minority faculty and recruitment of underrepresented minority students. Thus these guidelines were perceived as a chore rather than a moral imperative to open access and opportunity to all Californians. While Executive Order 340, issued in 1981, provided more guidance for recruitment and selection at the faculty and administrative ranks in compliance with federal and state affirmative action guidelines, the delay in issuing this policy negatively impacted the hiring of women and people of color while white attitudes in the general public toward affirmative action had started to sour in California and across the country.

Claudia Hampton and the other trustees of color were pushing for a model of educational access based on racial equity. Despite possible budget cuts looming, they were unwilling to "take their foot off the gas" regarding affirmative action. These trustees knew how tenuous the support for affirmative action was amongst the white members of the CSU board, including Chancellor Glenn Dumke. Dumke never offered an impassioned plea

---

34 Committee on Faculty and Staff Affairs Report, July 1980. CSU Board of
    Trustees Minutes of the Meeting of the Board of Trustees, Board of Trustees
    of the California State University Collection. Courtesy of the California State
    University Archives. California State University Dominguez Hills.
35 Committee on Faculty and Staff Affairs Report, July 1980.
36 Committee on Faculty and Staff Affairs Report, July 1980.
37 Committee on Faculty and Staff Affairs Report, July 1980.

for the CSU to embrace affirmative action as a moral obligation. It was not until he neared retirement that he offered an executive order to hold campuses accountable for implementing this policy. While Dumke did initiate the hiring of the system's first affirmative action officer, Herb Carter argues that Dumke only did so because of federal mandates requiring universities to develop a plan to enact affirmative action policy or risk losing federal funding.[38] Multiple race conflicts at the various CSU campuses meant that Dumke had to bring in personnel with specialized expertise who could quell racial tensions and create an affirmative action infrastructure to address university "diversity" hiring and campus climate issues. Dumke and other members of his staff, including Herb Carter, came to rely heavily on Claudia Hampton to convince her often reluctant conservative, white male colleagues to give affirmative action policy serious consideration. Herb Carter observed that "she [Claudia Hampton] had a unique ability to have people perceive her in ways that were comfortable, but they really didn't know her. Her values were her values, and she was not going to abort them. But she could have a conversation with you, and you could leave thinking she agreed with you."[39] It was this ability to charm and gain the trust of her fellow trustees that, in part, helped her to be so effective and influential as one of the main leaders on the board for several years. Hampton's ability to wear a mask of civility and play the game of boardsmanship belied the strategist and tactician underneath and allowed her to reveal her true thoughts and feelings only when securing opportunities and resources for underrepresented groups in the CSU system.

Strategy: Keeping a Finger on the Institutional Pulse

Hampton kept abreast of what was happening on the board by attending meetings outside of her regular committee assignments, and influenced policy discussions which might impact the implementation of affirmative action programs and policies.

Just as important as her relationship with influential board members was Hampton's very presence on the many standing and ad-hoc committees on which she served throughout her twenty-year tenure as a trustee. Hampton was a respected trustee because she was very involved in the board's business, not as a casual observer on the sideline, but as an active participant. As the appendix table indicates, Hampton was appointed to nine of the ten standing committees for the board, holding a leadership position as chair

---

38   Carter interview, 2018.
39   Carter interview, 2018.

or vice-chair in nearly all those appointments.[40] She also chaired multiple ad-hoc committees, including searches for campus presidents and person-nel review committees for campus presidents and Chancellor's Office Staff, and she chaired the search for a new chancellor. Hampton was even given a special commendation for her long-standing service as CSU representative for the California Post-Secondary Education Commission from 1977–1988. When board chair Wallace Albertson appointed Hampton to represent the CSU on the Commission for the Review of the Master Plan for Higher Education (henceforth "Master Plan Update"), Albertson told the board members in attendance: "As the most senior Board member, a past chair and as our representation since 1977 to the CPEC, Trustee Hampton is uniquely qualified to represent the system on this very significant project."[41] Subsequent board chairs also would refer to Hampton's many years on the board as evidence of her qualifications to make sound judgments on behalf of the board and the entire system. It is following her years as board chair that Hampton is elevated to "elder Black stateswoman"; even in situations where Hampton might have turned down an appointment because of a full schedule, trustees with less experience on the board than her would defer to her knowledge of board procedures and, most importantly, to her politi-cal savvy. Hampton's many years on the board allowed her to speak with authority, even on committees of which she was not a member.

Early in her tenure on the board, Hampton made it a point to attend meetings outside of her regular committee assignments so that she could gauge whether the affirmative action policies and programs she championed had funding and other types of support. In so doing, Hampton could keep her fingers on the institutional pulse by gaining broader institutional knowl-edge. She understood the inter-relationship of these committees and how a vote in one committee might affect the outcome of the same policy in another. She figured out pretty quickly that resolutions to establish, imple-ment, or expand affirmative action programs ultimately came down to fund-ing. Hence she regularly attended the finance committee meeting if it did not conflict with her other appointed committee meetings. The board meet-ing minutes from 1974 to 1981 show Hampton was present but did not speak unless it was to ask clarifying questions. This began to change at the end of her second term as board chair in 1981. During a discussion of newly

40   See appendix for Hampton's Trustee Committee Service and Leadership.
41   Chair Albertson's Report November 1984. CSU Board of Trustees Minutes of the Meeting of the Board of Trustees, Board of Trustees of the California State University Collection. Courtesy of the California State University Archives. California State University Dominguez Hills.

elected Governor George Deukmejian's proposed 2% reduction of the CSU budget in 1982, a fee increase for students was proposed during the finance committee meeting that Hampton attended. A hiring freeze was already being implemented, but Hampton raised her hand and asked to speak on behalf of students when she asked about the possibility of deferred payments to ease the burden on students?[42] The committee responded favorably to her question and added Hampton's suggestion to the resolution. The resolution to authorize a fee increase included Hampton's amendment, such that new fee increase payments could be spread over the academic year.

At the next finance committee meeting, trustees engaged in a lengthy discussion about fees versus tuition, with tuition referring to a fee for instruction. Hampton and Trustee Gomez-Quinones were concerned that if the CSU were to move to both tuition and fees, access for low-income and underrepresented groups would be severely impacted. The two urged postponement of the motion to initiate a tuition charge until the Chancellor's Office could explain how a new fee and tuition structure would impact access. Neither Hampton nor Gomez-Quinones served on the committee, but both understood that many good ideas regarding affirmative action died in the finance committee because of a lack of support. At the same time, a large majority of their white counterparts claimed to support the notion of access, but also pointed out that for the quality of instruction to be maintained and with the state having no money, the introduction of tuition might be a necessary step.[43] Ultimately, the committee voted in favor of both fees and tuition. However, Hampton and Gomez-Quinones did help to simplify the fee structure so that students would be charged one consolidated fee instead of several individually defined fees, to cover the costs of running the library or the student health center, for example. Although they were unsuccessful in blocking a charge for tuition, Hampton and Gomez-Quinones' intervention is yet another example of how the presence of people of color at the table is so vital to the interests of students, faculty, and staff of color in the system.

---

42 Finance Committee Report, January 1983. CSU Board of Trustees Minutes of the Meeting of the Board of Trustees, Board of Trustees of the California State University Collection. Courtesy of the California State University Archives. California State University Dominguez Hills.

43 Finance Committee Report, March 1983. CSU Board of Trustees Minutes of the Meeting of the Board of Trustees, Board of Trustees of the California State University Collection. Courtesy of the California State University Archives. California State University Dominguez Hills.

Strategy: Using Varied Committee Service to Shape Policy

*Hampton's long service on the board and her work on multiple board commit-
tees and special appointments enabled her to shape policy and influence votes on
the selection of important systems personnel.*

By 1982, Hampton was the board's most senior member after the retirement of Charles Luckman, who served continuously for twenty-two years.
As one of the longest-serving members, Hampton became even more influential, because she possessed a wealth of knowledge and institutional memory about the board culture and procedures. After serving two consecutive
terms as board chair, Hampton was placed again on the Organization and
Rules Committee as chair. In 1983, Hampton spearheaded the board's first
change to the rules of procedure since the board's inception in 1960, when
she called for a vote on a rule to limit the number of consecutive terms a
person could serve as chair of the board. When trustee Donald Livingston
requested a survey about the board's feelings on the matter, Hampton
politely but forcefully told Livingston and the rest of the committee that
the process for examining this proposed policy needed to be ready by next
meeting. Hampton gave Livingston a timetable to conduct his survey, but
she would not delay a vote to accommodate his request. With Livingston's
informal survey completed by the next meeting, the full board was ready to
vote, and the motion to limit a chair to three consecutive terms was carried.
It was unusual for the committee to vote so quickly on this important board
rule and procedural change. Trustees typically had to deliberate for two to
three meetings before votes are cast. Still, given that Hampton had multiple special committee appointments during this period, it seems that she
wanted to move the business along to more important discussions, such as a
review of the entire Rules and Procedures for the Board of Trustees, which
Hampton initiated.

It had been more than twenty years since the board's Rules and
Procedures were developed and updated. Given the appointment of a new
chancellor, W. Ann Reynolds, in early 1983, Hampton felt it was necessary
to define the board's role in serving on ad hoc and advisory committees in
addition to their normal work. During the discussion of rules and procedures, Hampton pointed out that some of the communications and materials sent to trustees from the Chancellor's Office conflated normal committee
work with committees designed to advise the Chancellor's Office when specific personnel matters arose. Hampton sought clarity and a provision in the
rules and procedure to disentangle this work, as personnel decisions are primarily the chancellor's responsibility. Hampton initiated this review process
because she juggled multiple committee assignments and special appointments. She was often called upon to also serve as chair with very little recognition from the Chancellor's Office regarding the amount of time needed

to serve in these varied roles. Additionally, it was bad practice to have board members, appointed to a special committee, discussing their work during regular committee work. Personnel matters, for example, often dealt with sensitive employee data that should not be discussed outside of that specific committee. Out of this review process, which lasted over several months, the Organization and Rules committee proposed the establishment of an as-needed personnel committee which would advise the chancellor on special and specific personnel matters.

Hampton was deeply embedded in the CSU, which ultimately served the institution well because no other trustee to that point had the same depth and range of experience, institutional memory, and influence that she had, which enabled her to put her varied committee assignments to purpose for her goals. For instance, in a single board year in 1983, Hampton chaired the Organization and Rules Committee, served as Vice Chair of the Educational Policy Committee, served on the Faculty and Staff Affairs committee, and continued in her role as the CSU representative for the California Post-Secondary Education Commission. In 1981, Board chair O'Connell had appointed Hampton as chair of the Criteria Committee, tasked with developing the criteria for the review and selection of the next chancellor. Six months later when that committee's work had concluded, O'Connell asked Hampton to chair the search committee for the next CSU chancellor with this work carrying on into early 1983. O'Connell also appointed Hampton to the Education 2000 Committee, a special sub-committee of the Educational Policy Committee in which Hampton served as vice-chair. This committee's charge was to develop a list of educational and academic options for the CSU to pursue and offer students in the future. Like the other special committees to which O'Connell had appointed Hampton, this extra committee work carried over for another two years. By the middle of 1983, Hampton was tapped yet again to chair another committee. This time, she was appointed chair of the evaluation and review committee for campus presidents and Chancellor's Office staff. Meeting minutes from these various appointments show that Hampton regularly raised questions about educational equity, affirmative action, and resources for low-income students.

Strategy: Finesse Process Obstacles

Hampton was able to leverage her many years of service to finesse process obstacles in policy or procedure and create new opportunities to extend support for affirmative action programs.

Hampton showed the greatest enthusiasm and had the most influence on the board with her work on the Educational Policy Committee. Given her background as a former teacher and school administrator, it is no wonder that Hampton was most interested in advocating for students. Hampton said of her interest in educational policy, "I have been a member of the educational policy committee ever since I have been on the board. So I started paying attention to those things. General Education. Teacher Preparation. I became the expert on educational issues before Mary Jane Pew got there. She was very interested and good with that. And gradually they not only accepted me as the resident expert, they would defer to me on those matters. And we worked out a turfdom arrangement that worked quite well. I had the reputation up until now to be the one interested in education."[44]

Being present during key policy/political discussions allowed Hampton to develop and use her influence in ways that explicitly supported students of color. Within two years on the board, Hampton was named vice chair of the Educational Policy Committee in 1976 and named chair two years later. Under her leadership, the committee debated and deliberated on a proposed special admission exception (aka the 4% rule), Title IX compliance and tackled the question of Mexican American student underrepresentation within the CSU, and access and retention of Black students within the CSU. Hampton spearheaded the development of a Mexican American teacher training program, a collaboration between the CSU and Los Angeles Unified School District, and she was involved in securing approvals to create affirmative action pilot programs for African American and Mexican American students at the Dominguez Hills and Fresno campuses, respectively. Over the course of her twenty years on the board, Hampton served on the Educational Policy Committee for approximately seventeen years and was directly involved with academic program reviews, modification of the freshmen admission requirements, and discussions on reducing remedial activity among the many topics dealing directly with student learning. As time went on, Hampton's participation on several special committees, namely as CSU representative on the California Post-Secondary Education Commission, and the commission to review the California Master Plan for Higher Education in 1985, helped to increase her influence on educational policy matters for the board of trustees. On these special commissions, Hampton often learned about new policy developments and educational trends across the state's different higher education institutions, ahead of the CSU Board of Trustees taking up these issues. For example, in 1983, ahead of Chancellor Reynolds suggesting an increase to student fees to offset impending budget cuts, Hampton learned during an emergency meeting of the CPEC that other institutions were considering a major fee increase in 1983–1984 based on the budget proposed by Governor Deukmejian. While presenting her CPEC report, Hampton advised the board to "pursue a balanced fee policy and have the CSU fee

---

44   Hampton, interview.

levels comparable to those of the University of California and community colleges."[45] This balanced fee policy, said Hampton, was one in which, if the need for continued access demanded increased fees, the only way this could happen was through increased student financial aid. In other words, Hampton argued that students should not bear the brunt of the state budget crisis without some assistance from both the federal and California state government. Chancellor Reynolds took Hampton's suggestion under advisement when she directed Dale Hanner, Vice Chancellor of Business Affairs to draft a fee increase proposal which addressed Hampton's concerns. Hanner and the finance committee responded with a proposal to increase student fees and make major reductions to library and custodial staff, along with the elimination of state support for summer session, while increasing student grants. Once the proposal was shared with the entire board, Hampton eagerly endorsed the plan and was able to get her colleagues to agree to a deferred payment plan to help ease the burden on students. This is just one example of Hampton's influence and power in shaping board policy. Through her acceptance of these special committee appointments, Hampton gained early access to information which she, in turn, used to her strategic advantage. She became one of the most actively engaged of all the trustees, which lent itself to her becoming one of the most well-respected members of the board, and as W. Ann Reynolds recounts, "I can't think of any issue of importance to the CSU that we were trying to get approval or funding for from the state that Dr. Hampton was not totally supportive of. She was right there on the issues."[46]

In 1982, Hampton was appointed to serve a two-year term in President Reagan's administration as a member of the President's Advisory Panel on the Financing of Elementary and Secondary Education. This panel, composed of parents, teachers, business persons, educational leaders, and elected officials, was mandated by Congress with the passage of the 1978 Educational Amendments to the Elementary and Secondary Education Act of 1965. Specifically, this panel was charged with providing counsel and guidance to the Department of Health, Education, and Welfare on the financing of special programs for educationally deprived children attending public schools. These programs aimed to increase mastery of basic skills, aid in the desegregation of school systems, and increase aid to bilingual, American

---

45 Trustee Hampton's Report on the California Postsecondary Education Commission. January 1983. CSU Board of Trustees Minutes of the Meeting of the Board of Trustees, Board of Trustees of the California State University Collection. Courtesy of the California State University Archives. California State University Dominguez Hills.

46 Reynolds, interview.

Indian, and female students.[47] Hampton's appointment to this presidential advisory panel was quite significant, because she was one of the first members of the California State University leadership to be invited to serve in an advisory role to a sitting U.S. president. While Glenn Dumke and later Ann Reynolds were able to visit with presidents for a brief meeting in their role as CSU Chancellor, neither was hand-picked to serve on a presidential panel. Furthermore, this appointment gave Hampton exposure to the world of educational policymaking beyond the CSU and California politics. Here she was interfaced with elected officials and laypeople across the country, while lending her input and expertise to the proposals submitted to the president for implementation. As a former elementary school teacher, an expert on school desegregation, and a leader in university governance, Hampton was uniquely qualified to serve in this role especially because she brought the added dimension of her affirmative action advocacy work. This appointment was extremely important in solidifying Hampton's reputation as the "elder Black stateswoman" on the board as she was the only trustee who could point to having influenced policy at the local, state, and national level regarding the education of under-represented populations in both K-12 and higher education.

Hampton's influence on board policy continued to grow after this federal appointment. She was subsequently nominated as vice chair and then chair of the board's Gifts and Public Affairs committee from 1981 to 1985. This committee, which has been renamed the Governmental Relations committee in recent years, was the place where trustees influenced policy at the state level. Members of the California Legislature submitted their proposed legislation related to higher education and workplace policy to the Gifts and Public Affairs committee for endorsement from the board. This gave trustees enormous power beyond their system governance duties as elected officials sought these endorsements to sway the public to vote in favor of their proposed bill or resolution. Those trustee board members who chaired this committee often corresponded or met face-to-face with state legislators to get clarification on board members' questions, ahead of committee meetings.

For Hampton, this appointment allowed her to influence the committees' potential endorsement of affirmative action related bills from members of the California Legislative Black Caucus (CLBC). Several members of the CLBC proposed legislation strengthening the state's affirmative action

---

47   Jimmy Carter, Education Amendments of 1978 and the Middle-Income Student Assistance Act Statement on Signing H.R. 15 and S. 2539 Into Law. Online by Gerhard Peters and John T. Woolley, The American Presidency Project https://www.presidency.ucsb.edu/node/243763.

infrastructure regarding public elementary, secondary, and higher education. As chair, Hampton ensured that these bills received full committee consideration. For example, Hampton encouraged her fellow committee members to endorse a state bill crafted by State Senator Dianne Watson (who was the first African American woman elected to serve in the California State Senate) to establish a University and College Opportunities program to improve the preparation of elementary and secondary students for matriculation into two- and four-year public higher education institutions. Trustee Blanche Bersch critiqued the bill's original wording as lacking sufficient reference to the under-representation of sex, ethnic, and economic backgrounds of students who could benefit from the program. Hampton endorsed the bill stipulating that the legislation must be written to be compatible with the CSU's student affirmative action program. The rest of the committee agreed and endorsed the bill. This is another example of how Hampton leveraged her influence to overcome process obstacles.

Strategy: Work with the Women and Manage the Men

To extend the reach of the CSU's affirmative action efforts, Hampton collaborated with women on major program or policy initiatives by using her skills at diplomacy and negotiation to bring reluctant male colleagues on board.

The appointment of a new chancellor was a significant undertaking no matter who chaired that committee, given the importance of the role, size, and complexity of the CSU system. But for the next chancellor to excel in the role, this person had to contend with the state's rapidly changing demographics. From 1970 to 1980, California's total population rose by 18.1%, making it the most populous state in the union with just under 24 million residents. In this ten-year period, there was a five percent (5%) increase in the number of non-white residents and a 3.5% decrease in white residents of the state.[48] This rise in the state's non-white population would have major implications for the implementation and enforcement of affirmative action, especially after the 1978 Bakke decision, which allowed race to be used as a factor in university admission but disallowed the use of racial quotas as a means of reaching racial parity in education and government contracting. Claudia Hampton, one of the board's most ardent advocates for the expansion of affirmative action, was tapped to be in charge of such a consequential selection process. This appointment spoke volumes about her influence over major board decisions. Serving as search committee chair for the Chancellor position helped ensure that candidates vying for the position would have

---

48   Data retrieved from usafacts.org on 8/17/2022.

to answer questions about their beliefs and plans regarding racial equity in hiring, student admission, and so on. Out of this exhaustive process, the committee recommended, and the board approved, the selection of the system's first woman chancellor, Dr. W. Ann Reynolds, who was set to begin in January 1983.

Before accepting the position of Chancellor of the California State University system, Reynolds had taught zoology at the University of Illinois College of Medicine before embarking on a career in higher education administration. First, she served as Dean of the Graduate College at the University of Illinois Medical Center before she was named as Provost at Ohio State University, where she stayed for three years. Those present during Reynolds' hiring process for the CSU Chancellorship, including Donald Gerth, recall her stating her unequivocal support for affirmative action and open access, which endeared Reynolds to Hampton. The two women, one black and one white, developed an early friendship that lasted even after Reynolds was forced to resign by the mostly white male trustees on the board in 1990. Their relationship was forged out of a type of interest convergence, where Hampton needed a chancellor who would demonstrate unwavering support for racial minorities and women through affirmative action policy and programs, while Reynolds needed Hampton's support to help her make inroads with the board, as Reynolds often had a difficult time working with people. Donald Gerth noted that prior to coming to CSU, Reynolds was dubbed "The Queen" by the faculty at Ohio State, because she did not like to work through committees to build consensus to get approval for her ideas. Reynolds also had a reputation for calling for the layoff of tenured faculty, which was a concern for some CSU Chancellor's search committee members. A few years into her tenure as CSU Chancellor, Reynolds was once again dubbed "Queen Ann" by members of the board of trustees, Chancellor Office staff, and the media.[49] Herb Carter, who generally spoke positively of Reynolds, who was his direct supervisor when he served at the Chancellor's Office as Executive Vice Chancellor, says "She [Reynolds] was an extraordinarily bright, very smart woman, had all the right values. Everything worked fine for her, but she had no sense how to deal with people. We would be in a meeting and a trustee would start to ask a question and before they could ask it, she would answer it, you know, and that just annoyed everybody."[50] Carter says that it became his job to

---

49　William Craven, "Commentary: The Real Issue Is One of Power. Chancellor W. Ann Reynolds has had ongoing intramural scrimmages with SDSU President Thomas Day since she was appointed. *Los Angeles Times* (San Diego County Edition), November 13, 1988, 2.

50　Carter, interview.

interface with the trustees because of Reynolds' frosty relationship with most of them. According to Carter, Claudia Hampton was the notable exception, says Carter, because "Ann was very emphatic about her commitment to people of color and to the need for education. So, she and Claudia concocted all kinds of ways to advance the cause of women and minorities."[51]

One such example of Reynolds and Hampton's collaboration still exists today. The Chancellor's Doctoral Forgivable Loan Program was established in 1987 (now known as the Chancellor's Doctoral Incentive Program or CDIP). Using proceeds from the California Lottery, Reynolds and Hampton devised a way to increase the number of women and minorities as CSU faculty by giving out "forgivable loans "of up to $30,000 per person for their doctoral studies. Loan recipients who completed their doctorate and returned to the CSU as faculty would have twenty percent (20%) of the loan forgiven each year of full-time postdoctoral teaching in the CSU. These loan recipients or CDIP fellows also received mentorship support and access to travel grants to attend conferences and workshops. Since the program's inception, over 2000 fellows have received funding and mentoring support, and sixty-nine percent (69%) who have earned doctorate degrees have obtained faculty positions at a CSU campus.[52] Reynolds and Carter developed the particulars of the program, and Hampton was instrumental in getting her colleagues on board.

Furthermore, due in part to the CSU's poor record of admitting and retaining African American students, Hampton convinced Reynolds to give a half million dollar grant to the 100 Black Men of Los Angeles, Incorporated's Young Black Scholars (YBS) program. Following Hampton's involvement with a 1983 CPEC study about the alarming number of African American students who did not meet the entrance requirements of the CSU or UC system upon high school graduation, 100 Black Men of Los Angeles responded by establishing the YBS program as a three-year pilot to provide academic workshops, enrichment activities, and support services to augment African American students' preparation for college. As Hampton was well known in Black Los Angeles political and social circles, she became friends with 100 Black Men of Los Angeles' founder, Dr. William H. Hayling, who was seeking support for the YBS pilot program in the mid-1980s. Herb Carter maintains that Reynolds and the board were convinced to approve this grant to the Young Black Scholars program because of Hampton's

---

51   Carter, interview.
52   Mission and History. The Chancellor's Doctoral Incentive Program. The California State University website. August 28, 2022. https://www.calstate. edu/csu-system/faculty-staff/cdip/Pages/mission-and-history.aspx.

"guile."[53] Securing this grant speaks volumes to how Hampton pursued opportunities and strategically used her connections.

After working with Reynolds to establish a minority faculty pipeline through the forgivable loan program, Hampton set about creating a pipeline for minority students graduating from Los Angeles area high schools, who were not adequately prepared for entrance into CSU or UC with establishment of the California Academy of Mathematics and Sciences (CAMS) on the campus of CSU Dominguez Hills. CAMS was Hampton's brainchild and a project that Ann Reynolds readily endorsed, despite Carter initially telling Hampton this idea would not work because it would be illegal to establish a minority-only high school. Hampton was undeterred and volunteered to speak with the Los Angeles School Board president, whom she knew personally. Hampton reportedly said the school would not discriminate but would give high preference to minority students who wanted to get more extensive training in the sciences. The president of the Los Angeles School Board shot down the idea. However, as luck would have it, Hampton was on a plane to Sacramento with the school board president for Long Beach Unified School District (LBUSD), where she mentioned the idea of a STEM school targeting minority students. Using her superior social intelligence and skills, Hampton turned this chance opportunity into something tangible and concrete. The LBUSD superintendent thought it was a great idea and now Hampton, Carter, and Reynolds were able to get the ball rolling. Carter says that Hampton's determination in bringing the CAMS idea to fruition is "a testimony to the leadership, compassion, and understanding of Claudia. She was always looking for ways to move the needle for minority kids and she was always looking for ways to do that so that she didn't antagonize or make a lot of enemies out of other people."[54]

Relying on the board's affection for Hampton, Reynolds was able to push through causes that she felt might otherwise be met with resistance. One might liken Hampton and Reynolds' dynamic to that of opposite personalities—one extroverted and the other introverted. Hampton enjoyed and even excelled at social interactions with her board peers, and while Reynolds displayed a gift for innovative policy and programming ideas, she often struggled to garner the support of the board. Before Reynolds' arrival, the Educational Policy Committee began discussing a resolution to modify the freshmen admission requirements to four years of English and two years of math for all graduating high school students. This change, if approved, would be the first major change to Title X (California's Code of Regulations governing education) since the creation of the 4% Special Admit Policy in

---

53   Carter, interview.
54   Carter, interview.

1978, and was aimed at improving students' preparation for college-level writing, quantitative reasoning, and critical thinking skills. While the admissions requirement discussion was underway, the Educational Policy and Finance committees were considering plans to substantially reduce "remedial activity" across the system by more than eighty percent (80%) within five years. Reynolds had appointed Ellis McCune, President of CSU Hayward, to chair a Task Force on Remediation and develop a plan in response to a CPEC report calling for eliminating remedial activity. Trustees Hampton and Ballesteros expressed concern about the CPEC report, given the CSU's emphasis on raising admission standards. Both cautioned that some groups would see these raised standards and a reduction in remedial classes and academic support services as an attempt to limit access. Assurances were made by Chancellor's Office staff that neither any future new admission requirements nor the reduction in remedial activity, would violate Title 5. To address whether the CSU should establish admission requirements for prospective students, the Chancellor's Office and the board had to first address the issue of funding for academic support services for the system's current student body.

Due in part to a petition by the Mexican American Legal Defense Fund (MALDEF) expressing concern about the low rate of transfer to the CSU from Black and Hispanic students who begin their educational careers at the community colleges, Chancellor Reynolds convened a blue-ribbon Commission on Hispanic Underrepresentation in March 1984, chaired by the CSU's first Mexican American campus president, Tomas Arciniega, from CSU Bakersfield. Within six months, the commission produced an initial report, "Hispanics and Higher Education: A CSU Imperative" that broadly outlined the barriers to Hispanic student matriculation and graduation from the CSU, as there had been a gradual steady increase of Hispanic students from 1973–1978 and then a sharp decline from then on. As a result of the increased pressure from outside groups, Reynolds went on record to state that "overcoming underrepresentation, especially of Hispanics, had become one of the highest priorities of her administration.[55] The report also contained 35 recommendations that dealt with pre-college advising and preparation, outreach, campus climate, and financial assistance. Ahead of the chancellor and trustees receiving the commission's full report, the Finance Committee was asked by the chancellor to consider a twelve-million-dollar request from Governor Deukmejian in the

---

55   Educational Policy Committee Report March 1984. CSU Board of Trustees
      Minutes of the Meeting of the Board of Trustees, Board of Trustees of
      the California State University Collection. Courtesy of the California State
      University Archives. California State University Dominguez Hills.

1985/1986 state budget for a Minority Underrepresentation line item, which included increased grants, scholarships, funding of the California Academic Preparation program, and remediation services for underrepresented groups attending a CSU campus.

It is not clear why the finance committee took the extraordinary step of moving so quickly on this matter, but what was clear was that the more conservative members of board took issue with a request to fund remediation activity throughout the system. For example, some of the more conservative trustees, such as Roy Brophy, were of the strong opinion that remediation should be handled at the elementary and secondary school levels. In contrast, trustee Claudia Hampton and Chancellor Reynolds wanted to reduce remedial activity, but not eliminate remediation services across the CSU campuses. While Reynolds argued that the need for these services was still great, particularly amongst underrepresented groups of students in the CSU, it was clear that Brophy believed that stringent admission standards should act as a gatekeeping mechanism to keep out those who needed access to remediation services. Brophy was basically making the argument about "quality students" one still hears today, where people think quality and minority are mutually exclusive and fail to recognize disadvantage by mistaking privilege for ability or intelligence. Universities often do not discover that a student needs remediation until the student has been admitted into the university, so it seems peculiar that Brophy would only take issue with the remediation part of the proposal, unless he did not want to see funds earmarked specifically to help underrepresented groups do well in the CSU. If the system wanted to continue to promote access while raising academic standards, funding for college preparation and remediation were simply non-negotiable. In the end, Governor Deukmejian included $7 million of the requested $12 million for minority underrepresentation, for which Chancellor Reynolds expressed her gratitude in her report: "We appreciate also the governor's recognition of our need for funds to address problems of minority underrepresentation and to increase the number of students from minority groups eligible to attend CSU."[56] Funding college preparation programs and remediation services proved to be far less controversial than raising CSU admission standards.

Buoyed by the 1978 Bakke decision, some GOP lawmakers in California began proposing legislation to eliminate all affirmative action programs beyond racial quotas such as Senate Constitutional Amendment (SCA) 39 in 1981. This bill would provide that "no business, public or private, could

---

56 Chancellor Reynolds Report. January 1985. CSU Board of Trustees Minutes of the Meeting of the Board of Trustees, Board of Trustees of the California State University Collection. Courtesy of the California State University Archives. California State University Dominguez Hills.

provide any benefits, detriments, privileges, or immunities, based on race, sex, creed, color, or national origin."[57] Even though this bill ultimately failed to get enough votes, there was a growing sense that the mood in Sacramento had shifted against affirmative action, and that given the CSU's dependence on state funding for its very survival, it would need to devise ways to appease state legislators, to remain in their good graces. Raising admission standards was viewed as one way to signal to lawmakers that the CSU had not abandoned academic excellence in their pursuit of educational access. Discussions about the potential modification of freshmen admission requirements began with the Educational Policy Committee holding information sessions for members so that they could become educated about the potential impact of these new requirements, which required all incoming freshmen students to have completed four years of English and two years of math to be eligible for admission into the CSU. Starting in 1982, the Educational Policy Committee took comments from minority constituent groups such as the RAZA Administrators and Counselors in Higher Education that voiced general support for increasing the admission requirements, but expressed concern about how this change might affect student affirmative action goals. Hampton, for her part, came out as an early supporter of the resolution, as long as the board continued receiving commentary from external groups raising concerns. At the committee's urging, the Chancellor's Office developed a questionnaire focused on the potential impact of these new requirements on student affirmative action admission, which was sent out to over 1100 school districts in California in early 1983. Unfortunately, only ten districts responded. Despite this low response rate, the committee moved forward with a vote authorizing the chancellor to appoint a CSU Admission Advisory Panel, to review and make recommendations for implementing new freshmen admission standards.

The timing of these discussions on increasing the admission requirements coincided with the establishment of the Commission on Hispanic Underrepresentation to address the low admission and matriculation rates of Hispanic students in the CSU. Issuing new admission standards at this time could open campus and system leadership to criticism for failing to consider how new admission criteria might negatively impact low income and underrepresented groups of students. To help allay concerns that these new requirements might disproportionately impact Hispanic and other underrepresented students, Hampton played a key role in helping Reynolds broker a deal with Harry Handler, then superintendent of the Los Angeles Unified School District, to create The Step to College program. This joint program

---

57 ACLU of Northern California News vol. 47, no. 1, 1982 January-February; PER ACLUN; California Historical Society.

was an early start initiative that would allow historically underrepresented students take college-level courses at their local Los Angeles area high school. CSU faculty would teach these courses, and they would form mentoring relationships with their students to encourage them to seek admission into one of the CSU campuses. Reynolds summed up the important role which Hampton played in helping the CSU build relationships with LAUSD like this: "We had some good K through 12 people throughout the state and she [Hampton] knew most of them. There would always be some conference and I would ask her to attend with me, and everyone was glad to see her. She could bridge a lot of our efforts with K through 12."[58] Hampton's support of Reynolds' efforts to diversify the student body through college preparation programs and improve teacher quality through CSU teacher preparation programs was vital in getting Reynolds' most ardent detractors on board.

Improving the quality of CSU teacher education programs was another priority of Reynolds' during her tenure as chancellor. She was fortunate to have a former schoolteacher and long-time school administrator in Claudia Hampton as one of her key allies in this endeavor. Despite the CSU being established primarily to prepare teachers for the state's growing populations, some trustees and campus presidents paid little attention to system's teacher training certificate and degree programs, focusing their energies and resources on turning the campuses into a university rather than teachers' colleges, according to Reynolds. "Sometimes many of the first few colleges, the older ones, had been established as teacher education institutions like San Jose State and even San Francisco and San Diego State. They weren't proud of that tradition. They were kind of trying to bury that and very much wanted to be considered as a university, although CSU was producing the majority of the teachers for the state of California, which is a wonderful thing to be doing."[59] Responding to the National Panel on Excellence in Education and the California Round Table on the Teaching Profession, Reynolds directed campus presidents to examine their teacher education programs by considering their existing admission and exit requirements and report their findings. She then directed Vice Chancellor for Academic Affairs Alex Sherriffs to organize two system-wide committees, one to assist the campuses with these reviews and the other to work with K to 12 leaders to improve the teacher education experience. Hampton supported these efforts. However, when Reynolds sought support from campus presidents and other trustees to ask Governor Deukmejian for funding to prepare and retain teachers who could work in areas with high concentrations

---

58 Reynolds, interview.
59 Reynolds, interview.

of minority students, Reynolds was met with resistance. She would call on Hampton to smooth things over with people like San Diego State University President Thomas Day, who had no interest in teacher education. Reynolds recalled that Hampton, ". . . was very good at talking to all of the presidents and could bring them around in a diplomatic way. She would tell them you might not get what you want this year, but I will help you get it next year."[60] Hampton's skill at diplomacy and negotiation with trustees, campus presidents and even Governor Deukmejian made the difference in Reynolds successfully pushing her agenda through. While Deukmejian was generally supportive of CSU's efforts to increase access to underrepresented groups through college preparatory programs, Reynolds said that one of her greatest achievements as chancellor was getting Deukmejian to approve multi-year funding for CSU's "Effective Education in Multicultural Settings" initiative. Starting in 1986, selected CSU campuses would establish centers (1) to attract and prepare teachers for work in predominantly minority areas, (2) to serve as research and development resources to advance and disseminate knowledge on effective educational practices for underrepresented minority students, and (3) to aid faculty in helping minority students succeed in high-demand fields in education. During a special board meeting to approve the 1985/1986 Trustee Support Budget, Reynolds asked Hampton to appeal directly to Governor Deukmejian, who was in attendance, to support this initiative in the upcoming budget, because Reynolds said, "I knew that his wife had a teaching degree and one of his daughters was studying secondary education at the time."[61] With Hampton's background in teaching, the appeal worked, and the CSU was awarded $7 million in 1985 and another $7 million the following year for teacher education. According to Reynolds, "This was the first time that the CSU was awarded more money from the governor than the UC (University of California) and they were very mad about it."[62]

Reynolds and Hampton successfully secured funding to expand college preparation and teacher education programs. Still, the issue of raising standards for freshmen admission proved to be a more difficult challenge to overcome, especially around the question of the impact on student affirmative action. No number of promises for additional support for college preparation programs targeting underrepresented groups could combat the impression that the chancellor and trustees were trying to make it more difficult for underrepresented students to gain acceptance into the CSU. During an Educational Policy Committee meeting in 1984, trustee Peevey "expressed

60   Reynolds, interview.
61   Reynolds, interview.
62   Reynolds, interview.

concern on the impact, at least in the short term, of the policy on minority enrollment in the system." Peevey asked "What was the record of Black
and Hispanic enrollment in the system in the last five years?"[63] Enrollment
records from that period 1977–1983 showed that Black student enrollment
went from 4.6 to 5.4% and Hispanic enrollment went from 5.2 to 8.1%,
both of which were higher than the national percentages for minority student enrollment in colleges and universities. Reynolds responded to Peevey's
query: "The (Hispanic Underrepresentation) commission chaired by
President Arciniega and other studies indicate that the two main barriers to
success for minority students in college has been the lack of financial support
and adequate preparation."[64] Reynolds' response, though correct, did not
address Peevey's central concern that if those new admission requirements
resulted in decreased Black and Hispanic student enrollment, the chancellor
and trustees would be accused of being racist in the court of public opinion.

Commentary from trustees like Roy Brophy, who was reappointed to
the board in 1983, added to the perception of that the board was hostile
to minority students, after groups like the RAZA Advocates for California
Higher Education Policy Committee asked that the board consider allowing
conditional admission for underrepresented students in the wake of the new
requirements. Brophy went on the record to say that he felt there was access
for all through conditional and special admission and "if there was discrimination, it is the discrimination that is an inevitable result of being unprepared and therefore the policy should be called "retention requirements"
rather than admission requirements."[65] Brophy's comments implied that
any discrimination that underrepresented minority students faced with being
denied admission into the CSU was the fault of minority students, rather
than public schools that failed them.

Siding with Brophy was Dr. William Vandament, CSU Vice Chancellor of
Academic Affairs, who stated, "When a school district puts greater emphasis
on academic subject matter, the number of minority students prepared for
college increases, and this creates and environment in which college preparation becomes the norm rather than the exception."[66] Certainly no one pres-

63 Educational Policy Committee Report November 1984. CSU Board of
   Trustees Minutes of the Meeting of the Board of Trustees, Board of Trustees
   of the California State University Collection. Courtesy of the California State
   University Archives. California State University Dominguez Hills.

64 Educational Policy Committee Report November 1984.

65 Educational Policy Committee Report May 1986. CSU Board of Trustees
   Minutes of the Meeting of the Board of Trustees, Board of Trustees of
   the California State University Collection. Courtesy of the California State
   University Archives. California State University Dominguez Hills.

66 Educational Policy Committee Report May 1986.

ent during these deliberations argued against the need for public schools to provide adequate preparation to minority students, but when certain trustees and Chancellor's Office staff suggested that minority students should not have the opportunity to attend the CSU because of institutional system failures, these comments give the impression that minority students lack the ability to do well in the university. Brophy and Vandament's comments so angered representatives from the California State Student Association (CSSA) that Damone Hall, the association's first African American president, had some choice words for Brophy, Chancellor Reynolds, and the Educational Policy Committee when he said: "We are now promised that if admission requirements are raised, life will be better. Why should we trust you? You are asking us to jeopardize what we have—which may or may not be anything—on a promise from a system that hasn't kept many of its promises. Your track record isn't too great."[67] Hall specifically referred to promises made to minority students to support them financially and with academic support services that rarely came to pass. The CSSA urged campus presidents and other system officials to work more aggressively and actively on the diverse needs of students, not simply raising admission standards as the sole means of retaining students to completion of their degrees.

Several months earlier, Hampton was on the record in stating her support for the new requirements, "There is evidence that the best avenue for social mobility for a minority student is through schooling. The only way to economic survival is to have an adequate, complete, and good education. I am supportive of this resolution with the understanding that there will be monitoring and self-correcting mechanisms built in."[68] She reiterated her support for the new requirements if two things could be guaranteed. First, Hampton wanted assurances that Black and Brown and other underrepresented students had access to a full range of college preparatory programs and services. Therefore, she lent her support, helping Reynolds broker deals with local school districts and helped community-based organizations get funding to expand their college prep programming. The other condition for Hampton's support was a stipulation in the resolution that called for a modification of the plan after careful monitoring, if data suggested that changes

---

67   Damone Hall, Annual Report of the California State Student Association, July 9, 1986. CSU Board of Trustees Minutes of the Meeting of the Board of Trustees, Board of Trustees of the California State University Collection. Courtesy of the California State University Archives. California State University Dominguez Hills.

68   Educational Policy Committee Report May 1986. CSU Board of Trustees Minutes of the Meeting of the Board of Trustees, Board of Trustees of the California State University Collection. Courtesy of the California State University Archives. California State University Dominguez Hills.

should be made in response to Hale's comments. By demanding these types of guarantees in exchange for her support, once again, Hampton assumed the role of conciliator between "the half that didn't want to do anything that helped minorities and the other half that wanted to give them everything in the university."[69] Some groups remained steadfastly opposed to these new requirements, but Hampton offered a way for the board to move forward and avoid major public backlash.

Reynolds received a favorable evaluation after her first year in 1984, but soon relations between Reynolds, several campus presidents, and trustees began to sour when Reynolds became embroiled in public battles with several campus presidents, was accused of having an explosive temper resulting in the verbal abuse of her subordinates at the Chancellor's Office, and was at the center of a pay raise controversy from which she was unable to recover. Through it all, Claudia Hampton remained one of Reynolds' most steadfast supporters. She noted in a statement following a 1987 attempt by some board members to oust Reynolds as chancellor, "Her [Reynolds'] accomplishments in providing educational leadership, instituting new academic programs, improving minority-ethnic access and raising the public image of CSU have been widely hailed."[70] Reynolds' management style might have been off-putting to some, but her success in increasing minority student admission, retention, and graduation rates silenced her critics at least for the time being. By 1987, some of the affirmative action programs that Reynolds created, with help from Hampton in securing votes from her board colleagues, began showing demonstrative signs of progress. For example, Hispanic student enrollment rose by fifty-five percent (55%) in a two-year period with similar increases for Asian and African American students. Degree attainment from the CSU also rose across these groups.[71]

It was Reynolds' decision to give herself a pay raise of forty-three percent (43%) and a twenty-one percent (21%) raise to campus presidents and vice chancellors that was ultimately her undoing, breaking a 1984 pledge she made to state legislators that discussions about executive compensation would be open and transparent. Unbeknownst to most of the trustees, Reynolds had secured the services of a private consultant to look at executive compensation in other higher educational institutions across the country. Reynolds' insistence on closed-door discussions of executive compensation

---

69 Carter, interview.

70 William Trombley, "Reynolds Receives Vote of Confidence from CSU Board" *Los Angeles Times*, May 13, 1987, 1.

71 Educational Policy Committee Report November 1984. CSU Board of Trustees Minutes of the Meeting of the Board of Trustees, Board of Trustees of the California State University Collection. Courtesy of the California State University Archives. California State University Dominguez Hills.

put the trustees in a very awkward position, having to answer to campus groups and the public, how she and twenty-six other staff members could justify such exorbitant increases, especially in the wake of hikes to student fees.

The trustees who failed to fulfill their oversight responsibilities regarding the salary question should share some of the blame for the controversy. The CSU had a reputation for having some of the lowest salaries for faculty, staff, and administrators in the country. The lack of competitive salaries had been noted as one of the chief reasons why the system failed to attract and retain top quality talent. Instead of doing the research and holding information sessions about executive compensation, the trustees authorized Reynolds to investigate the matter herself. Only when the public learned of the size of raises did the trustees try to save face by rescinding most of the raises and calling on Reynolds to resign or face a vote of no confidence. The trustees gave Reynolds what amounts to a blank check and allowed her to give herself and her subordinates a raise as she saw fit. Only after facing criticism from legislators and CSU faculty regarding the size of the raises did the trustees intervene, with most of their anger focusing on Reynolds' broken pledge of transparency—not over the actual size of the raises, because the trustees were very aware that CSU salaries were extraordinarily low to begin with.

Some trustees, like Claudia Hampton, believed that Reynolds deserved the raise given the size of the system. In a 2019 interview, Reynolds remarked "I should have been smart enough to turn it down (the raise). But I thought at the time that the increase did not make me equal to the UC president, but it was a significant increase. Well, in the face of this, I think, with the Lansdale problems things got very tumultuous. You know, what's a woman doing? You always kind of get a little bit of that. And that's basically what happened but Dr. Hampton was completely supportive of me through all of it."[72] Aside from Claudia Hampton and a few other loyal supporters, including trustees George Marcus and Robert Arndale, Reynolds had to face the board as the sacrificial lamb in the wake of public anger over the raises, because she failed to anticipate the political backlash that came with trying to right-size salaries for women, no matter how deserving that woman might be. Reynolds' failure to anticipate the backlash by giving herself a significant raise highlights a fundamental difference between Black and white women in academic leadership, where white women believe that being on the "inside" and having moral righteousness of their cause will be enough to weather criticism or rebuke. However, Black women in white academia are not under such illusions and instead rely on what sociologist Patricia Hill

---

72   Reynolds, interview.

Collins describes as an "outsider within" perspective to help them anticipate barriers along the way.[73]

Being an "outsider within" allows Black women like Claudia Hampton to avoid these potential pitfalls, by using sly civility to help craft a plan of action to help ensure their success. By all accounts, when it came to affirmative action and working to assist underrepresented groups to make progress within the CSU, W. Ann Reynolds displayed a high level of commitment and developed a proven record of success, but her downfall came because, unlike Claudia Hampton, she refused to play the game and, in the end, having the right values and vision was simply not enough. Shortly after Reynolds' resignation as chancellor, Hampton and the CSU system faced an even greater set of external challenges that ultimately worked to obliterate affirmative action in California for good.

Following an affirmative action progress report during the June 1989 CSU board of trustees meeting, Claudia Hampton declared that "the report indicated that the CSU was moving from a planning mode to an implementation mode" regarding increasing the number of ethnic minority students within the system.[74] As a strong advocate for affirmative action, Hampton regularly voiced her disappointment that the CSU seemed stuck in policy planning mode and lagged behind in implementing programs that produced results. In contrast to her predecessor, Chancellor W. Ann Reynolds implemented several system-wide educational equity programs, with help from Hampton, to increase the enrollment and retention of underrepresented groups of students. Reynolds also created an Educational Equity Advisory Council, a group of campus and system officials, faculty, staff, and students who would report to the Chancellor and trustees on the campuses' progress in achieving campus educational equity goals. The first meeting of the council was convened in 1986. From that point forward the council made annual presentations to the board, and these reports showed that the CSU had moved to an implementation mode. An analysis of five-year enrollment trends from 1984 to 1989 show that all racial groups had an increase in enrollment of first-time freshmen students, with significant gains among Hispanic (73.2%), Filipino (119.2%), Asian (61.3%), American Indian (45.8%), and Black (21.6%) students.[75] While the raw numbers were still

---

73   Patricia Hill Collins, *Black Feminist Thought: Knowledge, Consciousness, and the Politics of* Empowerment (New York, Routledge, 2008).

74   Affirmative Action Progress Report. June 14, 1989. CSU Board of Trustees Minutes of the Meeting of the Board of Trustees, Board of Trustees of the California State University Collection. Courtesy of the California State University Archives. California State University Dominguez Hills.

75   Progress Report on Campus Educational Equity Goals. Committee of the Whole. July 1990. CSU Board of Trustees Minutes of the Meeting of the Board of Trustees, Board of Trustees of the California State University

small for some groups, the growth percentages were impressive when you consider that during this same period the American Council on Education (ACE) reported that nationally the percentage of ethnic minority students attending colleges or universities had declined.[76] ACE speculated that this overall decline in the number of ethnic minority students eligible to be admitted in the nation's colleges and universities was due to higher college admission standards. Within the CSU, new admission standards were introduced in 1986 and required of all new freshmen by fall 1988. So in contrast to national trends, CSU minority enrollments rose. These increases could be partly atributed to better communication between K-12 and the CSU, systemwide and individual campus programs to prepare students for college admission, and the CSU's overall outreach efforts to diversify the classroom and the faculty.

During Reynold's tenure as chancellor, and with the approval of the trustees, the CSU had initiated six system-wide educational equity initiatives, seven teacher education/school improvement programs, and expanded the system's outreach programs beyond EOP to include the Step-to-College program in partnership with San Francisco and Los Angeles Unified School Districts, respectively. Likewise, grant-funded projects at several campuses helped underrepresented students to excel in science or math-based majors and careers. The educational equity programs listed above were in addition to existing federal and state mandated outreach, financial aid, and mentoring and tutoring programs.

Reynolds' success in increasing minority student admission rates and working to improve the CSU's teacher education programs was one of the reasons why trustees were split on whether Reynolds should be forced to leave following the controversy over executive compensation. Hampton told the Los Angeles Times in 1987 during the first attempt to remove Reynolds because of her management style: "Our admissions standards have been raised, our teacher training programs have been strengthened, our affirmative action and minority outreach efforts have been improved. I don't see how all that could have been accomplished if she (Reynolds) and (William) Vandament are such terrible administrators."[77] Reynolds stayed on for another three years, expanding her outreach and student affirmative action efforts to include a doctoral incentive program to help diversify the faculty

---

76   American Council on Education, *Status Report on Minorities in Higher Education* (Washington, DC: American Council on Education, 1990).

77   William Trombley, "Cal State Head Faces Moves to Remove Her." *Los Angeles Times*, March 21, 1987.

within the CSU, graduate equity fellowships, and the establishment of a summer bridge program for entering students.

To monitor the progress of these initiatives, Reynolds directed the Council of Presidents to prepare detailed plans for how Educational Equity Advisory Council recommendations would be implemented. Unlike her predecessor, Glenn Dumke, who never gave specific guidance or directives to campus presidents for implementing system-wide affirmative action admission or hiring programs, Reynolds built accountability mechanisms into each program she instituted. She noted in her resignation letter to the board the charge she was given by trustees when she was hired as chancellor in 1982 to "put in place outreach programs and campus commitment to encourage college access and success for underrepresented minorities . . . and to establish a faculty recruitment program designed to ensure both an outstanding faculty as well one more ethnically diverse."[78]

What Reynolds lacked in political savvy and a blunt management style, she made up for in commitment to her stated belief in educational equity and access for women and ethnic minorities within the system. Claudia Hampton believed that Reynolds was scrutinized because many people resented her displays of temper because they came from a woman. Hampton told reporters: "If she were a man, this behavior would be regarded as good leadership and assertiveness." "But because she is a woman, it is called "temper tantrum" or "shooting from the hip."[79] With Reynolds' departure, the CSU lost its most ardent affirmative action advocate besides Claudia Hampton. By all accounts, Reynolds, with significant help from Claudia Hampton, was able to carry out programs on her affirmative action priorities, and to date, no other chancellor before or after Reynolds has given the same level of attention and funding support to minority student and faculty concerns as W. Ann Reynolds. Shortly following Reynolds' department, the CSU system and public higher education across the state would find itself at an important crossroads with external forces working to upend everything Hampton had worked hard to establish so that all students could have access to a quality university education.

---

78   W. Ann Reynolds" Resignation Letter to the CSU Board of Trustees. April 12, 1990. CSU Board of Trustees Minutes of the Meeting of the Board of Trustees, Board of Trustees of the California State University Collection. Courtesy of the California State University Archives. California State University Dominguez Hills.

79   Trombley, "Moves to Remove."

Chapter Five

The Beginning of the End

Paul Bond, a staff writer for *The Daily Sundial*, the main student newspaper at CSU Northridge, wrote in a 1993 opinion piece entitled "Affirmative Action Is No Longer Effective" that "today, affirmative action means hiring quotas, lower standards and expectations for minorities, lawsuits where employers must prove their innocence (in direct conflict with the Constitution), race norming (artificially raising scores on aptitude tests for certain minority groups), and reverse discrimination."[1] To support his claims, Bond referenced the work of conservative African American scholars Thomas Sowell and Shelby Steele, arguing that affirmative action hurts African Americans. But more than simply name-dropping two African American opponents of affirmative action, Bond claimed that "currently, about three quarters of African American college students drop out before graduation, including thousands from elite colleges," without offering any evidence to support his claims.

Bond could get away with making such unsubstantiated claims about affirmative action, since public support for legislation and programming to promote educational equity started to wane in the early 1990s. Campus newspapers throughout the Cal State system, and mainstream dailies like the *Los Angeles Times* and *Washington Post*, regularly ran articles and opinion pieces during this period lambasting affirmative action and ethnic studies curricula as part of a multicultural movement that had gone too far. Critics of affirmative action claim that colleges and universities lowered standards and denied qualified white students access to the nation's colleges and universities in favor of less-qualified minority students. The end result of these special overtures to racial and ethnic minority students was a growing resentment by white students and working-class white voters, who saw affirmative action as a threat to their chances of getting an education and a good job. In this chapter I examine the impact of the culture wars on educational policy-making within CSU, culminating in the death of affirmative action with the

---

1   Paul Bond, "Affirmative Action is No Longer Effective" *Daily Sundial*, April 2, 1993.

passage of Proposition 209 in 1996, just two years after Claudia Hampton's death from lung cancer.

White resentment towards affirmative action had been a reality since the inception of this legislation, reaching fever-pitch with the Bakke decision in 1978. However, it was not until the early 1990s that the Republican Party began making race, multiculturalism, and affirmative action the centerpiece of their 1992 election campaign. Due to the volatile nature of race debates in the United States, even Democratic presidential contenders had to also address the race question. Jerry Brown and Bill Clinton, two of the main challengers for the Democratic nomination, offered contrasting and conflicting views on affirmative action during the 1992 debate for the Democratic Party's nomination. Brown made a more traditional civil rights appeal to entice black voters, by emphasizing the obligations of the white majority to minorities through social spending and unequivocal support for affirmative action. He also committed to having Jesse Jackson as his potential running mate. Bill Clinton, instead, offered a blend of a liberal opportunity message to appeal to black voters with a traditional conservative message of personal responsibility to appeal to working- and middle-class white voters.

Signs of growing racial conflict in the nation's colleges and universities began in the mid-1980s, when the Reagan administration began critiquing affirmative action as "reverse discrimination" and "quota systems," despite the Bakke decision, which had outlawed the use of racial quotas in college admissions more than a decade earlier. By the early 1990s, William Bennett, who served as the chairman of the National Endowment for the Humanities and later as Secretary of Education under Ronald Reagan, published a report in 1984 entitled To Reclaim a Legacy: A Report on the Humanities in Higher Education, where he claimed that "the humanities, and particularly the study of Western civilization, have lost their central place in the undergraduate curriculum."[2] Elsewhere, I have argued that "Bennett charged that sixties radicals were threatening a precious U.S. heritage in the name of a more inclusive curriculum as these 'radicals' were now deeply entrenched in the nation's colleges and universities as humanities faculty. This report and Bennett's critique of Stanford University's decision to add more works from women and people of color into a Western Civilization course required for all freshmen students, launched the Academic Culture Wars in 1985."[3] With the philanthropic support from conservative foundations and think

2   William J. Bennett, *To Reclaim a Legacy: A Report on the Humanities in Higher Education* (Washington, DC: National Endowment for the Humanities, 1984).

3   Donna J. Nicol, "Conservative Philanthropy's War against Race and Gender Studies in U.S. Higher Education," *HistPhil.com*, June 29, 2020.

tanks, the academic culture wars of the 1980s and 1990s constituted a period of sustained conflict and debate between the academic left and right about multiculturalism, affirmative action, and ethnic and gender studies in America's schools, colleges, and universities. This conflict eventually spilled over into national politics.

My contention is that "movement conservatives targeted ethnic and gender studies because these disciplines called into question who had the right to determine what constitutes U.S. values and specifically provided a critique of traditional politics, culture, and social affairs."[4] Along with affirmative action, ethnic studies programs were critiqued by conservative politicians and pundits as ill-conceived manifestations of the liberal welfare state. For example, conservative scholar and cultural critic Shelby Steele states that "affirmative action distorted our understanding of racial discrimination. By making Black the color of preference, these mandates have re-burdened society with the very marriage of color and preference (in reverse) that we set out to eradicate."[5] Media coverage of the debate over political correctness (P.C.), on which the 1990s Culture Wars were based, exploded from 101 articles in newspapers and journals in 1988 to over 3,989 articles in 1991, according to the National Council for Research on Women, which found that these debates were largely funded with conservative money.[6] As I have noted, "The PC conspiracy provided an irresistible opportunity for print media to attract readers with sensationalized headlines, graphics, and stories that play on the deepest fears of white, middle-class Americans" who feared being usurped by a vocal group of supposedly lesser-qualified racial minorities demanding access to the nation's universities and workforce.[7] This media coverage would soon impact politics at the local, state, and national levels as politicians looking to capitalize on increasing white resentment began to turn to conservative think tanks and academic change organizations such as the National Association of Scholars for talking points about affirmative action to help bolster their campaigns.

It is also important to note that the United States was in the middle of an eight-month economic recession starting in 1990, when the academic culture wars were in full swing, which contributed to accelerating white backlash and resentment against affirmative action. As with most economic

---

4   Nicol, "Conservative Philanthropy."

5   Shelby Steele. "A Negative Vote on Affirmative Action" *New York Times Magazine*, May 13, 1990.

6   Debra Schultz, *To Reclaim a Legacy of Diversity: Analyzing the Political Correctness Debates in Higher Education.* (New York: National Council for Research on Women, 1993).

7   Nicol, "Conservative Philanthropy."

downturns in the United States, racial prejudices became actualized, with white people expressing more explicit and implicit biases toward people of color (especially African Americans), justifying racial stereotypes, and regarding racial disparities between groups as acceptable and natural.[8] Anti-affirmative action proponents relied on racial stereotyping of Blacks. They resorted to racially scapegoating undocumented immigrants from Asian and Latin American countries to justify their racially charged rhetoric against affirmative action policies and programs. The Los Angeles Riots in 1992, which started in response to the acquittal of four Los Angeles police officers caught on video beating motorist Rodney King, also played a significant role in hardening white attitudes against social programs created in the 1960s to redress past discrimination. Many white people did not accept the premise that Black, Latino, and other racial groups clustered in urban, impoverished areas of Los Angeles and around the county were unfairly disenfranchised and thus clashes with law enforcement and destruction of property were not justified. In turn, affirmative action, and other measures to resolve minority problems, received scant support from white voters, who blamed the riots on Black and Brown folks' cultural pathology, rather than structural discrimination.

Within the California State University system, the recession, the Culture Wars, civil unrest, and debate over immigration all coalesced, putting pressure on trustees and other university officials to confront these very thorny issues on race and multiculturalism happening in the public domain. The outcome of these debates over immigration and affirmative action would have long-term consequences for the California State University by shifting the notion of access once again to be associated with a type of race neutrality or "colorblindness" that ignores systemic barriers that must be addressed, in order for true equality to occur.

Affirmative Action and the Looming Threat of Recession

The 1990–1991 economic downturn and the ensuing Culture Wars across the country upended any plans to expand or create new affirmative action and educational equity programming for the time being, forcing the CSU trustees to focus their attention away from monitoring affirmative action programs. However, Hampton and other affirmative action-minded trustees

---

8   Emily C. Bianchi, Erika V. Hall, and Sarah Lee, "Reexamining the Link between Economic Downturns and Racial Antipathy: Evidence That Prejudice against Blacks Rises during Recessions," *Psychological Science 29*, no. 10 (2018), 1584–1597. https://doi.org/10.1177/0956797618777214.

would soon fight to keep these programs alive. In the wake of the public relations fallout from the executive compensation fiasco, which led to Reynolds' forced resignation, CSU trustees were eager to remove any vestiges of the previous administration, including not retaining personnel hired and supervised by Reynolds. Trustees set aside Reynolds' recommendation to appoint Herb Carter as interim chancellor and voted to push Reynolds out earlier than noted in her resignation letter. Instead, the CSU trustees appointed CSU Hayward (now CSU East Bay) President Ellis McCune as interim chancellor. McCune served as president of CSU Hayward for 23 years from 1967 to 1990 and was well-liked and respected by faculty, students, staff, and administrators. Those who knew him believed he was the right person to bring stability to the Chancellor's Office and help repair the image of the CSU system.

During his eighteen months as acting chancellor, McCune and the board had to grapple with two major issues that would have an impact on the continuation of the system's affirmative action programming: the CSU budget and state legal orders on the issue of tuition for undocumented immigrant students. During his January 1991 report to the board of trustees, McCune spelled out the dire economic forecast facing the CSU, in which the system was expected to add 7,500 students in the coming year. Still, the Republican governor Pete Wilson's proposed budget for the CSU of $2.1 billion only represented a small increase of $800,000. Nearly half of the governor's proposed budget for the CSU had to go to mandatory spending to cover legislatively approved compensation increases, employee benefits, and student financial aid. These budget projections, however, were predicated on a twenty (20%) percent increase in student fees. But as McCune reminded the board, the trustees had already approved a 3% student fee increase. The California legislature passed the Maddy-Dills Act, which limited any increase in student fees to no more than ten percent (10%) in a single year. In essence, the CSU would not have enough money to hire over over 900 new employees needed across the system to support the projected student demand. McCune told the group: "The bottom line is that I really don't see how we're going to continue to offer the same level of service as we are now."[9] In fact, McCune warned trustees that layoffs were certainly a possibility and instructed his staff at the Chancellor's Office to look for ways to shore up the budget, including implementing an early retirement incentive program and selling the State University House, a home in Bel-Air donated

---

9   Report of Acting Chancellor Ellis McCune. January 16, 1991. CSU Board of Trustees Minutes of the Meeting of the Board of Trustees, Board of Trustees of the California State University Collection. Courtesy of the California State University Archives. California State University Dominguez Hills.

by businessman John Brown Cook, which netted a sales price of $3.61 million. Unfortunately, these efforts by McCune and his staff barely made a dent in the budget shortage, putting the search for a new chancellor on hold until the economic situation stabilized.

Amid this budgetary crisis, Claudia Hampton, in her role as chair of the Faculty and Staff Relations Committee, directed the Chancellor's Office staff to develop suggestions for modifying existing procedures for selecting presidents. Hampton told her fellow trustees that she "thought it was appropriate to restate the policy of the Board in this regard and said the review of procedures will recognize this fact."[10] Ever the strategist, Hampton used this downtime, brought on by the recession, to shore up the board's commitment to diversity regarding presidential appointments. She pointed out: "The CSU is committed to the principles of affirmative action and equality of opportunity in the selection of academic leaders within the system."[11] Few could argue with what Hampton was proposing and having this discussion before a new wave of presidential recruitment and selection got underway helped to ensure that the board kept the system's diversity goals at the forefront of their mind.

During the Faculty and Staff Relations Committee the following day, Hampton was able to secure an amendment to the existing procedure on the selection of presidents to include a provision on the Responsibility for the Appointment of Presidents that stated that "The CSU is committed to the principles of consultation with campus and community representatives and to affirmative action and diversity in the selection of campus presidents."[12] To the casual observer adding oversight for campus diversity activities and programming to a president's list of responsibilities might seem like a small addition. But before Hampton's suggested amendment, the only persons

---

10 Report of the Committee on Faculty and Staff Relations, May 15, 1991. CSU Board of Trustees Minutes of the Meeting of the Board of Trustees, Board of Trustees of the California State University Collection. Courtesy of the California State University Archives. California State University Dominguez Hills.

11 Report of the Committee on Faculty and Staff Relations, May 15, 1991. CSU Board of Trustees Minutes of the Meeting of the Board of Trustees, Board of Trustees of the California State University Collection. Courtesy of the California State University Archives. California State University Dominguez Hills.

12 Committee on Faculty and Staff Relations, "Modification of the Trustee Policy on Presidential Search," May 16, 1991. CSU Board of Trustees Minutes of the Meeting of the Board of Trustees, Board of Trustees of the California State University Collection. Courtesy of the California State University Archives. California State University Dominguez Hills.

held responsible for coordinating and meeting campus diversity goals were campus and system affirmative action/diversity officers. These middle management officers lacked the ability to enforce affirmative action policy, unless given express authority by the president. Now campus presidents would share the responsibility and could be held accountable to the chancellor and the trustees for failure to meet campus diversity goals.

Meeting system diversity goals would be a significant challenge in light of the budget crisis in California and across the country. The share of CSU revenue dropped by half a percentage point, resulting in a $231 million cut projected for the 1992/1993 budget. The timing of these cuts came just as the Asian Pacific American Advisory Committee (APAAC) presented the first comprehensive and in-depth study on Asian Americans in the CSU and the first time the trustees ever addressed issues of concern for Asian American students, faculty, and staff. Dr. Bob Suzuki, president of Cal Poly Pomona, chaired the committee and brought several points to the trustees' attention, including (1), Asian Pacific American students were the fastest-growing minority group in the CSU, representing over fifty different ethnic groups; (2) Asian Pacific American students reported the most concern for racial harassment and many complained about the inability to pass the exit writing exam; and, (3) Asians/Asian Americans comprise only eight percent (8%) of the faculty and staff and are very underrepresented in administrative and executive positions.

The APAAC committee offered twenty-nine recommendations across five broad categories: English proficiency assistance, racial harassment monitoring, student support services for APA students, outreach programs, and increasing affirmative action recruitment and hiring in all areas of APA underrepresentation. Trustees' responses to the report varied from those wishing to collapse all minority groups under an "umbrella group," thereby eliminating the need to look at each group individually, to other trustees rejecting this idea because Asian Pacific Americans experience the "model minority stereotype" in a positive way. Trustee Gloria Hom, a Chinese American educator from San Francisco, rightly pointed out that Asian Pacific Americans were the only group of ethnic minority students in the CSU to not receive lottery set-aside funding. Thus this report was important in highlighting and elevating the specific issues faced by Asian Pacific American students beyond the model-minority stereotype, such as the need for greater English language instruction, the development of Asian Pacific American Studies programs, and a process to monitor claims of racial harassment against Asian Pacific American students.

Based on the report's findings and recommendations, the Educational Policy Committee passed a resolution accepting the report and directed the chancellor to encourage campus leaders and faculty to pursue the goals of the recommendations, subject to available resources. Given the budget crisis, the inclusion of the "subject to available resources" clause of the resolution signaled that, for the time being, no dedicated funding would be set aside to ensure that these recommendations would be carried out. Instead, Asian Pacific American students would find themselves the target of increased racial harassment, both on and off campus, (along with Hispanic students) over the issue of tuition for undocumented immigrant students. Instead of expanding opportunities and services to Asian Pacific American students, the CSU essentially left this group to fend for themselves.

The recession also impacted the CSU's ability to enforce a fifteen-unit college preparatory course requirement for all graduating high school seniors seeking admission into the CSU. The board of trustees had directed the chancellor to implement this new requirement in ways that would be sensitive to underrepresented students and to monitor the impact of these requirements on the participation of ethnic minority students. During the discussion of the annual Admissions Advisory Council report in 1991, Claudia Hampton asked how many California high schools could not offer the full range of courses or sufficient sections of college preparatory courses due to state budget cuts, particularly in the visual and performing arts. When Chancellor's Office officials responded that ten to twelve schools were having difficulty in offering the full range of courses, Hampton asked if the system would consider building some flexibility into the admission process, considering that budget cuts adversely impacted students, especially those from underrepresented groups. Black and Brown students from large districts like Los Angeles and San Francisco comprised the largest proportion of conditionally admitted students.

The CSU increased the minimum number of units required for conditional admission shortly before the recession from ten to thirteen in 1990. This meant that students who were unable to take these college prep courses due to budget cuts, especially those students from large, urban, predominantly Black, and Latino areas, would find themselves denied access to the university through no fault of their own. Dr. Kerschner, Vice Chancellor of Academic Affairs, responded to Hampton's query and said he would refer the question to the Admissions Advisory Council for advice. While the other trustees and campus presidents voiced overall satisfaction with the results of this report, Hampton remained ever vigilant in standing up for ethnic minority students, who might otherwise be denied an opportunity to get a university education simply by having the misfortune of attending an under-resourced public high school.

Influenced by Claudia Hampton's call to review existing board policies, Marian Bagdasarian, chair of the Educational Policy Committee, appointed a subcommittee to focus on long-range planning for the CSU's teacher education programs, in light of this period of extensive budgetary constraints. With an extensive background in elementary and secondary education as a classroom teacher, school administrator, and adjunct lecturer in education, Claudia Hampton was asked to chair this new Subcommittee on the CSU's Relationship to School in late 1991 to assist the Chancellor's Office with planning around five major areas: meeting the needs of diverse student populations, strengthening the K-12 curriculum, recruiting, retaining and diversifying the new teacher pool, enhancing teacher preparation, and improving school leadership. Hampton's interventions as chair of this new subcommittee helped bolster support for students before they even entered the university. Even though the CSU campuses had established numerous programs, partnerships, and activities with public schools in California, the subcommittee sought input from the schools themselves on what these relationships should be. To that end, Hampton and her subcommittee members organized seminars that brought together school leaders and campus representatives, asking for input on what would constitute the characteristics of an optimal relationship between the CSU and these schools. The information gathered in these seminars would be combined with campus survey data on existing CSU–school partnerships to form a final report that would be used to encourage state lawmakers and business leaders to strengthen public elementary and secondary education.

As the single largest producer of teachers in the state, the CSU's relationship with K-12 schools is vital in addressing California's ongoing teacher shortage, especially in urban areas with high concentrations of Black and Latino students. However, since most of the CSU's funding comes from the state coffers, these teacher education programs were subject to the ebbs and flows of the state budget. Instead, newly appointed CSU Chancellor Barry Munitz, who was hired in late 1991, stated that the board's Institutional Advancement Committee would be focusing on encouraging "corporate California to give greater support to the CSU," utilizing the subcommittee's report to open up a conversation about the CSU in a variety of places that the system had not been able to contact before.[13] As Hampton noted at the beginning of her report, "the CSU was an enormous public resource," and it was incumbent on the board, the Chancellor's Office, campus leaders, and CSU faculty to highlight those successful programs with schools so that this important work did not go unnoticed.

---

13   Interim Report of the Subcommittee on the CSU's Relationship to the Schools. Committee of Educational Policy. July 14, 1992. CSU Board of Trustees Minutes of the Meeting of the Board of Trustees, Board of Trustees of the California State University Collection. Courtesy of the California State University Archives. California State University Dominguez Hills.

Hampton also worked with the campus presidents at CSU Los Angeles (Rosser), San Francisco State (Corrigan), San Diego State (Day), and CSU Hayward (Rees) to develop a special report and make a presentation to the Educational Policy Committee titled "Campus Initiatives with Inner City Schools." Since "meeting the needs of California's diverse student populations" was one of the main areas of concern for the subcommittee on the CSU's Relationship with Schools, Hampton shared with her board colleagues some information about urban community development efforts already underway and how this related to school/university cooperation. CSU campuses in Oakland, San Francisco, Los Angeles, and Hayward received federal and state funding to expand the CSU's capacity to serve students attending inner city schools who were also traditionally underrepresented in higher education. For example, CSU Los Angeles and San Francisco State were jointly awarded a three-year urban community service grant from the U.S. Department of Education.

A 1995 report by the American Association of State Colleges and Universities found that CSU Los Angeles regularly "sought collaborative strategies with different levels of government, community groups, and funding agencies" to encourage student participation in community service projects benefiting the community surrounding the CSU Los Angeles campus especially those having to do with inner-city school students.[14] The purpose of this presentation was to inform policy recommendation discussions of the subcommittee and to identify priority areas for improvement that the CSU could put in place beyond grant-funded projects. The ultimate goal was to ensure that all students, especially those from disadvantaged inner-city schools, had access to a quality education that would ensure their matriculation and success within the CSU.

At first glance, it would seem that Hampton's call for a review of board policies and convening a special subcommittee to review and develop a long-range plan to improve the CSU's relationship with schools would be part of the normal order of business for the trustees. However, given the on-going budgetary uncertainty facing the system along with a shift in the public's support against affirmative action and other measures designed to help racial and ethnic minority students, Hampton's insistence in securing provisions to ensure the board's commitment to the principle of educational equity and diversity was completely understandable.

In Hampton's role as chair of the Faculty and Staff Affairs committee, she also put the issue of gender equity on the agenda, when it was revealed

---

14 Joyce A. Scott and Meredith Ludwig, *Community Service at Urban Public Institutions: A Report on Conditions and Activities* (Washington, D.C. American Association of State Colleges and Universities, 1995).

that the CSU had no guidelines to address sex equity in employment, training, and benefits, nor clear procedures for addressing discrimination complaints. California enacted a California Sex Equity in Education Act (SEEA) in 1982, similar to federal Title IX law, and a state senate bill (SB 793) which went into law in 1987, requiring the California Department of Education and similar educational governing bodies, like the CSU board of trustees, to develop regulations to implement the SEEA. For reasons that are not altogether clear, given Chancellor Reynolds' interest in gender equity and women's issues, the CSU was slow to comply with this new legislative order. However, under Hampton's leadership, this new revision of the Education Code included an updated policy on "gender equity" that reaffirmed the CSU's commitment to nondiscrimination and affirmative action and created a sex equity coordinator position for individual campuses. The CSU did not have sex discrimination statutes in place for several years. Additionally, the issue of sex equity across employment and in the treatment of students, and related campus reporting procedures was sorely lacking. At this meeting, the trustees also reaffirmed support for "instruction approved to fulfill the general education breadth requirements recognize the contributions to knowledge and civilization that have been made by women."[15] Hampton used her considerable influence over the board to gently nudge her board colleagues toward shoring up the defense and support for affirmative action and educational equity programming as the culture wars were already deeply entrenched in academia by the late 1980s/early 1990s. Hampton, using her skills at strategy, pressed for the board to go on offense to "future proof" support, as anyone paying attention to the news could see that the CSU would not remain untouched by the effects of these culture war debates.

The Culture Wars in Academia

As I have previously written, "during the culture wars, affirmative action programs and ethnic and gender studies departments were targeted because these programs called into question who should have access to educational

---

15   Proposed Regulations Governing Gender Equity in the CSU, March 13,
     1991. A Report to the CSU Educational Policy Committee of the Board of
     Trustees. CSU Board of Trustees Minutes of the Meeting of the Board of
     Trustees, Board of Trustees of the California State University Collection.
     Courtesy of the California State University Archives. California State
     University Dominguez Hills. Campus Climate Report, 1991. CSU Board of
     Trustees Minutes of the Meeting of the Board of Trustees, Board of Trustees
     of the California State University Collection. Courtesy of the California State
     University Archives. California State University Dominguez Hills.

and economic opportunities, while simultaneously providing a critique of capitalism and traditional racial politics in the U.S.[16] In other words, conservative groups launched the culture wars as an economic protectionist policy using a racial capitalist approach that depends heavily on the media's use of racial dog-whistles to help turn the public against policies and programs that might help racial minorities, immigrants, and women. First, conservatives sought to withhold resources from "undeserving" minorities, thereby increasing privilege for white people. Second, especially for mega-rich wealthy conservative businesspeople, racial dog-whistling functioned as a divide-and-conquer strategy that redirected working-class white anger over the economy into racial resentment. All of these shifts in the 1990s, including welfare "reform" and the War on Drugs, utilized racial dog-whistling to subject these groups to more restrictions and more suffering. The result was that the nation's poor, often clustered in crowded urban cities, were cast as drains on American society and held responsible for the nation's economic and social problems. At the same time, "white individuals and predominantly white institutions use non-white people to acquire social and economic value."[17] Law professor Nancy Leong, author of *Identity Capitalists: The Powerful Insiders Who Exploit Diversity to Maintain Inequality*, argues that "racial capitalism is the process of deriving value from the racial identity of others."[18] Writer Michael Lind has even suggested that conservatives launched the culture wars as a method of diverting "the wrath of wage-earning populist voters from Wall Street and corporate America to other targets: the universities, the media, racial minorities, homosexuals, and immigrants."[19]

Galvanized by the publication of the Powell Manifesto, a secret document written by Associate Supreme Court Justice Lewis F. Powell in 1971 outlining academia's attack on capitalism, conservative groups built their own academic infrastructure using corporate funding from business tycoons Richard Scaife, Harry and Lynde Bradley, the Koch family, and the John Olin foundation, just to name a few. By 1973, the Heritage Foundation was established and, with funding from the Adolph Coors Foundation,

---

16   Donna J. Nicol. "Racism and the Roots of Conservative Philanthropy in the U.S." *Unpack the Past: Al Jazeera*, 22 Feb. 2022, www.aljazeera.com/features/2022/2/17/racism-and-the-roots-of-conservative-philanthropy-in-the-us.

17   Nancy Leong "Race and the Law: Racial Capitalism" *Harvard Law Review* 126, no.8 (June 20): 2013. https://harvardlawreview.org/2013/06/racial-capitalism/.

18   Leong, "Racial Capitalism."

19   Michael Lind, *Up from Conservatism: Why the Right is Wrong for America*. (New York: Free Press, 1996), 16.

served as the principal conservative think tank and funding intermediary for smaller conservative think tanks and educational policy institutes. Soon Heritage would be joined by the Madison Center for Educational Affairs, the National Association of Scholars, and the Castlerock Foundation, which funded Project 21, a conservative speakers bureau composed primarily of African American conservative scholars and activists, including Shelby Steele, Thomas Sowell, and Ward Connerly. These groups would be responsible for the explosion of news and opinion pieces featured in campus and national newspapers and books published by conservative scholars and political pundits focused on the political correctness debates and stories about unqualified minority and immigrant students being admitted to the nation's most prestigious colleges and universities at the expense of white students. The reports created by these groups fueled the backlash against affirmative action.

After circulating these reports railing against political correctness, multicultural education, and affirmative action, these groups could then sit back and watch this debate play out, while the unsuspecting public remained unaware that conservative think tanks, particularly the Heritage Foundation and the American Enterprise Institute, had become very savvy in the use of the media and manufactured these debates, using a technique called the media feedback loop. Stefanicic and Delgado detailed how this strategy worked in their book, *No Mercy: How Conservative Think Tanks and Foundations Changed America's Social Agenda*.[20] Conservative think tanks would publish various reports on controversial topics, usually those dealing with race and immigration, and send those reports to members of Congress whom they wanted to target. Simultaneously, these think tanks would send an executive summary to national newspapers that would, in turn, publish a small article or brief. These same think tanks would clip these briefs and send copies to the member of Congress who would assume that, because the story appeared in a newspaper, there was a groundswell of support for any legislation the think tank might be supporting. Many of these targeted officials would become sponsors of legislation proposed in these think tank reports. Likewise, these same members of Congress would use the think tank reports for talking points when news media interviewed them. In the absence of concrete data supporting their positions, anecdotal evidence of a single case might be repeated several times over.

Stefancic and Delgado found several instances where conservative scholars such as Thomas Short and conservative political pundits like Dinesh D'Souza and William Bennett relied on anecdotal evidence of cases in which faculty

---

20 Jean Stefancic and Richard Delgado, *No Mercy: How Conservative Think Tanks and Foundations Changed America's Social Agenda*. (Philadelphia: Temple University Press, 1996).

and students who expressed non-politically correct behavior or opinions, faced public condemnation and/or suppression. I have written that "Many of these claims could not be substantiated, but by using catchy phrases such as "reverse racism," "balkanization," or "dead white males," conservatives were able to generate a rhetoric that evoked an emotional response from the American public, one that rarely challenged the claims made by conservative critics of higher education."[21] Stefancic and Delgado maintain that the use of the media has been the single most important vehicle used by conservative groups to disseminate their political philosophy and agenda to a public unaware that the culture wars were strategic and calculated organizing efforts, that enabled wealthy, mostly white businessmen to control the discourse on race and equality within academia and eventually gain control over all of the media, the courts, and electoral politics. The ultimate aim of these conservative efforts was to expand their scope of power and influence to ensure that their brand of unrestricted capitalism would forever remain intact.

The Powell Manifesto, which explicitly called for an investment of corporate dollars to establish a conservative "counter-establishment" in defending against any critique of the free market system, used the language of war and other hyperbole to signal to American business leaders that if nothing was done to defend capitalism, the country would be overrun by liberals in all of the major social institutions (education, media, politics, and the courts) determined to limit corporate profit and power. [22] Instead, conservatives created a network of conservative think tanks, foundations, speakers' bureaus, and educational policy institutes in the 1970s and 1980s that worked methodically to shape public opinion against welfare recipients, affirmative action beneficiaries, non-white immigrants, or any government program that might specifically help these disadvantaged groups.

By the 1990s, using corporate foundation monies, conservative politicians and groups chipped away at affirmative action programs in public education and employment, severely limited access to welfare benefits, and cut public school funding, ushering in the charter school movement in 1991.[23]

---

21   Donna J. Gough (Nicol), "*Ideas Have Consequences: Conservative Philanthropy, Black Studies and the Evolution and Enduring Legacy of the Academic Culture Wars*, 1945–2005." Ph.D. dissertation, Ohio State University, 2007). Donna J. Gough is the maiden name of the author of this monograph.

22   Simon Blumenthal, *The Rise of the Counter-Establishment: From Conservative Ideology to Political Power* (New York: Times Press, 1986).

23   Barbara M. DeLuca and Craig R. Wood, "The Charter School Movement in the United States: Financial and Achievement Evidence from Ohio," *Journal of Education Finance* 41, no. 4 (Spring 2016): 438–450.

In the short-term, however, colleges and universities had to deal with the fallout brought on by these highly charged debates about diversity and multiculturalism. Within the Cal State system, these debates eventually led to controversial legislation that would have a devastating impact on everything that Claudia Hampton had worked so hard to protect over her twenty-year tenure as a CSU trustee.

The Material Consequences of the Culture War Debates

The immediate effect of the culture war debates on the CSU was not evident to trustees until members of the Educational Policy Committee were given a report on "Campus Climate in the California State University: Toward Appreciating Diversity" by Dr. Lee Kerschner, Vice Chancellor of Academic Affairs, at the November 1991 meeting. Kerschner reported to the committee that the Chancellor's Office had convened a panel of experts in January 1990 to review issues related to bias-related speech and behavior on CSU campuses. Panelists with expertise in intergroup conflict were asked: "to review campus climate within the CSU, assess the adequacy of existing system policies and practices, and develop recommendations which would supplement or improve the efforts already in place."[24] With reports of hate speech targeting ethnic and racial minorities, women, and gay students on the rise and playing out in classrooms across the CSU, the Chancellor's Office initially chose to quietly study the issue before informing the board. After months of deliberation, the group recommended an education-based approach to address climate issues on campus. An education-based approach was more ambitious than an incident-based one, but would involve the entire campus community in information gathering, consciousness-raising, heightened sensitivity, and multicultural curricular activity. The panel found that the system's incident-based approach was adequate for handling egregious cases of discrimination, but the group favored "the education-based approach because it emphasize[d] that procedures for responding to student and employee charges of abusive behavior should be easily understood, widely disseminated, and readily accessible."[25]

---

24   Campus Climate in the California State University: Toward Appreciating Diversity. November 20, 1991. A Report to the CSU Educational Policy Committee of the Board of Trustees. CSU Board of Trustees Minutes of the Meeting of the Board of Trustees, Board of Trustees of the California State University Collection. Courtesy of the California State University Archives. California State University Dominguez Hills.

25   Campus Climate in the California State University: Toward Appreciating Diversity. November 20, 1991. A Report to the CSU Educational Policy

Many reports of hate speech involved groups like the Young Americans for Freedom (YAF), a conservative youth activist organization started by conservative scholar and political commentator William F. Buckley, Jr. in 1960. YAF established chapters on California campuses in earnest in the 1980s with the election of Ronald Reagan to the presidency. The California-based chapters were described as "hellbent on more street action and fewer hallway debates over the theories of columnist Russell Kirk, novelist Ayn Rand, economist Ludwig von Mises and other rightist intellectuals who influenced Buckley's original cell."[26] Instead of debating political theory in the classroom, YAF members attending CSU, UC, and private universities preferred to shout down feminists and anti-apartheid activists, reserving most of their hostility for supporters of affirmative action.[27] I can attest to this myself, and did so, as you can see in this excerpt from a 2014 interview:

> Being one of the few Black students in the history department at CSU Fullerton in the 1990s was tough. I remember taking American History since 1945 with a professor who was a speechwriter for Richard Nixon. He required us to do a tour of the Nixon Library for a class assignment. The white conservative students loved him and would often make snide remarks about other liberal professors in the department. One day we were watching a video where Martin Luther King was making a speech, and the audience in the film responded using call and response. The College Republicans, or whoever those guys in the class claimed to be, heckled through the entire video and I had had enough. I shouted, "Do you mind? Folks are trying to listen, and you are being rude. The rest of us never do anything like this when that criminal Nixon is on the screen." The professor looked mortified that I shouted like I did but I glared at him as if I was daring him to say something, so instead, he walked back to their group and told them to calm down.[28]

Committee of the Board of Trustees. CSU Board of Trustees Minutes of the Meeting of the Board of Trustees, Board of Trustees of the California State University Collection. Courtesy of the California State University Archives. California State University Dominguez Hills.

26 Sigal Clancy, "Doing the Right Thing Founded a Generation Ago by William F. Buckley, The Young Americans for Freedom are Shock Troops for U.S. Conservatism" *Los Angeles Times*, April 29, 1990.

27 For a more detailed discussion of conservative student activism during the 1990s in California, see Wayne Thorburn, *A Generation Awakens: Young Americans for Freedom and the Creation of the Conservative Movement*, (Ottawa, IL: Jameson, 2010).

28 Donna J. Nicol, interviewed by Carie Rael. *Women in Politics and Activism Since Suffrage Project, Center for Oral and Public History*, CSU Fullerton, February 25, 2014.

Particularly on a campus like CSU Fullerton, located in the heart of conservative Orange County, California, racial conflicts over the lack of diversity on campus and debates about affirmative action and ethnic studies were commonplace during the Culture Wars of the 1990s. A commonly shared view among YAF members on affirmative action was, "I wasn't there for black slavery—why should I pay for it?" But more than asking questions that encourage thoughtful debate, YAF members had been accused of creating a hostile learning environment for students and faculty alike with their confrontation style. Former YAF national board member Richard Delgaudio was quoted as saying "No advance without confrontation," in describing the goal of YAF's brand of activism.[29]

Buoyed by the anti-multiculturalism rhetoric that had become commonplace as a result of the Culture Wars and increased funding from conservative donors like the John M. Olin Foundation, YAF and similar right-leaning campus groups, including the Intercollegiate Studies Institute and the Leadership Institute, saw their membership grow.[30] With this growth, these campus conservative groups were encouraged to disrupt the classroom and campus activities, leaving university officials scrambling to find ways to balance the free speech rights of groups like YAF with complaints that certain groups of students were targets of hate speech. For example, a measure to forbid offensive speech against members of racial or ethnic minorities and gay students was defeated at CSU Northridge. At CSU Fullerton, a human relations task force was stymied for two years in developing a policy on non-discrimination that would include references to hate speech. The faculty senate at San Diego State University issued a statement reaffirming their support for free speech on campus.

System officials initially tried to downplay the seriousness of what was happening on CSU campuses when Vice Chancellor of Academic Affairs Kerschner said, "We have sought, and are achieving, a pluralistic community within the CSU, perhaps more effectively than any other system," but he, later in his presentation, had to concede, saying "Yet, given our critical mass, we witness ethnic students (and women and students from the gay community and certain religious groups) becoming targets of abusive language, and not surprisingly, these students are the ones calling for changes in student conduct codes."[31]

---

29 Clancy, 1990.

30 Daniel George, "The Right Finds a Niche on Campus" *Insight on the News*, September 9, 2002.

31 Campus Climate in the California State University: Toward Appreciating Diversity. November 20, 1991. A Report to the CSU Educational Policy Committee of the Board of Trustees. CSU Board of Trustees Minutes of the Meeting of the Board of Trustees, Board of Trustees of the California State

To that end, the panel recommended the issuance of a "Principles of Campus Community" statement regarding expected behavior for all members of the campus community; the statement reaffirmed the right to free speech outlined in the U.S. and California constitutions but also encouraged students and employees in the CSU to practice "respect throughout the university for the dignity and rights of others, including the freedom from discrimination and harassment and the right to speak freely."[32] Through the passage of a resolution to create a campus code of conduct regarding diversity, trustees sought to convey their expectation that campus presidents would adopt a similar statement for their campuses and take the lead in implementing educational programs to help reduce the incidence of egregious behavior and foster better understanding and respect. It is difficult to assess how effective a trustee-endorsed statement on the "Principles of a Campus Community" was in reducing the incidence of hate speech on CSU campuses. It certainly was not enough to put an end to openly hostile language directed toward Asian Pacific American, Hispanic, and Black students in two separate, but related, system-wide issues: immigration status and affirmative action.

Since 1985, the CSU in compliance with an order of the Alameda County Superior Court, treated undocumented aliens as capable of establishing California residency for tuition purposes (commonly referred to as the Leticia A case). Five years later, the University of California was sued by a former employee at UCLA assigned to determine students' residency status (commonly referred to as the Bradford case). The plaintiff in the case, Bradford, asked the Los Angeles Superior Court to require the University of California to comply with then-California Attorney General John Van de Kamp's 1984 opinion, which stated, "the legislature did not intend to, and the subdivision does not permit undocumented aliens to establish residence for tuition purposes in California's public institutions of higher education."[33] The California Court of Appeals sided with Bradford, and with the refusal of the California Supreme Court to hear the case, the Court of Appeal's decision became the most recent ruling on the matter. In response to the Bradford decision, Assemblyman Richard Polanco introduced Assembly

---

University Collection. Courtesy of the California State University Archives. California State University Dominguez Hills.

32   Campus Climate in the California State University: Toward Appreciating Diversity. November 20, 1991. A Report to the CSU Educational Policy Committee of the Board of Trustees. CSU Board of Trustees Minutes of the Meeting of the Board of Trustees, Board of Trustees of the California State University Collection. Courtesy of the California State University Archives. California State University Dominguez Hills.

33   John Van de Kamp "Opinion of the California Attorney General 241," 1984.

Bill 592, which attempted to amend the education code to allow undocumented aliens to establish residency for tuition purposes. Although AB 592 passed both the California Assembly and Senate by large margins, Governor Pete Wilson vetoed the bill on June 12, 1991, triggering a battle between immigrant rights groups and anti-immigrant groups, with documented and undocumented Hispanic and Asian Pacific American students caught in the middle.

Despite undocumented students only constituting two-thirds of one percent (0.23%) of the total population of CSU enrollment, Wilson's veto of AB 592 inspired a new wave of anti-immigrant fervor in the state, culminating in the passage of Proposition 187 in 1994. Otherwise known as the Save Our State referendum, Prop. 187 sought to establish a state-run citizenship screening system and prohibit undocumented immigrants from using non-emergency health care, public education, and other services. Supporters of Proposition 187 maintained that their concerns about illegal immigration were economic, because the state could not afford to provide services for California's estimated 1.3 million undocumented residents, given that the state was still trying to recover from the 1990s recession.

Opponents of the bill, specifically civil and immigrant rights groups, maintained that the bill was racially motivated against Hispanic and Asian undocumented immigrants, who were scapegoated and blamed for all of California's economic woes. Proposition 187 opponents such as MALDEF argued, "presented a simple solution to economic problems to gain political traction, a formula used in most anti-immigrant proposals and by many politicians before and since the measure was enacted."[34] Lending credibility to MALDEF's critique of the bill, California Governor Pete Wilson ran a series of campaign ads, which included video clips of Mexicans running across Interstate 5 in an attempt to cross illegally into the United States, with captions that read "Two million illegal immigrants keep coming to California. The federal government won't stop them at the border, yet Californians are asked billions to take care of them."[35] Wilson took a page out of the Culture Wars playbook, as historian Timothy J. Henderson argues that "In a brilliant political move, Governor Pete Wilson of California revived his floundering 1994 electoral campaign by blaming the state's woes on the federal government's failure to control the border. His most effective tool for communicating this message was a television advertisement based on a video of illegal

---

34   Mexican American Legal Defense and Education Fund, October 24, 2019. "Proposition 187: The Granddaddy of Anti-Immigrant Measures," https://www.maldef.org/2019/10/proposition-187-the-grand-daddy-of-anti-immigrant-measures/.

35   Pete Wilson for Governor on Illegal Immigration TV Ad, 1994.

immigrants dashing across the board from Mexico into the southbound traffic at the San Ysidro port of entry. . . . Only a few years earlier, it should be recalled, Wilson had asked for a relaxation of controls so that Mexican workers could cross the board to apply for special agricultural workers' visas."[36] Wilson's ads portrayed Mexicans as criminals who mooched off the labor of hard-working California taxpayers, redirecting populist anger over the state's economy away from Wilson's policies, which included raised sales taxes on newspapers and snack food, more than double digit increases to student fees in the CSU and UC, and Wilson's reduction in education spending, which led to a budget impasse in 1992, resulting in teachers and other state workers not receiving paychecks for three months.

Wilson was deeply unpopular when he launched his re-election campaign, but in exploiting a growing anti-immigrant sentiment, Proposition 187 helped him snatch victory from the jaws of defeat with more than fifty-eight (58%) percent of California voters voting to approve the measure. Race played a significant role in the passage of Proposition 187, with over sixty-three percent (63%) of California's white voters supporting the bill, whereas Hispanic, Asian, and Black voters disapproved of the measure. Election officials and demographers noted that while Hispanic people made up twenty-eight (28%) of the state's population, only eight percent (8%) of Hispanic residents in California were registered to vote at the time. One of the long-term effects of the passage of Proposition 187 was that it motivated greater Hispanic political participation in future elections. In the short term, Wilson realized the power of racial capitalism to breed racial resentments that could be exploited to do away with policies and programs aimed at redressing historical and contemporary discrimination that conservatives despised. Essentially, Proposition 187 became a trial balloon to test conservatives' ability to mount an effective countermovement against multiculturalism in California, often considered the most liberal and progressive state in the union.

Proposition 209 and the End of Affirmative Action

The Culture Wars of the 1990s provide a dramatic contrast to the Civil Rights Movement when, despite opposition, affirmative action was implemented with the aid of federal and state pressure. If conservatives could succeed in California in rolling back all of the gains made to benefit racial and ethnic minorities, women, and immigrants since the Civil Rights Movement,

---

36   Timothy J. Henderson, *Beyond Borders: A History of Mexican Migration to the United States.* (Oxford, U.K. Wiley-Blackwell, 2011).

they could be successful in returning to the social status quo in other parts of the country. Building on conservatives' success in using anti-immigrant sentiment to pass Proposition 187, Wilson enlisted the support of his close friend Ward Connerly, a conservative African American businessman, to help put an end to affirmative action in California, once and for all. The 1992 Los Angeles Riots provided conservatives with the perfect opportunity to engage in racial capitalism by laying blame for the conditions in the inner city on bands of Blacks and Latinos engaged in looting and lawlessness. By stoking suburban white anger over the relatively small number of Blacks and Latinos who refused to comply with police to restore order, along with images showing the destruction of property and acts of physical violence in the aftermath of the riots, conservative anti-affirmative action activists were able to launch a full-fledged attack on affirmative action. The final result was the passage of Proposition 209 in 1996, which did away with state affirmative action law, which threatened the legacy of educational activism by Black women like Claudia Hampton.

The text for Proposition 209 (also known as the California Civil Rights Initiative) was authored by Glynn Custred, a CSU Hayward (now CSU East Bay) anthropology professor, with assistance from Tom Wood, the Executive Director of the National Association of Scholars (NAS), which is a conservative educational advocacy organization. At the height of the Culture Wars of the 1980s and 1990s, NAS leveraged more than $10 million in grants by different conservative foundations such as the John M. Olin, Harry and Lynde Bradley Foundation, and the Coors Family Foundation to support a wide range of programs related to higher education, including funds for conservative student newspapers, internships to train conservative student activists, and establishing endowed fellowships for conservative scholars. Custred was a member of the California chapter of NAS who has said, in interviews decades after the passage of Proposition 209, that his success with the bill was due to his "love of diversity."[37] Together Custred and Wood's bill sought to eliminate any consideration of race, sex, color, ethnicity, or national origin in public employment, public education, or public contracting. What Custred and Wood were proposing in Proposition 209 was to do away with over thirty years of affirmative action law in California, threatening a major upheaval in the way in which state agencies and institutions would do business. Both men were unknown figures in California politics who got a boost when people like Governor Pete Wilson and GOP presidential

---

37   James Varney, "Anthropologist Glynn Custred champions Proposition 209 in California," *Washington Times*, February 21, 2021. Retrieved 1/27/2023 https://www.washingtontimes.com/news/2021/feb/21/anthropologist-glynn-custred-champions-proposition/.

candidate Bob Dole endorsed the bill. However, when Proposition 209 received the endorsement of UC Regent Ward Connerly, an African American businessman who was a close personal friend of Pete Wilson, the public's support for the bill increased two-fold. Connerly became the public face of Proposition 209, and organizing anti-affirmative action became a lucrative business venture for Connerly. Using nearly $2m in funding from the Bradley Foundation, Connerly led the California Civil Rights Initiative Campaign, which helped put Proposition 209 on the California ballot.[38] After the passage of Proposition 209 in 1996, Connerly received an additional $4 million in conservative funding to spearhead anti-affirmative action legislation initiatives in other states.

Proposition 209 had a devastating impact on communities of color across California in government contracting, education, and employment across all state agencies, including the CSU system. In 1975, Claudia Hampton joined forces with the state's first Black Lieutenant Governor, Mervyn Dymally, to publicly censure the board's Building, Grounds, and Planning Committee for failing to adequately recruit minority contractors in specialized fields, such as architecture. It would take Hampton and Dymally another two years of lobbying and cajoling their peers on the board to pass a resolution outlining the specific affirmative action recruitment procedures for issuing government contracts throughout the system. But in one fell swoop, Proposition 209 rendered these and all other affirmative action procedures moot.

Asian, Black, Latino, and Native American student recruitment, enrollment, matriculation, and graduation were all negatively impacted by this blatantly racist policy in both the CSU and UC systems. Marketed to voters as a civil rights initiative, Proposition 209 also severely reduced non-white faculty participation in higher education. Within the California State University system, Proposition 209 was directly responsible for African American and American Indian student enrollments each dropping by half.[39] Since 1996, the California State University has stopped recruiting students and offering

---

38 Donna J. Nicol, "Activism for Profit: America's Anti-Affirmative Action Industry" *Al Jazeera,* February 28, 2021. https://www.aljazeera.com/opinions/2021/2/28/activism-for-profit-americas-anti-affirmative-action-industry.

39 According to data from EdSource, Native American student enrollment within the CSU has historically represented less than one percent (1%) of the CSU's total student enrollment for decades, but after the ban on affirmative action, that number dropped perilously low from 0.88 in 1996 to 0.18 in 2018. This anti-affirmative action legislation had an even greater negative impact on African American student, enrollment, going from 8.35 percent in 1996 to 4.32 percent in 2018. For more details on CSU enrollment by race and ethnicity, see Yuxuan Xie, "CSU and UC Freshmen Enrollment by Race and

scholarships based on race to relieve financial burdens. Thus the share of Black and Native American students has fallen quite dramatically.[40] In contrast to African American and Native American CSU student enrollment numbers dropping precipitously since 1996, Latino students have made the biggest gains in enrollment within the system's twenty-three campuses. From 1998 to 2018, Latino freshmen student enrollment within the CSU grew from 23.12 percent to 49.69 percent.[41] It is important to point out that Latino student increases within the CSU are a result of several factors, including the overall increase in the Latino population in California, which more than doubled from 7 million to 15 million people in the last twenty years, and the increase in the number of Latino high school graduates. Had the Latino population in California and the share of Latino high school graduates not increased so dramatically in such a relatively short space of time, there is little doubt that Latino student admissions and matriculation within the CSU would have either decreased or stagnated, like their African American and Native American counterparts, due to Proposition 209.

Proposition 209 further created "opportunity gaps" for students of color, where these students were more acutely impacted by circumstances beyond their control, such as financial issues, the quality of their high schools, and being first-generation college students. Prior to the ban on affirmative action, students of color could participate in the CSU's Equal Opportunity Program, which provided advising, tutoring, and mentoring services to underrepresented students who were admitted to the CSU to help with retention to graduation. From its inception in 1969 until the passage of Proposition 209 in 1996, race/ethnicity and income were the main criteria for admission into EOP. In some instances, students could be admitted into the CSU through the EOP program if they were short on one or two requirements for admission.

However, after affirmative action was banned, the very definition of what constitutes an underrepresented student shifted. Race/ethnicity was eliminated from the admission criteria. Now only first-generation, low-income students can participate. Students of color whose parents are able, based on income, to contribute at least $1,500 annually to their child's education or students whose parents earned a bachelors' degree, are now ineligible for admission into EOP through the CSU. Most EOP-based financial assistance

---

Ethnicity" *EdSource*, October 29, 2020. Accessed 6/6/23 https://edsource. org/2020/freshmen-enrollment-csu-and-uc-by-race-and-ethnicity/642182.

40   Thomas Peele and Daniel J. Willis, "Dropping Affirmative Action Had Huge Impact on California's Public Universities," *EdSource*, October 29, 2020. Accessed 6/6/23 https://edsource.org/2020/dropping-affirmative-action-had-huge-impact-on-californias-public-universities/642437.

41   Xie "CSU and UC Freshmen Enrollment."

in the form of tuition waivers or book grants has also been eliminated. In addition to narrowing students of colors' access to additional support services, Proposition 209 foreclosed the possibility of the CSU establishing scholarships and other financial aid programs targeting underrepresented racial/ethnic groups. The CSU could no longer use lottery funds to support a Young Black Scholars Program, or a teacher education program specifically geared toward increasing the number of Latino K–12 teachers in Los Angeles, like those that Claudia Hampton was able to make happen during her tenure on the CSU board. At CSU Dominguez Hills and Fullerton, campus leaders also discontinued the special admit (4%) option that campuses could use to help students who might be short one or two criteria to gain admission into the CSU. The special admit option was available to all students. Given that less than forty-three percent (43%) of Black high school graduates in California were CSU eligible in 2022, this option provided Black students with an alternative path into public higher education. Yet Black student enrollment at CSU Dominguez Hills, for example, has plummeted from thirty percent (30%) in 2010 to eleven percent (11%) in 2023, since the special admit option was eliminated.[42]

Proposition 209 has also impacted student persistence and graduation rates for students of color within the CSU. Fewer than half of all Black entering freshmen graduate with a degree within six years and less than 10 percent of Black students earn a degree in four years. With fewer Black students admitted to the CSU to begin with and reduced access to targeted scholarships and support services, Black persistent and graduation rates lag behind nearly every other ethnic/racial group with twenty-two percent (22%) gaps between Black students and their Asian and White counterparts, for the better part of twenty years. There is a ten percent (10%) gap between Black students' graduation rates and Latino students within the CSU. Despite having a high school graduation rate of eighty-two percent (82%) and a CSU eligibility rate that is higher than Black, Asian, and White students combined, Latino student graduation rates from the CSU peaked in 2015 at 57 percent (57%) and have remained unchanged ever since.[43]

Finally, the effects of Proposition 209 extend to the racial and ethnic makeup of the CSU faculty ranks, which does not come close to reflecting

---

42   CSUDH University Effectiveness, Planning and Analytics, Enrollment Data Dashboard, 2023; CSUDH Multicultural African American Student Success Working Group Reports, 2021; CSUDH Black Student Demands and President Willie Hagan Response, 2016; CSUDH Campus Climate Survey, 2019; CSUDH Anti-Racism in the Academy Task Force Report, 2023.

43   The CSU defines eligibility for admissions by the completion of a series of mandated courses taken in high school known as the "A-G requirements" with a grade of "C" or better in each course.

California's ethnic diversity. Although seventy-five percent (75%) of the student body within the CSU is made up of non-white students of color, more than sixty percent (60%) of the tenured faculty are white.[44] Even at the lecturer ranks, white faculty dominate with fifty-seven percent (57%) of the total lecturer pool.[45] Proposition 209 has made it even harder to recruit faculty who reflect the students that the CSU serves.

For example, in 1986, the Faculty and Staff Relations Committee of the CSU Trustees, where Claudia Hampton served as Vice Chair, called for the creation of an Ad Hoc Committee on the Procurement and Retention of High Quality Faculty that would review affirmative action recruitment initiatives across the various campuses. The goal was to increase the number of women and racial minority faculty in light of CSU's needed to hire approximately 8,000 new faculty in the next decade to keep pace with demand. The Chancellor's Office and the Board of Trustees gave campuses the express permission to be creative in using affirmative action recruitment strategies, such as setting aside funds to offer housing and relocation stipends to new minority faculty.[46] Within three years of convening this ad hoc committee, there were signs of progress in the recruitment of faculty of color when a 1989 Task Force Report on the Recruitment and Retention of a High Quality Faculty showed a twenty-seven percent (27%) increase in the number of minority tenure track faculty, bringing the total percentage of minority faculty to twelve percent (12%).[47] After Proposition 209, however, the percentage of CSU minority faculty hired on the tenure-track has remained virtually unchanged from the late 1980s (approximately 11.5% in 2022) even as the minority student population has grown exponentially. Banned from using race to recruit or make faculty hiring decisions has meant that students of color find it difficult to find mentors with whom they can connect with

---

44   CSU Faculty: Employee Profile, Fall 2022. Data from The California State University website, Accessed 6/1/2023. https://www.calstate.edu/csu-system/faculty-staff/employee-profile/csu-faculty.

45   CSU Faculty: Employee Profile, Fall 2022.

46   Chair Dale Ride Report, May 1988. A Report to the CSU Educational Policy Committee of the Board of Trustees. CSU Board of Trustees Minutes of the Meeting of the Board of Trustees, Board of Trustees of the California State University Collection. Courtesy of the California State University Archives. California State University Dominguez Hills.

47   Task Force Report on the Recruitment and Retention of a High Quality Faculty A Report to the CSU Educational Policy September 1989. Committee of the Board of Trustees. CSU Board of Trustees Minutes of the Meeting of the Board of Trustees, Board of Trustees of the California State University Collection. Courtesy of the California State University Archives. California State University Dominguez.

on a cultural level. The small number of minority faculty across the CSU has also put pressure on those minority faculty who do manage to get hired and retained. Personal narratives of CSU faculty of color are rife with stories about racial microaggressions from white faculty and administrators, cultural taxation, and emotional labor, pay and resource disparities, and significant barriers to promotion and tenure.

Anti-affirmative action forces moved with unprecedented speed to undo over thirty years of affirmative action law, the consequences of which have been devastating for "The People's University."[48] Today, the CSU system and campus leadership have had to scramble to find ways to address the ever-present and growing achievement gap for low-income and underrepresented minority students, made worse by the academic culture wars, Proposition 187, and Proposition 209. California's reputation for having one of the most accessible public higher education systems in the United States has been completely turned upside down since the passage of Proposition 209 and maybe that was the intent all along.

The student activists advocating for a progressive vision of higher education in California pushed to enhance access for a broader and more diverse student population. Claudia Hampton worked from within the system for twenty years to help see that progressive vision realized. Yet anti-affirmative action forces have proven to be formidable opponents, who have used the courts to weaken affirmative action with the 1978 Bakke decision; scapegoated immigrants for the state's economic crises with Proposition 187, and offered culturally racist/anti-Black analysis of urban ghetto life, particularly following the 1992 L.A. Riots, to justify ending affirmative action with Proposition 209. Had she lived to see the passage of Proposition 209, Claudia Hampton would likely have been appalled at witnessing the erosion of affirmative action in the CSU and might have wondered if all of her work to promote equal access to higher education had been in vain.

---

48 Donald R. Gerth, *The People's University: A History of the California State University*, (Sacramento, CA: Institute of Governmental Studies Press, 2010).

Conclusion

The Legacy and The Lessons

The Legacy

On April 12, 2018, I stood on a stage in Claudia Hampton Hall on the campus of CSU Dominguez Hills, ready to give a joint talk on the history of Black and Filipino solidarity with my colleague Dr. Mary Lacanlale from the Asian Pacific Studies Department. After I introduced myself to the audience, I asked, "Can anyone in here tell me about Dr. Claudia Hampton, the person whose portrait is on the wall?" The only responses I got were blank stares and heads shaking no in response to my question. "Well, before I get started with my presentation, I want to let you know who she was. Dr. Claudia Hampton was the first Black woman trustee in the Cal State system. She was responsible for making sure that folks like me can stand before you as an alum of Cal State Fullerton and Cal State Long Beach and chair of the Africana Studies department, presenting my research on my local family history about Black Filipinos living in the Compton-Carson area. I am working on a book about her. By the time I am done, I hope that more people know who she was and what she did for students of color in the system."

When I posed the question about who Claudia Hampton was to the audience, I underestimated how much more I would be learning about her and the political dynamics she faced in her twenty-year fight to save affirmative action. Though I was a CSU student during Hampton's years as trustee and have spent most of my professional career as CSU faculty on two campuses, if I had not stumbled across a photo of Hampton in a digital archive, I would have been completely clueless, just like the members of my audience, as to why my campus had a lecture hall named after Hampton. I found it peculiar how so few people on campus knew anything about her, since it took the passage of a faculty senate resolution to have a classroom named in her honor. I asked around to people who had been on campus for decades, some of whom were faculty when Hampton Hall was so named, and I could only identify one person who remembered her. On a campus like CSU Dominguez, I found the ignorance as to who Hampton was to be troubling as it speaks to a larger problem, where the work of women of color is often rendered invisible. Fortunately, evidence of Claudia Hampton's legacy as a civic leader and an educational activist can be found throughout the CSU system and the City of Los Angeles.

By the early 1990s, the CSU Board of Trustees experienced a personnel shift, where trustees appointed by George Deukmejian, who served as governor of California from 1983 to 1991, began to take over the leadership of the board. One of these Deukmejian appointees was a former attorney and vice president of California-based McMahan's Furniture Company, named William D. Campbell. Although Campbell was a life-long Republican and led the charge to oust embattled Chancellor W. Ann Reynolds in 1990, he became close personal friends with Claudia Hampton. She provided him with advice and counsel when he assumed the chairmanship of the board in 1990 and, in turn, he named her chair of the Committee on Committees (the committee that issues board assignments) in a nod to her institutional knowledge of the inner workings of the board. Campbell, at the urging of his wife Linda, established the Claudia Hampton Scholarship Fund by contributing $50,000 to start a million-dollar endowment for the fund, earmarked to support deserving but financially needy students from Los Angeles area public schools pursuing a college education in the CSU system.

Having a white Republican man and his wife establish a scholarship in honor of a Black woman from the opposite side of the political spectrum speaks volumes to the love and respect Hampton engendered from her peers on the board. The establishment of this scholarship would serve as a living memorial that cemented Hampton's legacy as one of the giants within the CSU system. In announcing the scholarship fund, Chancellor Barry Munitz said, "She has meant much to us at this institution, where she chaired this board, and the Los Angeles Unified School District, where she worked. Everybody in Los Angeles who knows her loves her; so, a thank you to Denny [Campbell's nickname] and a congratulations to Claudia."[1] Shortly after the Campbells' initial gift, the board added $100,000 from the CSU Lottery Revenue Fund.[2] Hampton was so loved and admired that Kathleen Carlson, who served as the first student member of the CSU Board of Trustees from 1976–1978, during Hampton's early days as a board member, became involved in the process to secure external support for the scholarship in Hampton's honor: "Actually, when I finish here, I'm going to meet

1   Report of Chancellor Barry Munitz. July 15, 1992. CSU Board of Trustees Minutes of the Meeting of the Board of Trustees, Board of Trustees of the California State University Collection. Courtesy of the California State University Archives. California State University Dominguez Hills.

2   Carol Chastang. "Nineteen Students Win Scholarships, and Namesake Feels Honored," *Los Angeles Times*, August 19, 1993.

with Dr. Douglas Petino, because the Equitable Foundation has supported the Claudia Hampton Scholarship Fund, so I'm going to talk to him about that."[3]

Before her death in 1994, Hampton was able to interview scholarship finalists and attend the scholarship banquet where the first group of recipients were presented with their awards as Hampton Scholars. The CSU has continuously awarded the Hampton Scholarship for over thirty years. In a true testament to Claudia Hampton's impact on students within the CSU, a year after her passing in 1994, student leaders from across the system met at CSU San Luis Obispo to discuss how they could honor Hampton's work in supporting inner city youth and the student movement. Board chair Jim Considine told those present at the board meeting:"We wouldn't have the incredible education and amount of quality that CSU provides if it wasn't for her [Hampton's] contributions on the board and the significant time she put into it."[4] He shared that students from across the system had collectively raised $2,000 to be donated to the Hampton Scholarship Fund to honor her memory. Understandably, Hampton's passing was difficult for many who had crossed paths with her in the CSU. Former trustee chair Roy Brophy was devastated, and W. Ann Reynolds made a special effort to attended Hampton's funeral services, even though she lived and worked in New York at the time.[5] Hundreds attended Hampton's funeral services and her life was memorialized in the local mainstream and Black press, respectively.

Yet the CSU was not the only institution to honor Hampton's legacy of service. In March 1992, Hampton was appointed to the board of directors for the California Community Foundation (CCF), where she served until her death in 1994. CCF is one of the largest non-profit philanthropic organizations in the nation by asset size and total giving. Established in 1915 by Los Angeles banker Joseph Sartori, CCF provides funds to support local non-profits in the areas of arts, education, healthcare, housing, and civic engagement. Recognizing Hampton's many years of service as an educator at the local, state, and national level, along with many years of civic engagement work encouraging African American women to participate in local and state politics, CCF awarded the South Bay Family Healthcare Clinic a $1.6

3 Kathleen Carlson, "Kathleen Carlson: A Student Trustee View," Oral History Project on the Origins of The California State University System, Phase II, Interviewed by Judson Grenier, November 22, 1994.
4 Report of the Chairman Jim Considine. May 10, 1995. CSU Board of Trustees Minutes of the Meeting of the Board of Trustees, Board of Trustees of the California State University Collection. Courtesy of the California State University Archives. California State University Dominguez Hills.
5 Carlson interview, 1994.

million grant to open the Dr. Claudia Hampton Clinic in 2003.[6] This was the first non-profit community clinic providing dental, family planning and reproductive services, and HIV testing and education to low-income residents of Hawthorne, Inglewood, and Lennox, California. The clinic provides these services regardless of a patient's ability to pay, ensuring healthcare access to all members of the community. Naming this particular clinic in honor of Claudia Hampton, given its mission to provide healthcare services to people in this greatest need, was a nod to her incredible legacy of advocating for those whom the "system" was not originally designed to support.

Further evidence of Hampton's legacy can also be found on the campus of CSU Dominguez Hills, where the California Academy of Mathematics and Sciences (CAMS) is located. This science-enrichment high school, administered by Long Beach Unified School District, was Hampton's brainchild and continues to appear on national lists of top-ranked public schools. CAMS has a majority-minority student body with over ninety-three percent (93%) students of color. Graduates of CAMS have been accepted in elite private colleges and universities and top-ranked public institutions, including Cal Poly San Luis Obispo, and CSU Long Beach.[7]

On a personal level, I consider myself a direct beneficiary of Hampton's legacy; one that lives on through those of us who benefitted from her willingness to serve and fight the good fight as the *Black Woman on Board*. Like hundreds of thousands of other low-income, female, and ethnic and racial underrepresented students across the system, I directly benefitted from Hampton's service on the board through special programs designed specifically to support non-white ethnic and racial students. I participated in a pre-college STEM enrichment program for African American high school students at CSU Dominguez Hills in 1990. While attending CSU Fullerton in 1992 for my bachelor's degree in history and Afro-Ethnic Studies, I was chosen to take part in a special peer-mentoring program through the Afro-Ethnic Studies Department, designed to help retain and graduate African American students. Through this program, I was able to connect with a faculty member in the department, who gave me my first job out of college as a data collector on a federal head start program grant and wrote one of my letters of recommendation for my doctoral studies. I was also a recipient of a State University Grant to attend CSU Long Beach to attend the master's

6   Daily Breeze Staff. "Inglewood Clinic to Serve Three Area Communities." *Daily Breeze* (Torrance, CA), October 22, 2003.

7   According to the 2022 U.S. News and World Report Ranking of Colleges and Universities in the United States, Cal Poly San Luis Obispo ranks second on their list of regional universities in the west, while CSU Long Beach ranks 137th on their national rankings. For more information on U.S. News Rankings, see https://www.usnews.com/best-colleges.

degree program in history. The State University Grant (SUG) program offered need-based grants to low-income students within the CSU. The program was established during W. Ann Reynolds' administration as chancellor in 1982–1983. Reynolds and the board's finance committee created the SUG program after Claudia Hampton pressed the board into adopting a balanced fee policy in which any fee increases would be offset by more access to need-based aid to students.

Hampton's lobbying on behalf of low-income students of color has enabled me to earn my bachelor's and master's degrees in the CSU, setting the stage for me to earn a doctorate degree in Educational Studies. I have, in turn, become the first woman of color to earn promotion and tenure in Women and Gender Studies at CSU Fullerton in 2014 and after transferring to CSU Dominguez Hills in 2017, earning early promotion to full professor as the first woman in the Africana Studies Department to achieve this rank. I owe a debt of gratitude to Dr. Claudia Hampton, and in writing this book, I hope to make others across the CSU system and around the county more aware of her many years of service and come to appreciate her efforts in ensuring that the CSU educates the nation's most ethnically, economically, and academically diverse student body in the nation.[8]

The Lessons

If someone had told me that the way I conduct myself as a Black woman in academic leadership would be forever changed as a result of researching and writing about Claudia Hampton's fight to save affirmative action, I would not have believed them. As I said in the introduction, I nearly walked away from this project because I had initially found Hampton's approach to trustee leadership and service to be irreconcilable with my own racial politics. However, as time went on and I became more deeply invested in this research, not only had I radically changed my perspective about Claudia Hampton's style of leadership, but I found myself utilizing many of her strategies in my work as the chair of the Africana Studies Department at CSU Dominguez Hills.

Early into my appointment as department chair, I was asked by the dean of my college to meet with a donor who planned to visit campus in order to decide whether or not they would continue funding a multi-dimensional archive, research, and performance project. In the past, funding from this donor provided students with internship and independent study

---

8   California State University, "The Impact of CSU: Diversity," Accessed January 20, 2023, https://www.calstate.edu/impact-of-the-csu/diversity.

opportunities in my department, funded a performance faculty position in the music department, and provided our campus library with access to unique archival materials. In order to continue reaping the benefits of this funding, it was critical that all parties involved had to make a good impression. After we had been introduced to one another, the donor asked about my research, and I proceeded to describe my project on Claudia Hampton as the first African American woman trustee in the CSU system. Without knowing anything about me or Claudia Hampton, the donor proceeded to caution me not to assume that simply because Hampton was the "first" Black woman trustee that she had faced racism or sexism. This donor was an African American first in their respective field who had been appointed as an attorney by a Republican president to a governmental agency in the 1960s/1970s and said they never experienced racial discrimination. Further, the donor said they were raised by parents who emphasized hard work as the way to "rise above" any misconceptions or negative stereotypes that others might have about them as a Black person. The donor then proceeded to say that scholars in my field of Africana Studies look for racism around every corner and that Africana Studies was not a rigorous field of study.

Frustrated by this donor's incorrect assumptions but keeping my students at the forefront of my mind as Claudia Hampton might have done in a similar situation, I politely explained how Hampton was appointed by Ronald Reagan when he served as governor of California. I also said that having Reagan's endorsement did not shield Hampton from direct encounters with racism, as demonstrated in the story I recounted of how a fellow white board member yelled, "there's a n----- in the woodpile" in response to something Hampton said in the middle of a board meeting. I shared with the donor that although the historical record showed that Hampton was able to run circles around many of her white colleagues because she used charm and her wits to great effect, she did experience pushback when she tried to implement and enforce affirmative action policies. Therefore, I was not "playing the race card," as the donor intimated with their commentary. The donor's response to my rebuttal was complete silence.

As luck would have it, an emeritus faculty member who brokered the original agreement with the donor was present and witnessed the exchange. Worried that I might have jeopardized the renewal of the donor's support, I turned to this emeritus faculty member and asked "Did you know Claudia Hampton? I know that both of you are AKAs."[9] This emeritus faculty mem-

---

9   AKA is the nickname for members of Alpha Kappa Alpha Sorority, Incorporated, which is one of the Divine Nine historically Black Greek Letter Organizations, founded in 1908 on the campus of Howard University in Washington D.C.

ber who taught at CSU Dominguez Hills for over forty years enthusiastically responded that she did know Hampton. She further shared how she first got to know Claudia Hampton when she served as chair of CSU Dominguez Hills' twenty-fifth anniversary celebration, where Hampton was presented with a Community Award. From there, the emeritus faculty member talked about attending trustee meetings in her role as dean of the college of humanities and fine arts where she would see Hampton and the two would make it a point to chat or go out to lunch during breaks. She confirmed my retelling of some of racist encounters that Hampton experienced on the board, which helped to mollify some of the tension in the room. The rest of the visit continued without a hitch and the commitment to continue funding this important program was renewed.

I do believe that my decision to ignore and not respond to insulting comments about the field of Africana Studies and my quick thinking in redirecting the conversation by engaging another person is reminiscent of how Claudia Hampton played the long game by making strategic short-term decisions in response to situations when so much was on the line. At risk with my exchange with the donor was funding to support scholarships and internships for CSU Dominguez Hills students; a faculty position in African American music and performance; funds to pay a part-time archivist to help maintain and enlarge an archive that houses books, films, oral histories, sound recordings, and other primary source materials; and the hiring of a director for the campus gospel choir. Like Claudia Hampton, I had to play the long game by using sly civility so that my students would not suffer and lose out on these opportunities. Reflecting back at this exchange, it became clear to me why I had to write the story of Claudia Hampton's twenty-year fight to save affirmative action within the CSU. It is a story peppered with so many lessons that could be instructive for those of us in academia, government, the business sector, or the military who work to advance the cause of equity and justice within these large-scale organizations.

One of the most important lessons one should take away from learning about the history of Claudia Hampton's fight to save affirmative action within the CSU system is about the power of university trustee boards to contribute to or obstruct structural change, especially around issues of inclusion, equity, and justice. As detailed in chapter 1, the CSU trustees chose when to insert themselves into the day-to-day operations of the university only after the 1960s campus protests became the popular means for students of color to get their voices heard. Following the SFSU student strike, the CSU trustees chose to focus heavily on monitoring ethnic studies programs around the system. Of particular interest was the number of students enrolled in ethnic studies courses, and whether or not ethnic studies courses were responsible for grade inflation for students enrolled in those classes.

The latter sentiment suggests that some trustees believed that ethnic studies courses were not as academically rigorous as other courses on campus.

The CSU Chancellor's Office continued to produce these reports on ethnic studies at the request of trustees until 1971 when a new five-year program review policy for all academic programs within CSU was put in place. Prior to the student strike, the trustees showed little interest in the curriculum, and no other academic programs were singled out for a program review in the way ethnic studies programs had been. But after the student strikes, the trustees sought a more hands-on approach in dealing with curricular matters, as a number of trustees expressed concern that Black Studies and other ethnic studies programs served as a breeding ground for radical, anti-government beliefs and ideas. Governor Reagan continued to openly question whether it was outside groups like the Black Panther Party and Students for a Democratic Society behind the protests that led to the formation of Black Studies.[10] Instead of further blocking the institutionalization of these student-driven academic programs and risk more clashes with angry students, the CSU trustees simply used the new review process to keep tabs on all CSU curricular programs.

What this all indicates is that if the trustees wanted to see affirmative action implemented or ethnic studies programs established throughout the CSU, they only needed to demand a report be drafted to study the issue/problem and then draft a resolution to be voted on to put that policy or program into effect. Instead, Claudia Hampton, along with her allies on the board had to outsmart, outplay, and outwit their fellow board members who lacked the moral or political will to ensure that the CSU would be open and accessible to all.

The need for universities to diversify their governing boards is another important lesson that emanates from this research. More than serving as a symbolic gesture that never equates to action, appointing underrepresented minority groups can be a critical step in helping university boards gather perspectives from people with diverse life experiences which is the basis for good policymaking. Although there were women on the board prior to Claudia Hampton's appointment, trustee records show that these women had never taken up a specific issue or policy related to women. Given the board was first established in 1960, it is likely that the rigid gender norms of the day made it difficult for these first women trustees, Margaret Bates, and Mabel Kinney, to raise gender-related issues on a predominantly white male

---

10   Minutes of the Meeting of the Board of Trustees of the Trustees of the State
      College, January 22, 1969, California State University Board of Trustees
      Committee Minutes and Agendas, Courtesy of the Department of Archives
      and Special Collections. University Library. California State University,
      Dominguez Hills.

board. Furthermore, without federal or state laws defining sex or gender as a protected class, it would be challenging for these women to gain much traction amongst their peers. Claudia Hampton's appointment to the board as the first Black woman trustee represented a fundamental shift in the composition of the board. Not only did she speak on issues of race, but over time as she became an influential power player on the board, she also addressed issues of gender.

In 1974, when Hampton was appointed to the board, race and gender were protected classes, although the Department of Housing, Education, and Welfare (HEW) was slow in enforcing federal non-discrimination and affirmation action law. Having Hampton's presence on the board during this time helped the system's first affirmative action officer, Herb Carter, secure approval of the system-wide employee affirmative action plan in record time. Following the California Legislature's passage of ACR-71 in 1974, which mandated that the state's public higher educational institutions create a plan for student affirmative action, Hampton used her service as the CSU representative to the California Postsecondary Education Commission to ensure that the CSU complied with this state policy. By joining forces with her allies on the board and in the Chancellor's Office, Hampton was able to speak on behalf of underrepresented groups, whereas many of her white colleagues simply lacked the life experience to speak on behalf of groups unlike themselves. Whether she was trying to ease the financial burden of increased tuition on low-income students by suggesting a payment plan option, or working to have the CSU sponsor a bilingual teacher education program for Hispanic students, Hampton's life experiences and perspective as a Black woman educator gave her a lens to work for equity and justice within the CSU that her board colleagues simply did not have.

It has only been within the last decade or so that university and even corporate boards have started to take seriously the need to diversify. As the current educational landscape has changed, where non-white students account for forty-five percent (45%) and women make up sixty percent (60%) of U.S. college and university enrollment, the need for increasing diversity on these boards has never been greater. Vicki Kramer and Carolyn Adams from the Association of Governing Boards of Colleges and Universities (AGB) note that "Trustees need to think as broadly and creatively as possible to solve current and emerging problems in ways that take into account the needs of their gender and racially and economically diverse stakeholders: students, faculty, and other employees, and members of their communities. Boardroom diversity is particularly important to achieving this."[11] The CSU Board of

---

11   Vicki W. Kramer and Carolyn T. Adams, "Increasing Diversity on the Boards of Colleges and Universities," Association of Governing

Trustees operated without this type of racial diversity for the first six years of its existence and without Claudia Hampton serving as the first *Black Woman on Board*, it is likely that the board would have continued to ignore the needs of the historically underrepresented. Ed Davis, in a news story about Hampton's appointment as board chair in 1979 wrote:"The importance of having Black representation on the board that governs these schools obviously is their sensitivity to the needs of Black people."[12] Thus her identity as a woman of color mattered, because she advocated for groups with similar backgrounds as herself, groups that would have remained marginalized and shut out from the academy had it not been for someone like Claudia Hampton as their champion.

Finally, this history teaches us the importance of making a space for oneself at the table instead of being a passive observer. Hampton knew that simply being on the board was not enough. By learning the culture of the board, developing her own list of goals and priorities, and then working strategically and tactically to attain those goals, Claudia Hampton was able to overcome any presumptions of racial or gender handicaps and delivered programs and services to groups who needed them the most. She enthusiastically embraced board service and leadership as a vehicle to facilitate the employment and enrollment of minorities and women within the CSU.

Through her active engagement and service on a high number of board committees, special commissions, task forces, and special board appointments, Hampton could confidently say "We are really getting the wheels going in the area of affirmative action, making information available to students who otherwise would not be attending one of the California State Universities."[13] In fact, at the time when these remarks were made, there were regional affirmative action programs underway at CSU Northridge, Long Beach, Los Angeles, and Dominguez Hills, which provided pre-college counseling to ethnic minority students. Funding for these special affirmative action programs came from the CSU Fund for Innovation and Improvement of Education, which began in 1972 to encourage CSU faculty to develop new and cutting-edge pedagogical pract o improve student learning. By the late 1970s, with substantial budget cuts on the horizon, the board's educational policy committee, chaired by Hampton, began to use this fund to shore up support for student affirmative action pilot programs across the system. None of this funding would have been possible without

---

Boards, September/October 2020, Volume 28, Number 5, Accessed January 19, 2023. https://agb.org/trusteeship-article/increasing-diversity-on-the-boards-of-colleges-and-universities/.

12   Ed Davis, "Black Heads CSUC," *Los Angeles Sentinel*, May 29, 1980, A8.

13   Davis, A8.

Hampton "leaning into" her role as the "affirmative action trustee" utilizing sly civility to influence her fellow board members to give their support for programming that benefitted underrepresented populations.

Hampton's twenty-year tenure on the board was a model of effective trustee service for future generations of university trustees. She readily embodied what the AGB refers to as the three principles of trusteeship: understand governance, lead by example, and think strategically.[14] Hampton became well versed in board governance because she quietly observed the board culture and identified the gaps where she could make an impact. Having chaired the board's Organization and Rules committee twice, her knowledge of board procedure enabled her to successfully lobby for changes to board policies. In championing equity and justice for all members of the CSU system, Hampton led by example, especially during times when her board colleagues were reluctant or even openly hostile to expanding opportunities for underrepresented groups of students, staff, and faculty. In order to be successful as the "affirmative action trustee," Hampton thought independently but acted collectively. She had her own agenda and goals, but her willingness to be flexible for the good of the system made her a leader that others were willing to follow. Finally, Hampton was a master strategist who listened with an open mind, focused on long-term outcomes, and cultivated relationships in order to shape the CSU into a model of public higher education that provided quality education to all.

Unfortunately, the issues facing Claudia Hampton as a university trustee in the 1970s echo those facing Black women education activists and leaders today: the re-litigation of affirmative action as a legal and moral principle; declining federal and state funding for public higher education; lack of representation of women and people of color in key educational decision-making posts, and white academe's long-standing belief in the presumed incompetence of Black women as students, scholars, and administrators. Contemporary Black and other marginalized women, especially those serving in advocacy and/or leadership roles, can learn from the ways in which Claudia Hampton used sly civility to address these issues. Hampton and her contemporaries understood the power of relationship-building and methodically building one's social capital in order to bring about change within the nation's major political and social institutions. By being on the inside as the *Black Woman on Board*, Hampton was able to effect change for countless numbers of students, faculty, staff, and administrators who might have otherwise been denied access to the largest public university system in the nation. Higher education in the United States today is facing a new series

14   Association of Governing Boards "Principles of Trusteeship" Accessed January 20, 2023, https://agb.org/principles-of-trusteeship/.

of challenges brought on by the presidency of Donald Trump, the COVID-19 pandemic, global summer 2020 protests following the police murder of George Floyd, and the backlash against efforts to diversify school and university classrooms, the corporate workforce, and even the nation's highest court. Claudia Hampton's story illuminates for all how Black women have worked, and continue to work, tirelessly to meet those challenges and advance educational opportunities for Black people and other marginalized groups by holding this nation and its institutions accountable for making good on its promise of liberty and justice for all.

Bibliography

Interviews

Canson, Virna. "Waging the War on Poverty and Discrimination in California through the NAACP, 1953–1974," Interviewed by Sarah Sharp, Regional Oral History Office, The Bancroft Library, University of California Berkeley, December 1984.

Carlson, Kathleen, "Kathleen Carlson: A Student Trustee View." Oral History Project on the Origins of the California State University System, Phase II, Interviewed by Judson Grenier, November 22, 1994.

Carter, Herbert. "Interview of Herbert Carter," Interview by Donna J. Nicol, March 9, 2018.

Gerth, Donald, R. "Interview of Donald Gerth," Interviewed by Donna J. Nicol, November 7, 2017.

Hampton, Claudia "Interview of Claudia Hampton" Interviewed by Sarah Sharp, 1984. Audio Cassettes (a/b), Government History Documentation Project: Bancroft Library Regional History Office. Donald R. Gerth Papers, Archives and Special Collections, California State University Dominguez Hills.

Reynolds, W. Ann. "Interview of Dr. W. Ann Reynolds." Interviewed by Donna J. Nicol, July 12, 2018.

Manuscript Collections

Baca, Herman Papers, Special Collections and Archives, University of California at San Diego.

California State University Archives, CSU Master Plan for Higher Education Collection, 1959–2004, Donald and Beverly Gerth Archives and Special Collections. University Library, California State University, Dominguez Hills.

California State University Board of Trustees, California State Board of Trustees Minutes and Agendas Collection, 1958–2006, Donald and Beverly Gerth Archives and Special Collections, University Library. California State University, Dominguez Hills.

California State University Archives, California State University Reports Collection, 1904–Present, Donald and Beverly Gerth Archives and Special Collections, University Library, California State University, Dominguez Hills.

Clark, Robert D. Papers, San Jose State University Office of the President. Special Collections and Archives, San Jose State University.

Gerth, Donald, R. Papers, 1946–2010, Donald and Beverly Gerth Archives and Special Collections. University Library. California State University, Dominguez Hills.

SFSC Strike Collection, J. Paul Leonard Library, San Francisco State University Archives, San Francisco State University.

Articles, Books, and Governmental Reports

American Civil Liberties Union. ACLU of Northern California News vol. 47, no. 1, 1982 January–February; PER ACLUN; California Historical Society.

American Council on Education, *Campus Disruption during 1968–1969*, Edited by Alan Bayer and Alexander Astin. Washington D.C.: American Council on Education, 1969.

Association of Governing Boards of Universities and Colleges. *Composition of Governing Boards*. Washington, D.C.: Association of Governing Boards of Universities and Colleges, 1985.

___. *Composition of Governing Boards of Public Colleges and Universities*. Washington, D.C.: Association of Governing Boards, 1997.

___. *Status Report on Minorities in Higher Education*. Washington, D.C.: American Council on Education, 1990.

___. "Principles of Trusteeship" Accessed January 20, 2023, https://agb.org/principles-of-trusteeship/

Bady, Aaron, and American Civil Liberties Union. ACLU of Northern California News, vol. 47, no. 1, 1982, January–February; PER ACLUN; California Historical Society.

American Council on Education, *Campus Disruption during 1968–1969*, edited by Alan Bayer and Alexander Astin. Washington D.C.: American Council on Education, 1969.

Association of Governing Boards of Universities and Colleges. *Composition of Governing Boards.* Washington, D.C.: Association Mike Konczal. "From Master Plan to No Plan: The Slow Death of Public Higher Education. Dissent, Fall 2012. Accessed May 30, 2023, http://www.dissentmagazine. org/article/from-master-plan-to-no-plan-the-slow-death-of-public-higher-education.

Barlow, William, and Peter Shapiro. *An End to Silence: The San Francisco State CollegeMovement in the 1960s.* New York: Pegasus, 1971.

Bayer, Alan W., and Alexander W. Astin. "Antecedents and Consequents of Disruptive Campus Environments." *Measurement and Evaluation in Guidance* 4, (1971): 18–30.

Belenky, Mary, F., Lynne A. Bond, and Jacqueline S. Weinstock, *A Tradition That Has No Name: Nurturing the Development of People, Families and Communities.* New York, Basic, 1999.

Bennett, William, J. *To Reclaim a Legacy: A Report on the Humanities in Higher Education.* Washington, DC: National Endowment for the Humanities, 1984.

Bhabha, Homi. *The Location of Culture.* London, Routledge, 1994.

Bianchi, Emily, C., Erika V. Hall and Sarah Lee. "Reexamining the Link between Economic Downturns and Racial Antipathy: Evidence That Prejudice against Blacks Rises during Recessions." *Psychological Science* 29, no. 10 (2018): 1584–1597. https://doi.org/10.1177/0956797618777214.

Biondi, Martha. *The Black Revolution on Campus.* Berkeley: University of California Press, 2012.

Blumenthal, Sidney. *The Rise of the Counter-Establishment: From Conservative Ideology to Political Power.* New York: Times, 1986.

Bond, Paul. "Affirmative Action Is No Longer Effective." *Daily Sundial,* April 2, 1993.

Bowser, Benjamin, P. *The Abandoned Mission in Public Higher Education: The Case of the California State University.* New York: Routledge, 2017.

California State Department of Education. A Master Plan for Higher Education in California, 1960–1975. Sacramento: California State Department of Education. Accessed January 31, 2023, http://ark.cdlib.org/ark:/13030/hb9c6008sn.

California State University, Faculty Profile. Fall 2022. Accessed 6/1/2023. https://www.calstate.edu/csu-system/faculty-staff/employee-profile/csu-faculty.

___. "The Impact of CSU: Diversity," Accessed January 20, 2023. https://www.calstate.edu/impact-of-the-csu/diversity.

California State University Dominguez Hills, unpublished university data.

California State University Northridge Special Collections Archive Blog. "A Look Back at School Desegregation and Busing in Los Angeles," February 27, 2018. Accessed January 3, 2023. https://library.csun.edu/SCA/Peek-in-the-Stacks/busing-desegregation-2

Carter, Jimmy. Education Amendments of 1978 and the Middle-Income Student Assistance Act Statement on Signing H.R. 15 and S. 2539 into Law. Online by Gerhard Peters and John T. Woolley, The American Presidency Project. https://www.presidency.ucsb.edu/node/243763.

Central YMCA College Board of Directors. "Spirit of the College." 1942. Print. Roosevelt University Archives.

Chancellor's Doctoral Incentive Program. The California State University website.

August 28, 2022. https://www.calstate.edu/csu-system/faculty-staff/cdip/Pages/mission-and-history.aspx.

Chastang, Carol. "Nineteen Students Win Scholarships, and Namesake Feels Honored." Los Angeles Times, August 19, 1993.

Chisholm, Shirley. Unbought and Unbossed. Boston: Houghton Mifflin, 1970.

Chronopolous, Themis. "Racial Turmoil at San Jose State: The Incident of the 1967 University of Texas at El Paso vs. San Jose State Football Game." Paper Presented to the Annual Meeting of the Popular Culture Association/American Culture Association. Philadelphia, PA, April 12–15, 1995.

Clancy, Sigal. "Doing the Right Thing Founded a Generation Ago by William F. Buckley: The Young Americans for Freedom Are Shock Troops for U.S. Conservatism." Los Angeles Times, April 29, 1990.

Cole, Johnetta, B. "Black Studies in Liberal Arts Education." Edited by Johnella Butler and John Walter. In Transforming the Curriculum: Ethnic and Gender Studies, 131–148. Albany, NY: State University of New York Press, 1991.

Congressional Research Service. The Higher Education Act (HEA): A Primer. Washington, DC, January 2, 2014.

Cooper, Brittney. Beyond Respectability: The Intellectual Thought of Race Women (Champaign, IL: University of Illinois Press, 2017).

Craven, William. "Commentary: The Real Issue Is One of Power: Chancellor W. Ann Reynolds has had ongoing intramural scrimmages with SDSU President Thomas Day since She Was Appointed. Los Angeles Times (San Diego County Edition), November 13, 1988, 2.

Crenshaw, Kimberle. "Mapping the Margins: Intersectionality, Identity Politics, and Violence against Women of Color." Stanford Law Review 43, no. 6 (1991): 1241–99.

Daily Breeze Staff. "Inglewood Clinic to Serve Three Area Communities." Daily Breeze (Torrance, CA), October 22, 2003.

Dallek, Matthew, The Right Moment: Ronald Reagan's First Victory and the Decisive Turning Point in American Politics. New York: Free Press, 2001.

Davis, Ed. "Black Heads CSUC," Los Angeles Sentinel, May 29, 1980, A8.

Deluca, Barbara, M., and Craig R. Wood. "The Charter School Movement in the United States: Financial and Achievement Evidence from Ohio." Journal of Education Finance 41, no. 4, (Spring 2016): 438–450.

Douglass, John, A. The California Idea and American Higher Education: 1850 to the 1960 Master Plan. Palo Alto: Stanford University Press, 2007.

___. "Revisionist Reflections on California's Master Plan @ 50" California Journal of Politics and Policy 3, no. 1 (January 2011): 1–36.

Dumas, Frederick, J. Presentation of the Council of Black Administrators. 1968. Box 421. Board Reports. Los Angeles Unified School District Board of Education Records, 1875–2012, Charles Young Research Library, Los Angeles, California.

Egner, Dick. "Negro Faculty Member Challenges Claims, San Jose State Race Prejudice Blasted." San Jose News, September 14, 1967.

___. "Militant Anti-Prejudice Move Threatens San Jose State Sports Program." San Jose News, September 15, 1967

Evans, Stephanie Y. Black Women in the Ivory Tower, 1850–1954: An Intellectual History. Gainesville: University Press of Florida, 2008.

Fanucchi, Kenneth, "Latin Educators Hit Appointment of Cal State Chief," Los Angeles Times, June 7, 1979, SG2.

Gaines, Kevin. "Racial Ideology in the Era of the "Negro Problem." In Freedom's Story, TeacherServe, National Humanities Center, Accessed 6/17/2022 http://nationalhumanitiescenter.org/tserve/free-dom/1865-1917/essays/racialuplift.htm.

Garcia, Mario T., and Sal Castro. Blowout! Sal Castro and the Chicano Struggle for Educational Justice. Chapel Hill, University of North Carolina Press, 2011.

George, Daniel. "The Right Finds a Niche on Campus." Insight on the News, September 9, 2002.

Gerth, Donald, R. "History of the California State Colleges." In An Invisible Giant: The California State Colleges, edited by Donald Gerth, 8–20. San Francisco: Jossey-Bass, 1971.

___. The People's University: A History of the California State University. Sacramento, CA: Institute of Governmental Studies Press, 2010.

Gerth, Donald, R. and Judson A. Grenier. A History of the California State University and Colleges. Carson, CA: California State University Dominguez Hills: Office of University Relations, 1981.

Gough (Nicol), Donna, J. *"Ideas Have Consequences: Conservative Philanthropy, Black Studies and the Evolution and Enduring Legacy of the Academic Culture Wars, 1945–2005."* PhD dissertation: Ohio State University, 2007.

Gnerre, Sam. "Sam Yakamoto: Former Carson Mayor and Unlikely Film Star," *South Bay History* (a Daily Breeze newspaper history blog). Accessed June 1, 2023, http://blogs.dailybreeze.com/history/2014/09/20/sak-yamamoto-former-carson-mayor-and-unlikely-film-star/

Grenier, Judson, A. *The Rainbow Years, 1960–1985: The First Quarter Century of California State University Dominguez Hills.* Carson: California State University Dominguez Hills Foundation, 1987.

Gross, Kali, N. "Examining the Politics of Respectability in African American Studies." *Benchmark Almanac* 43, no. 28, April 1, 1997. Accessed 6/17/2022. https://almanac.upenn.edu/archive/v43/n28/benchmrk.html.

Hale, Jon, N. *The Freedom Schools: Student Activists in the Mississippi Civil Rights Movement.* New York: Columbia University Press, 2016.

Hamilton, Charles, V. "An Advocate for Black Power Defines It." New York Times Sunday Magazine, April 14, 1968, SM22.

Haney Lopez, Ian. *Dog Whistle Politics: How Coded Racial Appeals Have Wrecked the Middle Class* (Oxford: Oxford University Press, 2014).

Harris, Angela P., and Carmen G. Gonzalez. "Introduction to *Presumed Incompetent: The Intersections of Race and Class for Women in Academia,* edited by Gabriella Gutierrez y Muhs, Yolanda Flores Niemann, Carmen G. Gonzalez, and Angela P. Harris. Utah State University Press, 2012. First edition.

Hayes, Floyd, W. "Taking Stock: African American Studies at the Edge of the 21st Century, *Western Journal of Black Studies* 18, no. 3 (1994): 153–163.

Heilbron, Louis. *The College and University Trustee: A View from the Board Room.* San Francisco: Jossey-Bass, 1973.

Henderson, Timothy, J. *Beyond Borders: A History of Mexican Migration to the United States.* Oxford. Wiley-Blackwell, 2011.

Higginbotham, Evelyn Brooks. *Righteous Discontent: The Women's Movement in the Black Baptist Church, 1880–1920.* Cambridge, MA., Harvard University Press, 1993.

Hill Collins, Patricia. *Black Feminist Thought: Knowledge, Consciousness, and the Politics of Empowerment.* New York, Routledge, 2008.

Holy, T.C. "California's Master Plan for Higher Education, 1960–1975: A Factual Presentation of an Important Development." *Journal of Higher Education* 32, no. 1 (January 1961): 9–16.

Howard Jarvis Taxpayer Association "Proposition 13." Accessed September 8, 2022. https://www.hjta.org/propositions/proposition-13/?gclid=Cj0KCQ jwpeaYBhDXARIsAEzItbEqGuxaG4DKMmaiAEBj3a3FWVs6J_9VAT6TjJ-JInxkgkyJxkvT1XBMaAqj0EALw_wcB

Kay-Hill, Herma, and Martha S. West. *Cases and Materials on Sex-Based Discrimination.* Eagan, MN: Thomson West, 2005.

Kerr, Clark, and Marian Gade. *The Guardians: Boards of Trustees of American Colleges and Universities: What They Do and How Well They Do It.* Washington, DC: Association of Governing Boards of Universities and Colleges, 1989.

Knox, Owen. "History of the Council of Black Administrators: Los Angeles Unified School District." Accessed January 9, 2023. http://www.lausd.k12. ca.us/orgs/coba/History.html._

Kramer, Vicki W., and Carolyn T. Adams. "*Increasing Diversity on the Boards of Colleges and Universities.*" Association of Governing Boards, September/ October 2020 28, no. 5. Accessed January 19, 2023. https://agb.org/ trusteeship-article/increasing-diversity-on-the-boards-of-colleges-and-uni-versities/.

Leong, Nancy. "*Race and the Law: Racial Capitalism.*" *Harvard Law Review* 126, no. 8 (June 2013). https://harvardlawreview.org/2013/06/racial-capitalism/.

Levin, Matt. "*What Is Proposition 13? Your Prop. 13 Cheatsheet.*" Prop. 13, The California Dream Series/CALMatters. Accessed September 8, 2022. https://projects.scpr.org/prop-13/history/.

Lind, Michael. *Up from Conservatism: Why the Right is Wrong for America.* New York: Free Press, 1996.

Lipman-Blumen, Jean. *Connective Leadership: Managing in a Changing World.* Oxford, Oxford University Press, 2000, 1st edition.

Longanecker, David, A. "Reconsidering Higher Education and the Public Good: The Role of the Public Spheres." In *Governance and the Public Good,* edited by William G. Tierney, 127–155. Albany: State University of New York Press, 2006.

Los Angeles Times, "Chicanos Protest Selection of Black to Head L.A. State." *Los Angeles Times,* May 27, 1979, B5.

Los Angeles Times Editorial Staff, "*The Real Issue at San Jose State.*" *Los Angeles Times,* September 28, 1967.

Los Angeles Unified School District. "District's Court Ordered Integration Programs." Accessed January 15. 2023. http://achieve.lausd.net/cms/ lib08/CA01000043/Centricity/Domain/263/Student%20Integration%20 Services%20Programs.pdf.

McGirr, Lisa, *Suburban Warriors: The Origins of the New American Right.* Princeton, NJ: Princeton University Press, 2001.

Meiklejohn, Alexander. *The Experimental College.* New York: Harper & Brothers, 1932.

Mexican American Legal Defense and Education Fund, October 24, 2019. "Proposition 187: The Granddaddy of Anti-Immigrant Measures." https://www.maldef.org/2019/10/proposition-187-the-grand-daddy-of-anti-immigrant-measures/.

Mohanty, Chandra. *Third World Women and the Politics of Feminism.* Bloomington: Indiana University Press, 1991.

National Park Service. "A History of Mexican Americans in California: World War II and Its Aftermath." November 17, 2004. Accessed December 15, 2022. https://www.nps.gov/parkhistory/online_books/5views/5views5d.htm.

Nava, Julian. *Julian Nava: My Mexican American Journey.* Houston: Arte Publico, 2002.

Nicol, Donna, J. "Activism for Profit: America's Anti-Affirmative Action Industry." *Al Jazeera*, February 28, 2021. https://www.aljazeera.com/opinions/2021/2/28/activism-for-profit-americas-anti-affirmative-action-industry.

___. "Conservative Philanthropy's War against Race and Gender Studies in U.S. Higher Education." *History of Philanthropy (HistPhil.com)*, June 29, 2020. https://histphil.org/2020/06/29/conservative-philanthropys-war-against-race-and-gender-studies-in-u-s-higher-education/.

___ "Racism and the Roots of Conservative Philanthropy in the U.S." *Unpack the Past: Al Jazeera*, 22 Feb. 2022, www.aljazeera.com/features/2022/2/17/racism-and-the-roots-of-conservative-philanthropy-in-the-us.

___. *Women in Politics and Activism since Suffrage Project.* Donna Nicol interviewed by Carie Rael. Center for Oral and Public History, CSU Fullerton, February 25, 2014.

Nicol, Donna, J., and Jennifer A. Yee. "Reclaiming Our Time: Women of Color Faculty and Radical Self-Care in the Academy," *Feminist Teacher: A Journal of the Practices, Theories and Scholarship of Feminist Teaching* 27, no. 2–3, (2017): 133–156.

O'Connor, Karen. *Women's Organizations' Use of the Courts.* Washington D.C.: Lexington, 1980.

Ogbar, Jeffrey. "Rainbow Radicalism: The Rise of Radical Ethnic Nationalism" in *The Black Power Movement: Rethinking the Civil Rights-Black Power Era*, edited by Peniel E. Joseph, 193–228. New York: Routledge, 2006 .

Orrick, William, H. *"Shut It Down! A College in Crisis: San Francisco State College."* Washington, DC: A report to the National Commission on the Causes and Prevention of Violence, 1969.

Peele, Thomas, and Daniel J. Willis. "Dropping Affirmative Action had Huge Impact on California's Public Universities." *EdSource*, October 29, 2020. Accessed 6/6/23. https://edsource.org/2020/dropping-affirmative-action-had-huge-impact-on-californias-public-universities/642437.

Perkins, Carol, O. "The Pragmatic Idealism of Mary McCleod Bethune" *Sage* 5, no. 2 (Fall 1988): 3–16.

Perlstein, Rick. *Nixonland: The Rise of a President and the Fracturing of America.* New York: Scribner, 2008.

Pottinger, J. Stanley. "Remarks at the Panel on Affirmative Action and Faculty Policy." New Orleans, LA: American Association of University Professors, May 5, 1972, 1–24.

Pusser, Brian. "The "New" New Challenge of Governance by Governing Boards." In *Governance and the Public Good*, edited by William G. Tierney, 19–41 . Albany: State University of New York Press, 2006.

Rael, Carie. *Taking Back Our Education: How Students Shaped California's Public Higher Education System, 1960–1996.* (MA Thesis, California State University Fullerton, 2015).

Rafferty, Max. "Educational Appeasement" *Oakland Tribune*, November 26, 1967.

Raines, Howell, "Voting Rights Act Signed by Reagan" *New York Times*, June 30, 1982. Accessed January 9, 2023. https://www.nytimes.com/1982/06/30/us/voting-rights-act-signed-by-reagan.html.

Rall, Raquel, Demetri L. Morgan, and Richard Chait "Does Your Board of Trustees Reflect Your Student Body?" *Washington Monthly*, August 27, 2023. Accessed September 16, 2023. https://washingtonmonthly.com/2023/08/27/does-your-board-of-trustees-reflect-your-student-body/.

Ramsey, Sonya Y. *Bertha Maxwell Roddy: A Modern Day Race Woman and the Power of Black Leadership.* Gainsville: University Press of Florida, 2022.

Rarick, Ethan. *California Rising: The Life and Times of Pat Brown.* Berkeley: University of California Press, 2005.

Roche, Jeff, "Cowboy Conservatism." In *The Conservative Sixties*, edited by David Farber and Jeff Roche., 79–92. New York, Peter Lang, 2003.

Ryan, William. *Blaming the Victim.* New York: Pantheon, 1971.

Sadler, Bernice, R. "Title IX: How We Got It and What a Difference it Made" *Cleveland State Law Review*, 55, no. 4, (2007).

Schultz, Debra. *To Reclaim a Legacy of Diversity: Analyzing the Political Correctness Debates in Higher Education.* New York: National Council for Research on Women, 1993.

Schuparra, Kurt. "A Great White Light": The Political Emergence of Ronald Reagan. Edited by David Farber, and Jeff Roche. In *The Conservative Sixties.* New York: Peter Lang, 2003.

Scott, Joyce A. and Meredith Ludwig. *Community Service at Urban Public Institutions: A Report on Conditions and Activities.* Washington, DC American Association of State Colleges and Universities, 1995.

Steele, Shelby. "A Negative Vote on Affirmative Action." *New York Times Magazine,* May 13, 1990.

Stefancic, Jean, and Richard Delgado. *No Mercy: How Conservative Think Tanks and Foundations Changed America's Social Agenda.* Philadelphia: Temple University Press, 1996.

Thorburn, Wayne. *A Generation Awakens: Young Americans for Freedom and the Creation of the Conservative Movement,* Ottawa, IL: Jameson, 2010.

Trombley, William. "Cal State Head Faces Moves to Remove Her." *Los Angeles Times,* March 21, 1987.

___. "Reynolds Receives Vote of Confidence from CSU Board" *Los Angeles Times,* May 13, 1987, 1.

Vaca, Nicholas, C. *Presumed Alliances: The Unspoken Conflict between Latinos and Blacks and What It Means for America.* New York: HarperCollins, 2004.

Van de Kamp, John. "Opinion of the California Attorney General 241," 1984.

Varney, James. "Anthropologist Glynn Custred champions Proposition 209 in California," *Washington Times,* February 21, 2021. Accessed 1/27/2023 https://www.washingtontimes.com/news/2021/feb/21/anthropologist-glynn-custred-champions-proposition/.

Walker, Jesse. "The Five Faces of Jerry Brown," *American Conservative,* November 1, 2009.

West, Martha, S. "The Historical Roots of Affirmative Action" *Berkeley La Raza Law Journal* 10, no. 2 (2015): 607–630.

White, Newman, I. "The White Man in the Woodpile: Some Influences on Negro Secular Folk-Songs." *American Speech* 4, no. 3 (1929): 207–15.

Whitson, Helene. *"On Strike! Shut It Down! A Revolution at San Francisco State: Elements For Change, edited by Joan Borrelli.* San Francisco, Calif.: J. Paul Leonard Library, San Francisco State University, 1999.

___. *"Strike! A Chronology, Bibliography, and List of Archival Materials concerning the 1968–1969 Strike at San Francisco State College.* Washington DC: Educational Resources Information Center, 1977.

Wiggins, David, K. "The Future of College Athletics is at Stake: Black Athletes and Racial Turmoil on Three Predominantly White University Campuses, 1968–1972" *Journal of Sport History* 15, no. 3 (1998): 304–333.

Willliams, Gareth, "Higher Education: Public Good or Private Commodity?" *London Review of Education* 14 no. 1 (April 2016): 131–142.

Williamson, Joy Ann. "In Defense of Themselves: The Black Student Struggle for Success and Recognition at Predominantly White Colleges and Universities. *Journal of Negro Education* 68, no. 1 (1999): 92–105.

Wing, Adrien, K., ed., *Critical Race Feminism: A Reader*. 2nd edition. New York: New York University Press, 2003.

Woodyard, Chris. "Latin Teacher Proposal OKd by College Trustees," *Los Angeles Times*, July 26, 1978, C1.

Xie, Yuxuan. "CSU and UC Freshmen Enrollment by Race and Ethnicity" *EdSource*, October 29, 2020. Accessed 6/6/23 https://edsource.org/2020/freshmen-enrollment-csu-and-uc-by-race-and-ethnicity/642182.

Appendix

Hampton's Trustee Committee Service and Leadership

Table 1. Claudia Hampton's Committees Membership/Leadership, 1974–1994.

Standing Committees	Years Served	Leadership Role(s)
Educational Policy	1974–1978, 1981–1994	Vice Chair 1976/77, 1983/84 Chair 1977/78, 1988/89, 1990/91, Chair 1993/94
Organization and Rules	1974/75, 1981–1984, 1993–1994	Chair 1982/83, Chair 1993/94
Audit	1976–1977, 1984/85, 1988/89	Vice Chair 1984/85
Faculty and Staff Affairs	1974–1977, 1981–1983, 1985–1989, 1990–1993	Vice Chair 1986/87 Chair 1990–1993
Committee on Committees	1976–1979, 1984/85, 1989/90, 1991/92	Chair 1978/79, 1989/90, Chair 1991/92
Gifts and Public Affairs/ Governmental Relations	1981/82, 1983–85, 1986/87, 1991/1992, 1993/94	Vice Chair 1981/82, Chair 1983–1985, Vice Chair 1993–1994
Collective Bargaining	1985/1986	
Personnel	1985–1988, 1991/92, 1993/94	Chair 1985/86, Vice Chair 1991/92
Finance	1988/89, 1990	
Institutional Advancement	1993/94	

Table 1. Claudia Hampton's Committees Membership/Leadership, 1974–1994 (*continued*)

CSU BOT Ad Hoc Committees	Years Served	Leadership Role(s)
Task Force on Off Campus Instruction	1975/76	Chair 1975/76
Criteria (Selection of New Chancellor) Chair of Search Committee for Selection of New Chancellor	1981–1983	Chair 1981–1983
Directions 2000 (Educational and Academic Options for the Future)	1981/82	
Committee to Review Executive Council of Presidents and Chancellor's Office Staff	1983/84	
Committee to Review Procedures to Evaluate Chancellor and Vice Chancellors	1984/1985	Chair 1984/85
Committee to Select President of Stanislaus Campus	1984	Chair 1984
Committee to Select President of Dominguez Hills Campus	1977, 1987	Chair 1977
Committee to Review Honorary Doctorate Applications	1988	
Committee to Select President of Fullerton Campus	1989	
Committee to Select President of the Pomona Campus	1990	

Table 1. Claudia Hampton's Committees Membership/Leadership, 1974–1994 (*continued*)

Special Appointments	Years Served	Leadership Role(s)
CSU Rep for the California Postsecondary Education Commission	1977–1988 Primary 1989/90, 1990/91, 1992/93 Alternate	
Appointed to President Reagan's Advisory Panel on Financing of Elementary and Secondary Education (Federal)	1982	
Appointed to a Committee to Evaluate the President of University of New Mexico Highland by the American Association of Colleges and Universities (Out of State)	1984	
Recommended for Appointment as Director of the CSU Foundation	1984	
Appointed CSU Rep for the 1985 Revision of the California Master Plan for Higher Education	1985	Chair of Community College Subcommittee
Appointed to the Selection Panel for the Trustees Award for Outstanding Achievement	1990	
Subcommittee on CSU's Relationship to the Schools	1992/93	Chair 1992/93

Index

Note: Illustrations are indicated by page numbers in *italics*.

San Jose State College/University, 21,
28–33, 29n3, 30n7, 36–37, 60
Scaife, Richard, 176
scholarship, 192–93
Schools and Community Relations
Unit, 8–9, 11, 91
SDS. *See* Students for a Democratic
Society (SDS)
Second Great Migration, 10, 12, 48,
129
segregation, 1–2, 7–8, 10–11, 28, 48,
93
Senate Constitutional Amendment 39,
154–55
Senn, Milton, 72–73
sexual harassment, 106
Sharp, Sarah, 2, 95
Shelley v. Kraemer, 13, 48, 129
Sheriffs, Alex, 71, 93–95, 104, 108
Short, Thomas, 177
SJSC. *See* San Jose State College
(SJSC)
sly civility, 3–4, 18–21, 89–90, 96,
105, 107, 112, 114, 124, 127,
162, 197, 201
Smith, Gilbert, 100
Smith, Robert, 58–59
sororities, 4n5, 12
South Bay Family Healthcare Clinic,
193–94
Sowell, Thomas, 165, 177
Sparling, Edward J., 6
"special admit," 70, 70n18, 152–53
SSS. *See* Student Support Services
(SSS)
Stanford University, 166
State University Grant (SUG), 195
State University House, 169–70
Steele, Shelby, 165, 167
Stefancic, Jean, 177–78
Stennis, Willie, 138–40
Step to College program, 155–56

Stetson, Jeffrey, 140
student housing, 28–29
Student Non-Violent Coordinating
Committee (SNCC), 32
Student Support Services (SSS), 45
Students for a Democratic Society
(SDS), 2, 33, 198
Suburban Warriors (McGirr), 12
SUG. *See* State University Grant
(SUG)
Summerskill, John, 52, 57
Suzuki, Bob, 171
Swim, Dudley, 51

Talent Search, 45, 138
Taylor, Sidney, 106
teacher education, 156–57
teacher shortage, 173–74
"telephone network," 102–4, 125
Third World Liberation Front
(TWLF), 55, 55n75
Title IX, 65, 146, 175
Title VII, 64–65, 106
Toyada, Shoichiro, 100
TRIO programs, 45
Trump, Donald, 202
TWLF. *See* Third World Liberation
Front (TWLF)
Tyndall, Robert, 139

UBSA. *See* United Black Students for
Action (UBSA)
United Black Students for Action
(UBSA), 28–32
United Professors of California
(UPC), 73
University of California Berkeley, 37
University of California system, fund-
ing of, 36
University of Maryland College Park,
65
University of North Carolina, 4n5

www.ingramcontent.com/pod-product-compliance
Lightning Source LLC
Chambersburg PA
CBHW070151310326
41914CB00089B/811